Automated Trading with R

Quantitative Research and Platform Development

Chris Conlan

Apress®

Automated Trading with R: Quantitative Research and Platform Development

Chris Conlan
Bethesda, Maryland
USA

ISBN-13 (pbk): 978-1-4842-2177-8   ISBN-13 (electronic): 978-1-4842-2178-5
DOI 10.1007/978-1-4842-2178-5

Library of Congress Control Number: 2016953336

Managing Director: Welmoed Spahr
Acquisitions Editor: Susan McDermott
Developmental Editor: Laura Berendson
Technical Reviewers: Stephen Nawara, Jeffery Holt
Editorial Board: Steve Anglin, Pramila Balen, Laura Berendson, Aaron Black, Louise Corrigan,
    Jonathan Gennick, Robert Hutchinson, Celestin Suresh John, Nikhil Karkal, James Markham,
    Susan McDermott, Matthew Moodie, Natalie Pao, Gwenan Spearing
Coordinating Editor: Rita Fernando
Copy Editor: Kim Wimpsett
Compositor: SPi Global
Indexer: SPi Global
Cover Image: Designed by Freepik

For my family.

Contents at a Glance

Contents

About the Author

Chris Conlan began his career as an independent data scientist specializing in trading algorithms. He attended the University of Virginia where he completed his undergraduate statistics coursework in three semesters. During his time at UVA, he secured initial fundraising for a privately held high-frequency forex group as president and chief trading strategist. He is currently managing the development of private technology companies in high-frequency forex, machine vision, and dynamic reporting.

About the Technical Reviewers

Dr. Stephen Nawara earned his PhD in pharmacology from Loyola University – Chicago. During the course of his dissertation, he gained five years of experience analyzing biomedical data. He currently works as a data scientist and R tutor. He specializes in applying high-performance computing and machine-learning techniques to automated portfolio management.

Professor Jeffrey Holt has served as the Program Director of the University of Virginia's MS in Data Science and chair of the Department of Statistics, where he is currently the director of the undergraduate program. He received his PhD in Mathematics from the University of Texas. His research concerns analyzing the effects of sampling methods in ecological studies. He teaches classes in machine learning, data manipulation, and mathematics for UVa undergraduate and graduate students.

Acknowledgments

I am grateful to Professor Jeffrey Holt for seeing this book through, from inception to completion. I offer my sincere appreciation to Professor Holt, Gretchen Martinet, and Paul Diver (of the Department of Statistics at the University of Virginia) whose dedicated teaching has inspired me to share my knowledge.

I am thankful to Dr. Stephen Nawara, a gifted programmer and fantastic business partner, for his extraordinary commitment to quality and clarity in his many revisions of this text.

Further, I would like to thank the R developer community and package contributors for donating their time and expertise to maintaining and extending the R language.

Lastly, I cannot thank my family enough for their continual love and support throughout the development of this text and my life as a whole.

Introduction

This book will cover the broad topic of *automated trading*, starting with mathematics and moving to computation and execution. You will gain unique insight into the mechanics and computational considerations taken in building a backtester, strategy optimizer, and fully functional trading platform.

The code examples in this text are derived from deliverables of real consulting and software development contracts. At the end of the book, we will bring the concepts together and build an automated trading platform from scratch. This book will give a prospective algorithm trader everything he needs except a trading account, including full source code.

Definitions

Trading strategies are predetermined sets of rules a trader uses to make trading decisions. Trading strategies use the following tools and techniques:

- *Manual execution* involves the trader placing his trades manually. This can be

  - Calling the brokerage

  - Placing an order through E*Trade, Tradestation, or other brokerage platforms

  - Pit trading

- *Computer automation* involves the trader authorizing a computer to place trades on his behalf. Many retail brokerage platforms and trading software have incorporated this functionality into their platforms, but they are typically very limited. Most brokerages have an API for more customized implementation through the trader's programming language of choice.

  - Tradestation Easy Language, Metatrader

  - Charles Schwab API

  - Black-box algorithms

- *Indicators* are functions of relevant data that inform the trader by interacting with rule sets.

  - MSI

  - Moving averages

  - Custom indicators

- *Rule sets* are logical filters of the indicator that trigger trading decisions. The indicator combined with the rule set comprises the trading strategy.

  - "Buy if the indicator rises above 80."

  - "Short if the indicator crosses two standard deviations below its mean."

  - "Cover short if the indicator crosses zero and the position is net short."

Strategy development is the art of building, testing, optimizing, and maintaining trading strategies. Major topics in strategy development include the following:

- *Backtesting* involves simulating past performance of a given strategy, often with specific parameters of interest. A backtest will yield the performance metric the developer aims to maximize. Backtests may be performed thousands or millions of times in order to optimize parameters in the strategy.

- *Strategy optimization* attempts to determine a strategy in the present that will maximize a performance metric in the future. Optimization methods make trade-offs between computation speed and search completeness.

  - Exhaustive search

  - Gradient methods

  - Genetic search

- *Performance metrics* can be any function of a return series or equity curve that the developer attempts to maximize.

  - Total return

  - Sharpe Ratio

  - Total Return to Max Drawdown Ratio

- *Parameter updating* is part of maintaining a strategy that utilizes real-time performance data to optimize performance. Traders use faster optimization methods and more local searches at this stage.

Scope of This Book

There are a lot of steps in turning a trading idea into a fully automated trading strategy. This book will discuss, from start to finish, the development process through R. With this discussion, this book will cover a broad range of topics in programming, high-performance computing, numerical optimization, finance, and networking.

There will be examples at every step, including full source code in Appendix A. This source code represents the total work product of the topics discussed in the book.

If you have brokerage accounts with the API clients covered in this text, you can plug in your username and password and start trading right away. Obviously, it is important that traders understand what is happening inside their scripts before they begin trading.

Programming in R

R is a language of choice for many data scientists and statisticians at every level. It has a large and rapidly growing community and more than 7,000 contributed packages as of the time of writing. Packages include software suites for data management, machine learning, graphics and plotting, and much more. Installing a new package takes a few seconds and opens up a ton of capabilities within R. If a trader wants to experiment with Lasso regression as an indicator, he can install the glmnet package and run Lasso regression with one line of code.

You are not required to have prior experience with R but will benefit from it. Most concepts will be discussed with complementary mathematics, so they can be read and learned without necessarily executing the code. Please see the book's website, r.chrisconlan.com, for instructions on downloading and installing R and RStudio.

High-Performance Computing

Any program that works can probably work even faster. In high-performance computing, we aim to minimize computation time by taking full advantage of a computer's resources in an organized fashion.

Most programs we run utilize only one core in our computers. Unless they are doing some very heavy lifting, this is probably best. When we write programs that do a lot of number crunching, we may benefit from distributing the load over multiple cores, known as *parallelizing*. We will see that some jobs are easy to parallelize, and some are not. We will also see that some jobs make huge speed improvements with parallelization, and others are made slower.

Sometimes programs might run very slowly because our computers run out of memory (RAM) and need to access memory on our hard drives (disk space). Storing and fetching information from the disk is a very slow process. We will see how memory management can lead to speed improvements by preventing our data from spilling out of RAM into disk.

Numerical Optimization

Some readers may recall finding the minimum or maximum of a function using basic calculus. This is known as *analytical optimization*. In analytical optimization, we analyze the mathematics to find a solution on paper.

Numerical optimization, on the other hand, involves using high-performance computing and search algorithms to estimate minima or maxima. Some of these algorithms will draw on calculus by estimating high-dimensional derivatives (or gradients), and others will search in an unguided grid-like fashion. We use these algorithms as opposed to calculus because we do not know the form of the performance function or its derivatives.

We will make our biggest speed improvements here by reducing the number of parameters in our trading strategy and selecting the best-suited algorithm to find the maximum of the performance function.

Finance

When building a backtesting algorithm, we must estimate the impact of many real-world financial phenomena to make sure we produce accurate estimates of strategy performance. We will discuss various estimation methods for commissions, margin, slippage, and others in order to produce accurate performance projections in backtesting.

We will address questions like the best time of day to trade, how to find the optimal trading frequency given account constraints, and which risk model validation metrics to use.

Networking

Data providers supply data to all sorts of players in the financial world in real time. Brokerages take messages from clients and execute orders on their behalf. How do traders get their data? And how do brokers get their messages?

To get the data, we will send computer-generated messages to data providers, and they will respond with the data we request. These computer-generated messages work with the providers through an application programming interface (API). With an API, our computers can talk to their computers in a predefined language they understand. It may be through a very long URL or a form of formatted message.

To give brokerages our orders, we will do the same. Most platform-based brokerages have APIs by which traders can program computers to trade on their behalf. Brokerages sometimes require different request and message formats to add security. We will discuss various file transfer and message transfer formats and why certain services use them.

Material Overview

This book will be broken into three major parts. Part I will further clarify the objectives and goals of the book and discuss some interesting analytic problems in strategy trading. Part II will focus on developing the core functionality of the platform. This is where the majority of R programming happens. Part III brings the platform into a production environment by extending and scheduling the platform built in Part II. It will also discuss how our platform measures up to the competition and where to go next to further your education and/or career in strategy development.

Part I: Problem Scope

- *Chapter 1, "Fundamentals of Automated Trading"*: We will continue defining the problem scope of automated trading by mathematically defining the equity curve and return series. We will introduce some popular risk-return metrics and explore their characteristics on simulated equity curves and the S&P 500.

Part II: Building the Platform

- *Chapter 2, "Networking Part I"*: We begin by fetching, storing, and loading the data we will use for analysis and trading throughout the book. We will use URL-based APIs and MySQL-style APIs to build an ASCII database of .csv files of stock data. We will discuss efficient updating, storage, and loading into memory for analysis.

- *Chapter 3, "Data Preparation"*: Here we take the data loaded in Chapter 2 and apply a handful of use-specific cleaning methods. We discuss these methods and generate additional data for use in analysis in later chapters.

- *Chapter 4, "Indicators"*: We discuss the theory and usage of indicators in trading strategies. We introduce the concept of information latency and compute a handful of indicators as examples. You will grow very comfortable with apply-style functions that are the cornerstone of time-series computations in R.

- *Chapter 5, "Rule Sets"*: We discuss the theory and usage of rule sets in trading strategies. We introduce and standardize important terminology for discussing and programming rule sets. We give a lot of attention to which types of indicators work well with which types of rule sets.

- *Chapter 6, "High-Performance Computing"*: This chapter serves as a broad introduction to high-performance computing and a specific guide on high-performance computing in R. This will extend your familiarity with apply-style functions to multicore computing.

- *Chapter 7, "Simulation and Backtesting"*: We will use our combined knowledge thus far to generate simulated trade results from our data, indicators, and rule sets with high-performance methods from Chapter 6.

- *Chapter 8, "Optimization"*: This chapter places Chapter 7 inside a for loop to discover optimal parameters for trading strategies. We spend a lot of time discussing optimal methods for parameter discovery.

- *Chapter 9, "Networking Part II"*: This chapter covers a handful of popular brokerages and how to send orders to them through API calls.

Part III: Production Trading

- *Chapter 10, "Organizing and Automating Scripts"* : We establish CRON jobs in both UNIX and Windows to run your trading strategies automatically on a schedule.

- *Chapter 11, "Looking Forward"*: We discuss the challenges that large-scale funds and high-frequency funds face, what program languages they may use, and generally how to advance a career in automated trading.

Learning Resources

- *Setting up R and RStudio*: `r.chrisconlan.com`
- *Community discussion*: `r.chrisconlan.com`

Risk Disclosure

Apress Media LLC and the author warn there is a high level of risk associated with automated trading in any asset class, and it may not be suitable for all investors. Automation can work against you, as well as to your advantage. Before deciding to invest in automated trading, you should carefully consider your investment objectives, level of experience, and risk appetite. The possibility exists that you could sustain a loss of some or all of your initial investment, and therefore you should not invest money that you cannot afford to lose. There are risks associated with the use of online deal execution and trading systems including but not limited to software and hardware failure and Internet disconnection. You should be aware of all the risks associated with automated trading and consult with an independent financial advisor if you have any doubts.

Apress Media LLC and the author shall not be responsible for any loss arising from any investment based on any recommendation, forecast, or other information provided. Apress Media LLC and the author will not accept liability for any loss or damage, including without limitation to any loss of profit that may arise directly or indirectly from use of or reliance on such information.

The materials printed in this book are solely for informational purposes. No offer or solicitation to buy or sell financial assets, trading advice, or strategy is made, given, or in any manner endorsed by Apress Media LLC and the author. You are fully responsible for any investment or trading decisions you make, and such decisions should be based solely on your evaluation of your financial circumstances, investment/trading objectives, risk tolerance, and liquidity needs.

PART 1

■ ■ ■

Problem Scope

CHAPTER 1

■ ■ ■

Fundamentals of Automated Trading

The fundamental goal of trading is to maximize risk-adjusted return. When developing strategies, we will simulate trading performance in an attempt to maximize risk-adjusted return in simulation. There are many ways to measure risk-adjusted return. They involve examining the shape of the *equity curve* and the *return series*.

Equity Curve and Return Series

The *equity curve* is the trading account value plotted against time. It can otherwise be thought of as cash on hand plus the equity value of portfolio assets plotted against time. We want it to rise linearly if we trade with a uniform account size or exponentially if we reinvest gains. The *return series* is the list of returns on the account at each trading period. The return series depends only on which assets are traded when, not the trading account size, so it will be the same whether or not we reinvest gains.

Figure 1-1 shows an example of an equity curve generated by a strategy that is long up to ten S&P 500 stocks at a time with a trading account of $10,000, trading once per day, without reinvesting gains. A gray reference line is plotted for an equivalent investment in the SPY S&P 500 ETF, a tradable fund that closely mimics the behavior of the S&P 500.

Electronic supplementary material The online version of this chapter (doi:10.1007/978-1-4842-2178-5_1) contains supplementary material, which is available to authorized users.

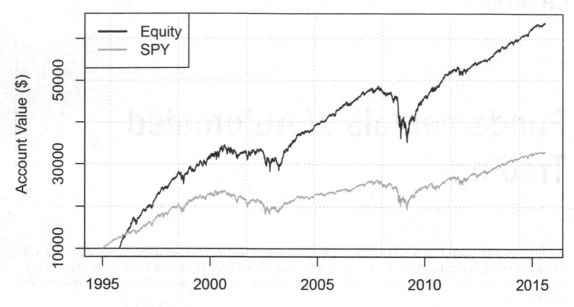

Figure 1-1. *Example equity curve*

The return series is the portfolio gain or loss as a percentage of tradable capital at each trading period. Figure 1-2 shows the daily return series of the equity curve in Figure 1-1.

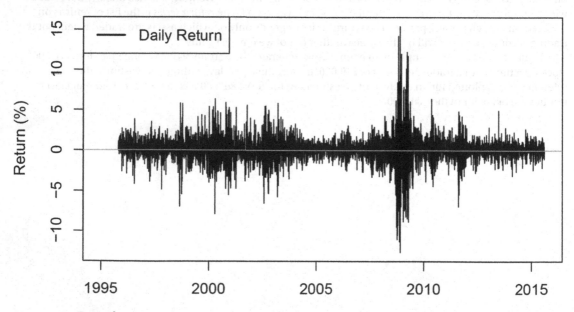

Figure 1-2. *Example return series*

Characteristics of the Equity Curve

We will introduce some notation to study characteristics of the equity curve.

We define P_{t_0} to be the dollar value of the portfolio before adjustment and P_{t_1} to be the dollar value of the portfolio after adjustment for t in $0, 1, 2,..., T$, where $t=0$ represents the beginning of simulation and $t=T$ represents the current time.

We assume that portfolio adjustments (or trades) happen instantaneously in time. The change in P from t_0 to t_1 represents change due to adjustment, while the change in P from $(t-1)_1$ to t_0 represents change due to movement of market prices of the assets in the portfolio. Chronologically, t evolves as $t_0, t_1, (t+1)_0, (t+1)_1, (t+2)_0, ..., T_0, T_1$, with transitions from t_0 to t_1 happening instantaneously when an algorithm automatically adjusts the portfolio.

We define C_0 as initial cash, C_{t_0} and C_{t_1} as uninvested cash at t_0 and t_1, and K_t as trading costs incurred during instantaneous adjustment from t_0 to t_1. The equity curve at time t_0 is equal to the following:

$$E_{t_0} = C_{t_0} + P_{t_0} = C_0 + \sum_{i=1}^{t} \left(P_{i_0} - P_{(i-1)_1} - K_{i-1} \right)$$

Note that $C_0 = C_{t_0}$ for $t=0$. Further, we note that the difference between E_{t_0} and E_{t_1} is the total of trading costs incurred during the adjustment period, from t_0 to t_1.

$$E_{t_1} = E_{t_0} - K_t.$$

When we plot the equity curve and perform risk-return computations on it, we use only E_{t_1} for t in $0, 1,..., T$. The choice of E_{t_1} over E_{t_0} is intended to reflect the impact of commissions in the equity curve.

Characteristics of the Return Series

We define Vt to be the tradable capital at time t_0. This is a value set by the trader. The total cash invested by the trader cannot exceed Vt at any given time. We define $t(i_1)$ and $t(i_0)$ to be the times t_1 and t_0 at which trade i was initiated and exited, respectively. Trade i is considered to be active at time t if $t(i_1) \leq t_1 < t(i_0)$. We say that $i \in I_t$ if i is active at t_1. We define ji as the asset initiated in trade i. Further, allow P_{t_0} and P_{t_1} to be subsettable by asset such that $P_{t_1, j}$ represents the value of asset j in the portfolio at time t_1.

If we make 15 trades in the instantaneous adjustment period occurring from t_0 to t_1, there will be 15 new i's subsettable to t for these transactions. This allows us to make infinitely many overlapping trades and describe them using our notation.

The tradable capital must meet the following condition for all t in $0, 1,..., T$:

$$V_t \geq \sum_{i \in I_t} P_{t(i_1), j_i}$$

where Vt is determined during or prior to $(t-1)$ based on information available at that time.

Verbally, this means the sum of the initial purchase prices of all active trades is less than or equal to the tradable capital. Note that there is no restriction regarding the relationship between Vt and P_{t_0} or P_{t_1}. This is because P_{t_0} and P_{t_1} represent the current market value of the portfolio rather than the initial purchase price. The previous equation may seem like a trivial definition, but Vt will serve as the denominator in our return series equation. It is necessary to define Vt in this way to

- Enforce determination of the value of V_t algorithmically before the adjustment period occurs in t_0 to t_1.

- Penalize the return series for allocating more capital than is invested. In this sense, allocated capital is treated the same as invested capital even if it remains uninvested.

- Allow for flexibility in tradable capital rather than enforce strict constancy or compounding.

The return series at time t is defined as follows:

$$R_t = \frac{P_{t_0} - P_{(t-1)_1} - K_{t-1}}{V_{t-1}}$$

This definition of the return series is a direct consequence of the definition of V_t and benefits greatly from it.

The classic definition of the return series at t is the percentage change in the equity curve from t-1 to t. Our definition allows us to honestly measure performance without imposing unrealistic assumptions on our financial behavior. The classic definition of the return series fails in many scenarios:

- If cash withdrawals or deposits are made to the trading account after t=0

- If earnings are not strictly reinvested

Many of the risk-return metrics we will discuss and utilize in this book impose no specific rules on how to calculate the equity curve and return series. Note that we have presented them in this chapter in a way that is both honest and realistic. Traders and investors should be wary when comparing metrics of their own strategies to metrics of strategies developed by others. Failing to honor the aforementioned relationships can give risk-return metrics an unrealistic upward bias.

Risk-Return Metrics

The goal of strategy development is to build a strategy that maximizes future risk-adjusted return. We will attempt to do this by backtesting performance and selecting the model with the best risk-adjusted return for use in rea-time trading. There are many measures for risk-adjusted return. We will compute a lot of them during backtesting but optimize our strategy to maximize a single metric. Table 1-1 summarizes some useful risk-return metrics mathematically. R code will be discussed later in this chapter.

Table 1-1. *Common Risk-Return Metrics*

Metric	Formula	Notes
High-Frequency Sharpe Ratio	$Sharpe = \dfrac{\bar{R}}{\sigma_R}$, where $\bar{R} = \dfrac{R_1,\ldots R_T}{T}$ and $\sigma_R = \sqrt{\dfrac{1}{T-1}\sum\left(R_t - \bar{R}\right)^2}$	Requires that returns are normally distributed if used for inference.
High-Frequency Jensen's Alpha	α, where the regression equation $R_t = \alpha + \beta R_{t,b} + \varepsilon_t$ is estimated, where $R_{t,b}$ is the return of a benchmark index at t	Requires that returns are normally distributed if used for inference. Commonly used to assess fund performance. Rewards consistently good performance over purely superior performance.
Pure Profit Score	$PPS = \dfrac{E_{T_0} - V_0}{V_0} R^2$ where R^2 is the R-squared value of regression $\dfrac{E_{t_0}}{V_t} = \alpha + \beta t + \varepsilon_t$	Scales return on initial tradable capital by linearity of equity curve standardized for level of reinvestment.
Net Profit to Max Drawdown Ratio	$NPMD = \dfrac{E_{T_0} - V_0}{MD}$, where $MD = max\left(E_{k_0} - E_{l_1}\right)$ for $k < l < T$	Simple but effective nonparametric risk-return metric. Maximum drawdown is the largest loss, from any point to any later point, in the equity curve.
High-Frequency Burke Ratio	$Burke_n = \dfrac{\bar{R}}{\left(\dfrac{1}{T}\sum_{i=1}^{n}MD_i^2\right)^{\frac{1}{2}}}$	MD_i represents the ith largest maximum drawdown. The denominator is a form of partial variance accounting for very large losses. $n=T/20$ is favorable.
Lower and Higher Partial Moments of Order n	$LPM_n\left(R_b\right) = \dfrac{1}{T}\sum_{t=1}^{T} max\left[R_b - R_t, 0\right]^n$ $HPM_n\left(R_b\right) = \dfrac{1}{T}\sum_{t=1}^{T} max\left[R_t - R_b, 0\right]^n$	The lower partial moment (LPM) is considered superior to standard deviation for performance ratios because it is affected only by returns below R_b, the minimum accepted return. R_b can be set to zero, the risk free rate, or the mean return.
Generalized Omega of Order n	$\Omega_n\left(R_b\right) = \dfrac{\bar{R} - R_b}{\left(LPM_n\left(R_b\right)\right)^{\frac{1}{n}}}$	Sortino Ratio for $n=2$, Kappa(3) for $n=3$, linearly equivalent to Shadwick and Keating Omega for $n=1$.
Improved High-Frequency Sharpe Ratio	$SR = \dfrac{\bar{R}}{\left(LPM_n(0)\right)^{\frac{1}{2}}}$	Accounts only for negative semivariance against a mean zero return. Denominator penalizes only for volatile losses.
Upside Potential Ratio of Order (n_1, n_2)	$UPR_{n_1,n_2}\left(R_b\right) = \dfrac{HPM_{n_1}\left(R_b\right)^{\frac{1}{n_1}}}{LPM_{n_2}\left(R_b\right)^{\frac{1}{n_2}}}$	$UPR_{1,2}(R_b)$ developed by Sortino in 1999, after he developed the Sortino Ratio in 1991. $UPR_{2,2}(0)$ has many desirable properties.

7

Characteristics of Risk-Return Metrics

In this section, we will simulate equity curves to study the characteristics of risk-return metrics in Table 1-1. This will help us determine which risk-return metrics to focus on when we optimize strategies.

We will generate our equity curve using SPY returns and random numbers with a constant tradable capital of $10,000. If you want to simulate the same random numbers as in this text, copy the set.seed line. We will be defining only E_{t_0} for the sake of simplicity.

Listing 1-1 installs an API package called quantmod that fetches stock data. We will be covering APIs, time-series packages, and quantmod in a later chapter, so you can ignore it for now. For now, you should make sure you are connected to the Internet and select a download mirror if prompted. The following code snippets will assume that you have installed quantmod and called it through the library function. We have wrapped it in suppressWarnings() because it is very verbose. quantmod warnings and xts warnings can generally be ignored.

Listing 1-1. Loading SPY Data

```
# Checks if quantmod is installed, installs it if unavailable,
# loads it and turns off needless warning messages
if(!("quantmod" %in% as.character(installed.packages()[,1])))
  { install.packages("quantmod") }
library(quantmod)

options("getSymbols.warning4.0"=FALSE,
        "getSymbols.auto.assign"=FALSE)

# Loads S&P 500 ETF data, stores closing prices as a vector
SPY <- suppressWarnings(
  getSymbols(c("SPY"),from = "2012-01-01"))
SPY <- as.numeric(SPY$SPY.Close)[1:987]
```

Now that we have acquired and prepared our data, we can begin simulating equity curves and studying risk-return metrics. All of the remaining code in this chapter is relevant to your understanding of the topics and content discussed in it. Listing 1-2 randomly generates two more equity curves based on SPY and plots the results in Figure 1-3. Veteran R users may notice that there are faster methods for performing many of the computations in this chapter. This is intentional for instruction. We will simulate equity curves and return series by adding a small constant plus a random effect to the return series of the SPY S&P 500 ETF.

Listing 1-2. Simulating Equity Curves

```
# Set Random Seed
set.seed(123)

# Create Time Index
t <- 1:(length(SPY)-1)

# Tradable Capital Vector
Vt <- c(rep(10000, length(t)))

# Benchmark Return Series
Rb <- rep(NA, length(t))
for(i in 2:length(t)) { Rb[i] <- (SPY[i] / SPY[i - 1]) - 1 }
```

```r
# Benchmark Equity Curve
Eb <- rep(NA, length(t))
Eb[1] <- Vt[1]
for(i in 2:length(t)) { Eb[i] <- Eb[i-1] * (1 + Rb[i]) }


# Randomly Simulated Return Series 1
Rt <- rep(NA, length(t))
for(i in 2:length(t)){
  Rt[i] <- Rb[i] + rnorm(n = 1,
                         mean = 0.24/length(t),
                         sd = 2.5 * sd(Rb, na.rm = TRUE))
}


# Randomly Simulated Return Series 2
Rt2 <- rep(NA, length(t))
for(i in 2:length(t)){
  Rt2[i] <- Rb[i] + rnorm(n = 1,
                          mean = 0.02/length(t),
                          sd = .75 * sd(Rb, na.rm = TRUE))
}


# Randomly Simulated Equity Curve 1
Et <- rep(NA, length(t))
Et <- Vt[1]
for(i in 2:length(t)) { Et[i] <- Et[i-1] * (1 + Rt[i]) }

# Randomly Simulated Equity Curve 2
Et2 <- rep(NA, length(t))
Et2 <- Vt[1]
for(i in 2:length(t)) { Et2[i] <- Et2[i-1] * (1 + Rt2[i]) }

# Plot of Et1 against the SPY Portfolio
plot(y = Et, x = t, type = "l", col = 1,
     xlab = "Time",
     ylab= "Equity ($)",
     main = "Figure 1-3: Randomly Generated Equity Curves")
grid()
abline(h = 10000)
lines(y = Et2, x = t, col = 2)
lines(y = Eb, x = t, col = 8)
legend(x = "topleft", col = c(1,2,8), lwd = 2, legend = c("Curve 1",
                                                          "Curve 2",
                                                          "SPY"))
```

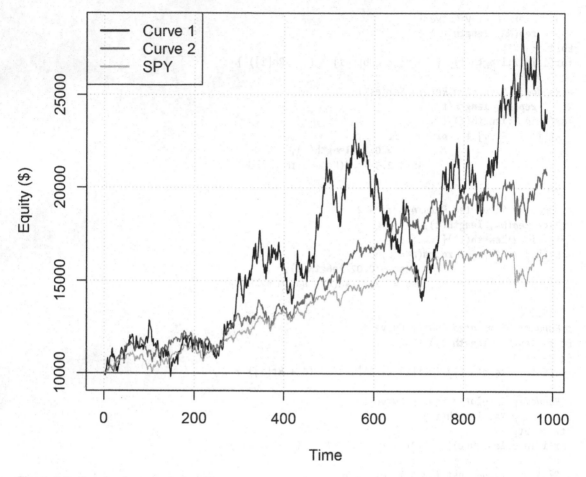

Figure 1-3. *Randomly generated equity curves*

The randomly generated equity curve is intended to behave like a real equity curve of a strategy that trades members of the S&P 500. We will use R to study the equity curve and return series using methods in Table 1-1.

Sharpe Ratio

The Sharpe Ratio is one of the best-known metrics for measuring strategy performance. It was developed in 1966 by William F. Sharpe and has been a long-recognized fund and strategy performance metric. It is widely known that the Sharpe Ratio has theoretical shortfalls, but it is still utilized for off-the-cuff benchmarking in conversation and reporting.

The Sharpe Ratio established an important framework for measuring fund and strategy performance. The idea of maximizing *excess return divided by risk* is echoed in most of our performance metrics in Table 1-1. For the Sharpe Ratio, it is specifically *mean excess return divided by standard deviation of returns*.

The High-Frequency Sharpe Ratio neglects to subtract the benchmark/risk-free return in the numerator, using only $\bar{R}$ instead of $\bar{R} - R_f$. It acknowledges that typical benchmark returns, like the 90-day T-Bill, are negligibly small when shortened to frequencies of daily or shorter. This metric exists to solidify that high-frequency traders ought not to use the original Sharpe Ratio. Proponents of the original Sharpe Ratio argue that the benchmark return should be the average of trading costs. This is a valid argument, and it is the reason our definition of the return series already includes trading costs.

Listing 1-3 computes High-Frequency Sharpe Ratios for the randomly generated equity curves.

Listing 1-3. High-Frequency Sharpe Ratio

```
# Use na.rm = TRUE to ignore NAs at position 1 in return series
SR <- mean(Rt, na.rm = TRUE) / sd(Rt, na.rm = TRUE)
SR2 <- mean(Rt2, na.rm = TRUE) / sd(Rt2, na.rm = TRUE)
SRb <- mean(Rb, na.rm = TRUE) / sd(Rb, na.rm = TRUE)
```

Listing 1-4 plots the equity curves against the computed values of the Sharpe Ratios in Figure 1-4. In the rest of the book, plotting code will be included only if it introduces new or instructive plotting concepts. The following is a good template for comparing equity curves with performance metrics and will not be printed when used in the future.

Listing 1-4. Plotting Equity Curve Against Performance Metrics

```
plot(y = Et, x = t, type = "l", col = 1,
     xlab = "",
     ylab= "Equity ($)",
     main = "Figure 1-4: Sharpe Ratios")
grid()
abline(h = 10000)
lines(y = Et2, x = t, col = 2)
lines(y = Eb, x = t, col = 8)
legend(x = "topleft", col = c(1,2,8), lwd = 2,
       legend = c(paste0("SR = ", round(SR, 3)),
                  paste0("SR = ", round(SR2, 3)),
                  paste0("SR = ", round(SRb, 3))))
```

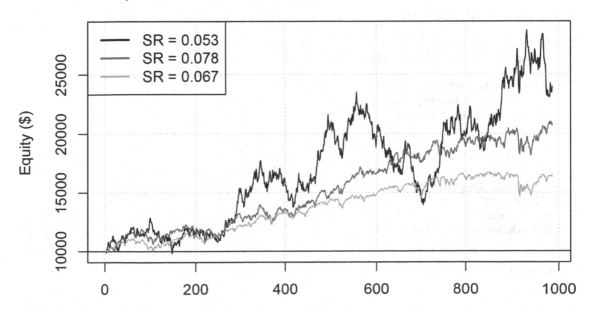

Figure 1-4. Sharpe Ratios

We are quick to notice that the first equity curve with the highest overall return has the lowest Sharpe Ratio because of its high variance of returns. Curve 2 makes about twice as much as the SPY portfolio with only slightly higher variance, making it the best according to the Sharpe Ratio.

As we move forward, keep in mind the theoretical shortfalls of the Sharpe Ratio:

- The denominator penalizes large gains as well as large losses.

- Inference methods using the Sharpe Ratio require returns to be normally distributed. Financial assets are known to exhibit highly non-normal returns.

- The denominator standardizes against the mean return, but the numerator standardizes against a separate benchmark rate or zero. Performance ratios are known to benefit in robustness from the consistent application of benchmarking figures in both the numerator and the denominator.

Maximum Drawdown Ratios

Maximum drawdown simply represents the most dollars in equity a strategy lost from any point to any point in the future. This figure is a candidate to replace standard deviation in the denominator of the Sharpe Ratio. It is a one-sided measure of risk and behaves like a variance term when the top n maximum drawdowns are aggregated in some way.

The formula is short when expressed mathematically, but programmatically, there are a lot of computations to make in order to compute all drawdowns and then find the n highest. We will define a function here to use throughout the chapter. Notice that in the formula in Table 2-1 we use E_{k_0} and E_{l_1}, before and after the adjustment period, to account for trading costs, which means we normally need to supply two vectors, E_{t_0} and E_{t_1}. We will use our single equity curves representing E_{t_0} for simplicity here.

In the following example and Listing 1-5, we use the following:

$$MD = max\left(E_{k_1} - E_{l_1}\right) \text{ for } k < l < T$$

Listing 1-5. Maximum Drawdown Function

```
MD <- function(curve, n = 1){

  time <- length(curve)
  v <- rep(NA, (time * (time - 1)) / 2)
  k <- 1
  for(i in 1:(length(curve)-1)){
    for(j in (i+1):length(curve)){
      v[k] <- curve[i] - curve[j]
      k <- k + 1
    }
  }

  m <- rep(NA, length(n))
  for(i in 1:n){
    m[i] <- max(v)
    v[which.max(v)] <- -Inf
  }

  return(m)

}
```

The argument *curve* is for the equity curve. The function returns a vector of length n containing the n highest drawdowns, with a default of $n=1$. We will demonstrate computation of the Net Profit to Maximum Drawdown Ratio and the Burke Ratio using this function.

$$NPMD = \frac{E_{T_0} - V_0}{MD}.$$

$$Burke_n = \frac{E_{T_0} - V_0}{\left(\dfrac{1}{T} \displaystyle\sum_{i=1}^{n} MD_i^2 \right)^{\frac{1}{2}}}.$$

The High-Frequency Burke Ratio is an attempt at an improvement on the Sharpe Ratio utilizing the squared sum of the n highest drawdowns as a variance metric. These ratios are not highly standardized, so we can use either mean return or total dollar return in the numerator. In Listing 1-6, we will use total dollar return to compare easily with the Net Profit to Max Drawdown Ratio (NPMD Ratio). Additionally, we will use $n=T/20$. We compare the results in Figure 1-5.

Listing 1-6. Maximum Drawdown Ratios

```
NPMD <- (Et[length(Et)] - Vt[1]) / MD(Et)

Burke <- (Et[length(Et)] - Vt[1]) /
        sqrt((1/length(Et)) * sum(MD(Et, n = round(length(Et) / 20))^2))
```

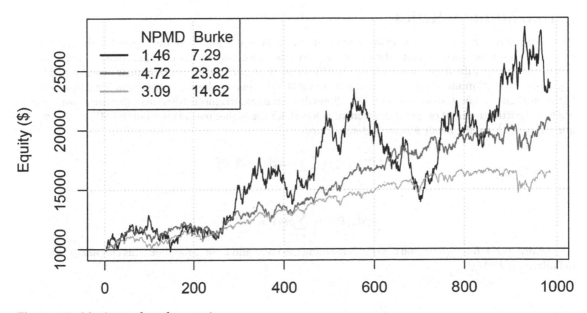

Figure 1-5. *Maximum drawdown ratios*

In Figure 1-5, curve 2, the second most profitable curve, is again the best performer, and by a factor of three against curve 1, the black curve. The NPMD and Burke Ratios are almost exactly proportional for these equity curves. This will not always be the case, especially where we have longer time spans and multiple periods with massive drawdowns. Maximum drawdown ratios address all of the theoretical shortfalls of the Sharpe Ratio in that:

- The denominator penalizes only large losses and ignores all gains.

- Maxima and minima are nonparametric measurements, meaning they make no assumptions about normality or distribution.

- Both the numerator and the denominator standardize against zero.

Issues with maximum drawdown ratios primarily concern robustness and comparison.

- Maximum drawdown ratios tend to over-reward low drawdown simulations by ignoring that a higher maximum drawdown for the given strategy may not have occurred yet. This is a natural consequence of utilizing a single maximum drawdown as opposed to a distributional descriptor of downward spikes.

- maximum drawdown ratios strongly penalize high-variance strategies when compared to low-variance strategies. The Sharpe Ratio for curve 2 is about 50 percent higher than for curve 1, while the NPMD and Burke Ratios for curve 2 are more than three times as high as for curve 1. This is not an issue when we are only attempting to find a maximum, but when comparing two strategies, investors may not see curve 2 as three times better than curve 1.

Partial Moment Ratios

Partial moments are also attempts at improvements on the Sharpe Ratio. They are inspired by the statistical concept of *semi-variance*, meaning the average squared deviations of only observations that are above or below the mean, or the upper semivariance and lower semivariance, respectively. In their mathematical expression, partial moments rely on a *max* function in the summand where one argument is a difference between R_t and R_b and the other is zero. The allows the summand to ignore differences that are above R_b for the lower partial moment or ignore differences below R_b for the higher partial moment (HPM). $LPM_2(\bar{R})$ and $HPM_2(\bar{R})$ are the lower and upper semivariances.

$$LPM_n(R_b) = \frac{1}{T}\sum_{t=1}^{T} max[R_b - R_t, 0]^n.$$

$$HPM_n(R_b) = \frac{1}{T}\sum_{t=1}^{T} max[R_t - R_b, 0]^n.$$

Listing 1-7 defines a function in R for computing the HPM and LPM throughout this chapter. It will default to the $LPM_2(0)$.

Listing 1-7. Partial Moment Function

```
PM <- function(Rt, upper = FALSE, n = 2, Rb = 0){
  if(n != 0){
    if(!upper) return(mean(pmax(Rb - Rt, 0, na.rm = TRUE)^n))
    if(upper) return(mean(pmax(Rt - Rb, 0, na.rm = TRUE)^n))
  } else {
    if(!upper) return(mean(Rb >= Rt))
    if(upper) return(mean(Rt > Rb))
  }
}
```

It is perhaps easier to see through the R code the effects of different degrees of partial moments.

- $n=0$ is the success or shortfall probability for UPM or LPM, respectively. In other words, it is the probability that R_t is greater than R_b for the UPM and is less than R_b for the LPM. It assumes $0^0 = 0$, which is not the case in R, so this is easier to compute as follows:

```
# For LPM
mean(Rb >= Rt)
```

Notice how this is manifest in the function declaration in Listing 1-7. This gives the generalization some mathematical elegance.

- $n=1$ is the mean of returns in excess of R_b or less than R_b, for the UPM and LPM, respectively.

- $n=2$ is the upper or lower semivariance assuming a mean R_b.

- $n=3$ is the upper or lower semiskewness assuming a mean R_b. This is the foundation of Kaplan and Knowles's Kappa(3) developed in 2004, which is equal to $\Omega_3(R_b)$.

The two important partial moment ratios are the Generalized Omega, shown here:

$$\Omega_n(R_b) = \frac{\bar{R} - R_b}{\left(LPM_n(R_b)\right)^{\frac{1}{n}}}$$

and the Upside Potential Ratio, shown here:

$$UPR_{n_1,n_2}(R_b) = \frac{HPM_{n_1}(R_b)^{\frac{1}{n_1}}}{LPM_{n_2}(R_b)^{\frac{1}{n_2}}}$$

The Generalized Omega expressed as $\Omega_2(0)$ is the Improved High-Frequency Sharpe Ratio, or otherwise a high-frequency Sharpe Ratio that utilizes the LPM. It specifically utilizes the $LPM_2(0)$, which is equivalent to the semivariance under the assumption of a mean zero return.

The Upside Potential Ratio uses two degree parameters, n_1 and n_2, for the UPM and LPM, respectively. $UPR_{1,2}(0)$ was developed by Sortino in 1999 and is mathematically similar to the Sortino Ratio, in that it utilizes the mean of positive observations as opposed to the mean of all the observations. $UPR_{2,2}(0)$ is, in my opinion, a robust improvement on Sortino's original ratio. Instead of computing an average return and dividing it by a penalization factor, $UPR_{2,2}(0)$ measures the ratio of positive volatility to negative volatility. It will strongly favor strategies that are able to short a market crash rather than avoid it. Additionally, equal degrees in the numerator and the denominator make it a great candidate for gradient optimizations.

Listing 1-8 computes the Improved High-Frequency Sharpe Ratio (or $\Omega_2(0)$) and the Upside Potential Ratio expressed as $UPR_{2,2}(0)$. Keep in mind the defaults of the partial moment function declared in Listing 1-7 when reading the following code.

Listing 1-8. Partial Moment Ratios

```
Omega <- mean(Rt, na.rm = TRUE) / PM(Rt)^0.5
UPR <- PM(Rt, upper = TRUE)^0.5 / PM(Rt)^0.5
```

See Figure 1-6. Notice that $UPR_{2,2}(0)$ is the first ratio to favor curve 1, the most profitable curve, over curve 2, the second most profitable curve. The many upward spikes in its path contribute to this phenomenon. Per the formulation of the *UPR*, if a catastrophic loss is corrected with a gain of equal magnitude, the ratio will move closer to 1 but not fall below it. Some investors may see this as a desirable quality because it rewards aggressive but calculated risk-taking.

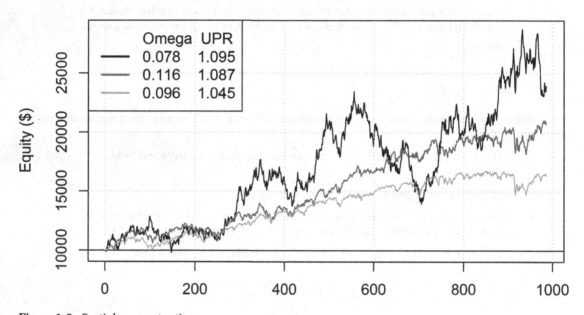

Figure 1-6. *Partial moment ratios*

Regression-Based Performance Metrics

In the spirit of maximizing risk-adjusted return, we seek equity curves that are smooth and linear with a steep upward slope. These three qualities are analogous to low volatility, long-term consistency, and high returns. Linear regressions allow us to fit the best possible straight line through a set of data. Regression-based metrics assess strategy performance allowing us to compare returns between indices and measure the straightness of equity curves.

Jensen's Alpha is a well-known statistic that is the α term in the regression equation

$$R_t = \alpha + \beta R_{t,b} + \varepsilon_t$$

where $R_{t,b}$ is the return of a benchmark, like the S&P 500, at time t. α will represent the y-intercept of the fitted line. It strongly rewards good performance at times when the benchmark is performing badly. In Listing 1-9, when we run the regression, we will also find the β value of the portfolio. This is the same β that is well-known in finance for measuring volatility-scaled correlation between assets. We will not use β for optimizing strategies, but it is interesting nonetheless.

Listing 1-9. Regression Against Benchmark

```
# Scatterplot of Rt against Rb
plot(y = Rt, x = Rb,
     pch = 20,
     cex = 0.5,
     xlab = "SPY Returns",
     ylab= "Return Series 1",
     main = "Figure 1-7: Return Series 1 vs. SPY")
grid()
abline(h = 0)
abline(v = 0)

# Compute and store the regression model
model <- lm(Rt ~ Rb)

# Plot the regression line
abline(model, col = 2)

# Display alpha and beta
legend(x = "topleft", col = c(0,2), lwd = 2,
       legend = c("Alpha Beta R^2",
                  paste0(round(model$coefficients[1], 4), " ",
                         round(model$coefficients[2], 2), " ",
                         round(summary(model)$r.squared, 2))))
```

See Figure 1-7. Because of the symmetric way we randomly generated our equity curves, the α is essentially zero. We built our initial examples by adding a small constant plus a random effect to every return. The regression finds that there is no deliberate avoidance or outperformance of the benchmark index, which is truly the case here.

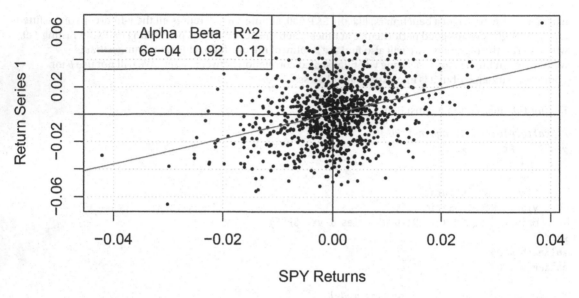

Figure 1-7. *Return series 1 vs. SPY*

We will run the regression again, temporarily adding a small constant to all negative returns to demonstrate how Jensen's Alpha works.

```
# Creates vector of same length without first NA value
RtTemp <- c(0, Rt[-1])
```

```
# Adds 0.01 to all negative values and runs regression
RtTemp[RtTemp < 0] <- RtTemp[RtTemp < 0] + 0.01
model <- lm(RtTemp ~ Rb)
```

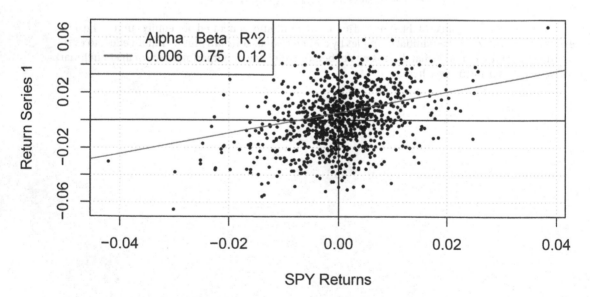

Figure 1-8. *Return series 1 (altered) vs. SPY*

We see in Figure 1-8 that Jensen's Alpha is ten times higher when the strategy is able to reduce the impact of losing days by an average of 1 percent. Jensen's Alpha will prefer risk management on down days to outperformance on good days. Pure Profit Score (PPS) describes risk and return by multiplying the total account return by the R^2 of a regression of a linearized equity curve against time. The equity curve is linearized by dividing it by the tradable account V_t, and time is the integer vector 0, 1,..., T. Note that V_t is constant in our simulation, so linearization is trivial in this case. Listing 1-10 implements the following equations:

$$PPS = \frac{E_{T_0} - V_0}{V_0} R^2$$

$$\frac{E_{t_0}}{V_t} = \alpha + \beta t + \varepsilon_t$$

Listing 1-10. Perfect Profit Score

```
# Create linearized equity curve and run regression
y <- Et / Vt
model <- lm(y ~ t)

# Compute PPS by pulling "r.squared" value from summary function
PPS <- ((Et[length(Et)] - Vt[1]) / Vt[1]) * summary(model)$r.squared
```

Note that in Figure 1-9, α, β, and R^2 refer to summary statistics on the regression between the return series and the SPY returns, as is computed for Jensen's Alpha. *PPS* utilizes the R^2 term from a separate regression between the equity curve and t.

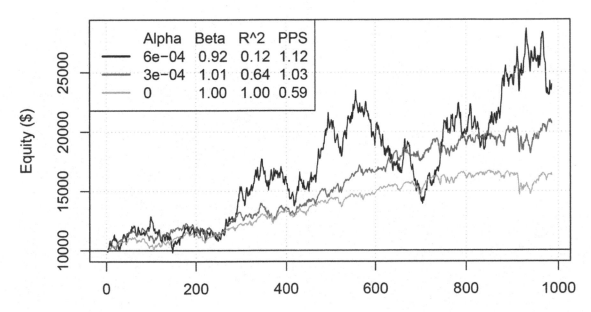

Figure 1-9. *Regression statistics (vs. SPY)*

This is the second metric of many we have covered that favors curve 1 over both curve 2 and the SPY portfolio. Every metric has a different personality. Investors should study them to choose one that is robustly applied and favors their investing style.

Optimizing Performance Metrics

The fundamental goal of trading is to maximize risk-adjusted return. The fundamental goal of strategy development is to build a strategy that maximizes risk-adjusted return during trading. We will accomplish this with cross-validation methods specific to time-series. We simulate lack of knowledge of future stock prices by splitting the data into training and testing sections, with the goal of maximizing the performance metric in the testing section given only the information in the training section.

Chapter 8 will rigorously outline this procedure and make use of the performance metrics covered in this chapter.

PART 2

Building the Platform

CHAPTER 2

■ ■ ■

Networking Part I

In Part 2 of this book, we will be introducing topics in order of appearance in the source code of our trading platform. This chapter will discuss acquisition, storage, and updating of data using free APIs. Our trading platform will contain various processes that run automatically throughout the day, and our data needs to be in our R environment for us to work with it. We may want to run R and RStudio to do unrelated jobs between those times, which means we need a way to store the data in files in our computer so that they can be fetched when the analysis starts. In this chapter, we will explore various ways to fetch, store, and load data. We will ultimately settle on the most efficient method to execute the following algorithm. This algorithm will be referred to as "the algorithm" throughout the chapter.

- Process 1: Initial Acquisition and Storage
    1. Fetch the list of desired stocks.
    2. If all the desired stocks are present in storage directory,
        a. End Process 1 and proceed to Process 2.
    3. If the desired stocks are missing from storage directory,
        a. Fetch missing stock data as far back in time as desired.
        b. Store data on the directory in the drive for access by other processes.
        c. Clear the R environment.
        d. End Process 1 and proceed to Process 2.
- Process 2: Loading Data into Memory (R Environment)
    1. Fetch the names of all files in the storage directory.
    2. Load data from the drive into the R environment.
    3. If data is up to date,
        a. Proceed to step 5.
    4. If data is not up to date,
        a. Fetch missing data.
        b. Append new data to the existing data in the drive.
        c. Append new data to the existing data in the R environment.

C. Conlan, *Automated Trading with R*, DOI 10.1007/978-1-4842-2178-5_2

5. Prepare data in memory.

    a. Compute the date template.

    b. Organize data according to date template.

    c. Organize data in the zoo object with the uniform date attribute.

Yahoo! Finance API

Yahoo! Finance has a popular, simple, and free API for fetching historical stock data. We will learn to use it as an introduction to APIs and assess its feasibility as a data source for our trading platform.

Documentation for the Yahoo! Finance API is becoming increasingly hard to locate as the years go by, leading some longtime users to refer to it as a hidden API. Fortunately, it is straightforward and well-understood by developers with past experience. This section will present a useful but possibly incomplete guide to the Yahoo! Finance historical quote API for CSV data. Yahoo! has not made any express commitments to continue supporting this API, but I have no lack of confidence it will continue to run as it has for more than a decade.

There are many ways to interact with APIs in the world of programming. The Yahoo! Finance CSV API allows us to query a database by supplying and transmitting parameters to a URL. URL-oriented APIs will consist of a base URL followed by a list of parameters starting with a question mark and separated by ampersands. For n parameters represented by p_i and n values represented by v_i

$$\text{API URL} = \text{Base URL} + ? + \text{``}p_1=v_1\text{''} + \& + \text{``}p_2=v_2\text{''} + \& + ... + \& + \text{``}p_n=v_n\text{''}$$

where plus signs represent string concatenation. The Yahoo! Finance historical quote API is outlined in Table 2-1.

Table 2-1. *Yahoo! Finance CSV API*

Component	Example	Argument Notes
Base URL	http://ichart.yahoo.com/table.csv	icharts is a subdomain of yahoo.com that hosts the API.
p_1	s=GOOG	Stock symbol.
p_2	a=5	Zero-indexed month of start date, from 0 to 11.
p_3	b=5	Calendar day of start date, from 1 to 31.
p_4	c=2011	Calendar year of start date.
p_5	d=8	Zero-indexed month of end date.
p_6	e=20	Calendar day of end date.
p_7	f=2012	Calendar year of end date.
p_8	g=d	Frequency. "d" = daily, "w" = weekly, and "m" = monthly.
p_9	ignore=.csv	Static parameter required by API.

Setting Up Directories

Before we get started with code examples in this chapter, it is important that you set up some of the key folders and directories for the platform. Navigate to the proper locations on your computer and create the following:

- A root directory for the project. Mine will be a folder in my home directory.

- A subdirectory of the root for storing .csv files with stock data.

- A subdirectory of the root for storing custom R functions.

Modify Listing 2-1 to store the paths as character variables.

Listing 2-1. Setting Path Variables

```
rootdir <- "~/Platform/"
datadir <- "~/Platform/stockdata/"
functiondir <- "~/Platform/functions/"
```

URL Query Building

The following query URL will call a .csv file of Google stock prices from January 1, 2014, to January 1, 2015: http://ichart.yahoo.com/table.csv?s=GOOG&a=0&b=1&c=2014&d=0&e=1&f=2015&g=w&ignore=. csv. Try following the link on a computer. It will automatically download a .csv file that can be opened with spreadsheet software or any text editor. Our programming challenge is to execute the algorithm automatically in R for many stocks. We will do this by building URL queries in R using string concatenation and accessing many stocks at a time using loops.

Listing 2-2 declares a function that calls the Yahoo! Finance API with a reduced set of parameters based on what we commonly use. Notice that the start date defaults to January 2000 and the ending date has no default. When the parameter *current* evaluates to true, its default, the end date parameters, (d, e, f), are automatically reassigned to the current date. Additionally, we have *tryCatch* to handle errors. If the stock symbol is not found or there is no Internet connection, the function will return NULL. Finally, we make sure to source the function in the functions folder of the root directory. Make sure to create a root directory for the platform and create a functions folder or subdirectory. We will commonly source small R objects and functions for accessibility later.

Listing 2-2. Yahoo! Finance CSV API Function

```
yahoo <- function(sym, current = TRUE,
                  a = 0, b = 1, c = 2000, d, e, f,
                  g = "d")
{
  if(current){
    f <- as.numeric(substr(as.character(Sys.time()), start = 1, stop = 4))
    d <- as.numeric(substr(as.character(Sys.time()), start = 6, stop = 7)) - 1
    e <- as.numeric(substr(as.character(Sys.time()), start = 9, stop = 10))
  }

  require(data.table)
```

```
tryCatch(
suppressWarnings(
fread(paste0("http://ichart.yahoo.com/table.csv",
             "?s=", sym,
             "&a=", a,
             "&b=", b,
             "&c=", c,
             "&d=", d,
             "&e=", e,
             "&f=", f,
             "&g=", g,
             "&ignore=.csv"), sep = ",")),
  error = function(e) NULL
  )
}
```

```
setwd(functiondir)
dump(list = c("yahoo"), "yahoo.R")
```

Running the following code will store a data frame GOOGL in your R environment with Google's daily closing price from 01-01-2000 (MM-DD-YYYY), or when it was first sold, through the current date.

```
GOOGL <- yahoo("GOOGL")
```

Data Acquisition

For Process 1, we want to fetch a list of desired stocks, make sure they are all in a directory, and get them from Yahoo! Finance if they are not present. Listing 2-3 pulls a list of S&P 500 stocks from my web site and converts the list to a character vector.

Listing 2-3. List of S&P 500 Stocks

```
# Up-to-date at time of writing (May 2016)
url <- "http://trading.chrisconlan.com/SPstocks.csv"
S <- as.character(read.csv(url, header = FALSE)[,1])
```

We will save it in our directory so that we do not need to download it again.

```
setwd(rootdir)
dump(list = "S", "S.R")
```

In Listing 2-4, we are going to point R to a directory containing .csv files of stock prices. We will check to see whether the directory contains files with names equal to the vector S with .csv concatenated to it. We will then load the nonmatched files with the Yahoo! Finance API. On the first run-through, all of the files will be missing, and they will all be loaded.

Listing 2-4 also contains a mechanism for checking whether we supplied any invalid stock symbols to R in the character vector S. These will be stored as an R object after execution if the program discovers that the stock has no data in the Yahoo! Finance API. This will help prevent unnecessary API calls in future runs. If the S&P 500 has not been modified since the time of writing, the invalid vector should remain empty.

Listing 2-4. Initial Directory Loader

```
# Load "invalid.R" file if available
invalid <- character(0)
setwd(rootdir)
if("invalid.R" %in% list.files()) source("invalid.R")

# Find all symbols not in directory and not missing
setwd(datadir)
toload <- setdiff(S[!paste0(S, ".csv") %in% list.files()], invalid)

# Fetch symbols with yahoo function, save as .csv or missing
source(paste0(functiondir, "yahoo.R"))
if(length(toload) != 0){
  for(i in 1:length(toload)){

  df <- yahoo(toload[i])

  if(!is.null(df)) {
    write.csv(df[nrow(df):1], file = paste0(toload[i], ".csv"),
              row.names = FALSE)
  } else {
    invalid <- c(invalid, toload[i])
  }
 }
}

setwd(rootdir)
dump(list = c("invalid"), "invalid.R")
```

This marks the end of Process 1. We will clear the R environment and move on to Process 2. We run rm() to remove selected R objects from the environment, but this does not necessarily remove them from memory on our machines. We will run gc(), which stands for *garbage collection*, after rm() to make sure memory occupied by cleared objects is made available.

```
# Clears R environment except for path variables and functions
rm(list = setdiff(ls(), c("rootdir", "functiondir", "datadir", "yahoo")))
gc()
```

Loading Data into Memory

We will be fetching the names of all the files in datadir to load into memory. We will use the package data.table used in the yahoo function to read .csv files quickly. This package provides the fread() function, which has significant speed advantages over read.csv() when .csv files are large and well-formed. Listing 2-5 stores each stock's history as a data frame within a single list, DATA.

The vector S will now represent all the files successfully downloaded into the data directory. Throughout this text, S will be used to represent stocks we have data on as opposed to the full list of May 2016 S&P 500 symbols.

Listing 2-5. Loading Data into Memory

```
setwd(datadir)
S <- sub(".csv", "", list.files())

require(data.table)

DATA <- list()
for(i in S){
  suppressWarnings(
  DATA[[i]] <- fread(paste0(i, ".csv"), sep = ","))
  DATA[[i]] <- (DATA[[i]])[order(DATA[[i]][["Date"]], decreasing = FALSE)]
}
```

The fread() function takes an astonishing six seconds on a home computer to read and organize 200MB of stock data. You may have noticed that we sorted the data by date after loading. This will be important later when we start appending data from different sources.

Note on Coding Style

The coding style of this text is intended to be moderately self-explaining with a few major conventions. We will use all capitals for large lists and data frames, as is the case with the DATA variable in Listing 2-5. Looping variables are lowercase single letters. Scalars and vectors are camel case with the exception of certain major algorithmic objects, which can be single letters for the sake of brevity and legibility. Such is the case with the vector S. All variables, package, names, and classes other than large data objects will be in code font in the text.

Updating Data

Listing 2-6 will check to make sure the data is up to date by checking the most recent date of each symbol. The Yahoo! Finance API updates at about 4:15 p.m. EST after each trading day. This is 40.25 hours away from midnight the day before. Midnight is the default time assigned by R for dates supplied without timestamps. We have supplied dates with a daily resolution, so we consider midnight of the night before as the time of reference. If the difference between the most recent time in our data and the current time is greater than 40.25 hours, then 4:15 p.m. EST of the following day has passed and we update the data.

If readers are in a time zone other than EST, consider adjusting the 40.25 figure to reflect this or running the following to set the default time zone to EST:

```
Sys.setenv(TZ='EST')
```

Additionally, the program checks whether it is the weekend, and there is no new data with the weekend and span Booleans. If both of the days following the most recent day and the current day are weekend days and they are less than 48 hours part, we will consider it the weekend and not update the data. The updating script will effectively prevent meaningless and empty queries by exploiting known behaviors of the API. Logically, this can cause misfires on Mondays during the morning, and more can be done to completely prevent unnecessary calls. Fortunately, eventual automation of this process will altogether eliminate the need for these precautions.

In the case of unnecessary calls, which are occasionally unavoidable, we exploit the ordering of the data and the default response of fread() to ensure no duplicate rows are added to our environment or database. This speeds up the updating process substantially by eliminating the need to computationally verify uniqueness and order.

Listing 2-6. CSV Update Method

```
currentTime <- Sys.time()
for(i in S){
  # Store greatest date within DATA for symbol i
  maxdate <- DATA[[i]][["Date"]][nrow(DATA[[i]])]
  if(as.numeric(difftime(currentTime, maxdate, units = "hours")) >= 40.25){

    # Push the maxdate forward one day
    maxdate <- strptime(maxdate, "%Y-%m-%d") + 86400

    weekend <- sum(c("Saturday", "Sunday") %in%
                     weekdays(c(maxdate, currentTime))) == 2

    span <- FALSE
    if( weekend ){
      span <- as.numeric(difftime(currentTime, maxdate, units = "hours")) >= 48
    }
    if(!weekend & !span){
      c <- as.numeric(substr(maxdate, start = 1, stop = 4))
      a <- as.numeric(substr(maxdate, start = 6, stop = 7)) - 1
      b <- as.numeric(substr(maxdate, start = 9, stop = 10))
      df <- yahoo(i, a = a, b = b, c = c)
      if(!is.null(df)){
        if(all(!is.na(df)) & nrow(df) > 0){
          df <- df[nrow(df):1]
          write.table(df, file = paste0(i, ".csv"), sep = ",",
                      row.names = FALSE, col.names = FALSE, append = TRUE)
          DATA[[i]] <- rbind(DATA[[i]], df)
        }
      }
    }
  }
}
```

We have successfully executed all but the final steps in the algorithm using the Yahoo! Finance API. After running Process 1 once to fill the data directory, our program takes about 15 seconds to check and update the data on a regular day. This is sufficient for most purposes, including programming a trading platform.

With this API, we are limited to stocks on the Yahoo! Finance (most publicly listed U.S. stocks), and we have to perform one web query per stock when loading and updating. Users run the risk of missing stocks if they lose an Internet connection momentarily and the code is large and complex. We will investigate other methods of data acquisition and ultimately combine these components with our Yahoo! Finance API script for a smoother and more secure execution.

YQL Web Service

YQL (Yahoo! Query Language) is a versatile MySQL-style API that streamlines data collection from XML, HTML, and Yahoo!-owned database resources. The goal of YQL is to facilitate general-purpose web scraping. Collection and merging are performed on YQL servers and delivered to the user in XML or JSON.

We will use YQL to update stock data because it has many desirable properties when used to access data internal to Yahoo! We cannot solely rely on YQL to execute Process 1 of the algorithm because it does not allow for large file downloads. To best take advantage of YQL, we will make 5 downloads of about 101 stocks each. YQL tends to throw errors and deliver incomplete data if we request more than 15 trading days at one time (in batches of 101 stocks), so we will use this process with the intention to update the data daily. If the user ever finds he has not updated his stock data for about 10 days, he can use the updating method in Listing 2-6 to bring it up to speed. This decision-making process will be automatically handled in the final source code detailed in Appendix A. Table 2-2 details the structure of the YQL API.

Table 2-2. *YQL API Structure*

Component	Example	Argument Notes
Base URL	http://query.yahooapis.com/ v1/public/yql	The base URL for the free YQL API. Allows for maximum of 20,000 requests per day.
p_1	q=select * from yelp.review. search where term='pizza'	MySQL-style query that accesses a web site or predefined datatables.org resource.
p_2	diagnostics=false	Will YQL include diagnostics in the XML? Often true in testing and false in production.
p_3	env=store://datatables.org/ alltableswithkeys	We specify this argument when accessing a datatables.org predefined table.

URL and Query Building

The URL for this request will be much bigger than ones we sent to fetch .csv data. We will first illustrate with a smaller example. We will focus on construction of the *q* argument. The other arguments are straightforward.

The *q* argument is for a MySQL-like query. It will typically begin with select * from followed by a table name and subsetting arguments. For example, the following

```
base <- "http://query.yahooapis.com/v1/public/yql?"
begQuery <- "q=select * from yahoo.finance.historicaldata where symbol in "
midQuery <- "( 'YHOO', 'GOOGL') "
endQuery <- "and startDate = '2014-01-01' and endDate = '2014-12-31'"
endParams <- "&diagnostics=true&env=store://datatables.org/alltableswithkeys"

urlstr <- paste0(base, begQuery, midQuery, endQuery, endParams)
```

will pull Yahoo! and Google stock prices for the year 2014. Copy and paste urlstr to your browser to see the XML output.

We will use the XML package in R to handle the output. Users familiar with XPath will quickly understand how we pull information from the XML tree downloaded through YQL. XPath is a universal tool, much like regular expressions, used in many programming languages that allows us to access values in an XML tree in a similar fashion to UNIX file paths.

In Listing 2-7, we will programmatically generate midQuery based on the vector S. Through experimentation, we have found that YQL typically cooperates with queries of 120 stocks or less. We will request 101 stocks at a time to account for variability in name length and cover the vector S in five downloads. We sacrifice some flexibility with dates using YQL because we must request the same date range for all 101 stocks. We will find the earliest date in the 101-stock batch no greater than a month from today and discard any duplicates if found.

Listing 2-7. YQL Update Method

```r
setwd(datadir)
library(XML)

currentTime <- Sys.time()

batchsize <- 101

# i in 1:5 for this example
for(i in 1:(ceiling(length(S) / batchsize)) ){

  midQuery <- " ("
  maxdate <- character(0)

startIndex <- ((i - 1) * batchsize + 1)
endIndex <- min(i * batchsize, length(S))

# find earliest date and build query
for(s in S[startIndex:(endIndex - 1)]){
  maxdate <- c(maxdate, DATA[[s]][[1]][nrow(DATA[[s]])])
  midQuery <- paste0(midQuery, "'", s, "', ")
}

maxdate <- c(maxdate, DATA[[S[endIndex]]][[1]]
            [nrow(DATA[[S[endIndex]]])])

startDate <- max(maxdate)

if( startDate <
    substr(strptime(substr(currentTime, 0, 10), "%Y-%m-%d")
          - 28 * 86400, 0, 10) ){
  cat("Query is greater than 20 trading days. Download with csv method.")
  break
}

# Adds a day (86400 seconds) to the earliest date to avoid duplicates
startDate <- substr(as.character(strptime(startDate, "%Y-%m-%d") + 86400), 0, 10)
endDate <- substr(currentTime, 0, 10)

# Yahoo! updates at 4:15 EST at earliest, check if it is past 4:15 day after last
isUpdated <- as.numeric(difftime(currentTime, startDate, units = "hours")) >=
  40.25

# If both days fall in the same weekend, we will not attempt to update
weekend <- sum(c("Saturday", "Sunday") %in%
              weekdays(c(strptime(endDate, "%Y-%m-%d"),
                        c(strptime(startDate, "%Y-%m-%d"))))) == 2

span <- FALSE
if( weekend ){
  span <- as.numeric(difftime(currentTime, startDate, units = "hours")) < 48
}
```

```r
if( startDate <= endDate &
    !weekend &
    !span &
    isUpdated ){

# Piece this extremely long URL together
base <- "http://query.yahooapis.com/v1/public/yql?"
begQuery <- "q=select * from yahoo.finance.historicaldata where symbol in "
midQuery <- paste0(midQuery, "'", S[min(i * batchsize, length(S))], "') ")
endQuery <- paste0("and startDate = '", startDate,
                   "' and endDate = '", endDate, "'")
endParams <- "&diagnostics=true&env=store://datatables.org/alltableswithkeys"

urlstr <- paste0(base, begQuery, midQuery, endQuery, endParams)

# Fetch data and arrange in XML tree
doc <- xmlParse(urlstr)

# The next few lines rely heavily and XPath and quirks
# of S4 objects in the XML package in R.
# We retrieve every node (or branch) on //query/results/quote
# and retrieve the values Date, Open, High, etc. from the branch
df <- getNodeSet(doc, c("//query/results/quote"),
                 fun = function(v) xpathSApply(v,
                                               c("./Date",
                                                 "./Open",
                                                 "./High",
                                                 "./Low",
                                                 "./Close",
                                                 "./Volume",
                                                 "./Adj_Close"),
                                               xmlValue))

# If the URL found data we organize and update
if(length(df) != 0){
# We get the attributes from the same tree, which happen
# to be dates we need
symbols <- unname(sapply(
    getNodeSet(doc, c("//query/results/quote")), xmlAttrs))

df <- cbind(symbols, data.frame(t(data.frame(df, stringsAsFactors = FALSE)),
            stringsAsFactors = FALSE, row.names = NULL))

names(df) <- c("Symbol", "Date",
            "Open", "High", "Low", "Close", "Volume", "Adj Close")

df[,3:8] <- lapply(df[,3:8], as.numeric)
df <- df[order(df[,1], decreasing = FALSE),]

sym <- as.character(unique(df$Symbol))
```

```
for(s in sym){

  temp <- df[df$Symbol == s, 2:8]
  temp <- temp[order(temp[,1], decreasing = FALSE),]

  startDate <- DATA[[s]][["Date"]][nrow(DATA[[s]])]

  DATA[[s]] <- DATA[[s]][order(DATA[[s]][[1]], decreasing = FALSE)]
  DATA[[s]] <- rbind(DATA[[s]], temp[temp$Date > startDate,])
  write.table(DATA[[s]][DATA[[s]][["Date"]] > startDate],
                  file = paste0(s, ".csv"), sep = ",",
                  row.names = FALSE, col.names = FALSE, append = TRUE)
}
}
}
}
```

Listing 2-7 accomplishes the same updating procedure as Listing 2-6, but instead of making 500 data requests, it makes 5. It is much less prone to failure by connection loss but spends more time organizing data. As long as we are capable of using YQL, we will continue using it to help reduce traffic to Yahoo! and speed up our platform.

Note on Quantmod

Quantmod is a popular package for pulling historical stock prices from Yahoo! Finance and other APIs, including Google Finance and Bloomberg.

As a general programming paradigm, developers sacrifice flexibility by relying on prebuilt packages. In this section, we will discuss why Quantmod was considered but not chosen as a financial data management tool for our platform.

Background

Quantmod is a staple in academia. It is convenient for a classroom of students who are not necessarily R experts to be able to download finance data with a single line of code. Quantmod was designed specifically for this purpose.

```
getSymbols(c("SPY"), from = "2012-01-01")
```

Comparison

Unfortunately, academic time-series analysis has a tendency to analyze single series or small groups of series rather than hundreds at a time. Consequently, Quantmod was built without consideration for robust batch-fetching of stock data. If you run the previous line of code, you will see that Quantmod loads the data, converts it to an xts object, and then assigns it the variable SPY. Auto-assignment can be turned off for single-stock requests, but it will be required if we pull multiple stocks. This forces us to completely forfeit our ability to organize data and access it programmatically through lists and data frames.

If we were to attempt to execute the algorithm using Quantmod, we would end up with 500 separate variables in our R environment. Additionally, it would force us to pause for one second between each request. This is Quantmod's way of being courteous to Yahoo! We have gone a step above in speed and courtesy by utilizing YQL for updating. To illustrate how Quantmod completes 5 percent of our workload, you can run the following line of code:

```
getSymbols(S[1:25], from = "2000-01-01)
```

If an error related to auto.assign is thrown, it may have been altered from its default value of TRUE through the options() function. Specify auto.assign = TRUE in the previous function call to remedy this.

Organizing as Date-Uniform zoo Object

This is the last step in executing the algorithm. We want to allow our platform to pull data and run strategies for a multitude of symbols in any number of countries, so we need to make sure the dates line up and account for days off in each respective country. Listing 2-8 will use the merge function to accomplish this. This function is computationally expensive, so we will attempt to save time by checking whether the dates already match before using it. In the case where all the symbols being analyzed are on major American stock exchanges, we will not utilize the merge function because the dates will already match.

Listing 2-8. Organizing as Date-Uniform zoo Object

```
library(zoo)

# Compute the date template as a column of a data.frame for merging
# Considers date are strings in YYYY-MM-DD format
datetemp <- sort(unique(unlist(sapply(DATA, function(v) v[["Date"]]))))
datetemp <- data.frame(datetemp, stringsAsFactors = FALSE)
names(datetemp) <- "Date"

# Double-check that our data is unique and in ascending-date order
DATA <- lapply(DATA, function(v) unique(v[order(v$Date),]))

# Create 6 new objects that will hold our re-organized data
DATA[["Open"]] <- DATA[["High"]] <- DATA[["Low"]] <-
  DATA[["Close"]] <- DATA[["Adj Close"]] <- DATA[["Volume"]] <- datetemp

# This loop will sequentially append the columns of each symbol
# to the appropriate Open, High, Low, etc. object
for(s in S){
  for(i in rev(c("Open", "High", "Low", "Close", "Adj Close", "Volume"))){
    temp <- data.frame(cbind(DATA[[s]][["Date"]], DATA[[s]][[i]]),
                       stringsAsFactors = FALSE)
    names(temp) <- c("Date", s)
    temp[,2] <- as.numeric(temp[,2])

    if(!any(!DATA[[i]][["Date"]][(nrow(DATA[[i]]) - nrow(temp)+1):nrow(DATA[[i]])]
           == temp[,1])){
      temp <- rbind(t(matrix(nrow = 2, ncol = nrow(DATA[[i]]) - nrow(temp),
                             dimnames = list(names(temp)))), temp)
```

```
        DATA[[i]] <- cbind(DATA[[i]], temp[,2])
      } else {
        DATA[[i]] <- merge(DATA[[i]], temp, all.x = TRUE, by = "Date")
      }

      names(DATA[[i]]) <- c(names(DATA[[i]])[-(ncol(DATA[[i]]))], s)
    }
    DATA[[s]] <- NULL

    # Update user on progress
    if( which( S == s ) %% 25 == 0 ){
      cat( paste0(round(100 * which( S == s ) / length(S), 1), "% Complete\n") )
    }

}

# Declare them as zoo objects for use with time-series functions
DATA <- lapply(DATA, function(v) zoo(v[,2:ncol(v)], strptime(v[,1], "%Y-%m-%d")))
# Remove extra variables
rm(list = setdiff(ls(), c("DATA", "datadir", "functiondir", "rootdir")))
```

Note on zoo Objects

The zoo package and corresponding zoo class is one of the options we have for manipulating time-series data in R. Other options include the xts class and the ts class from their respective packages. We use zoo because it is a minimal format that affixes and maintains a vector of dates to time-series data. The vector of dates is necessary to declare the zoo object. From then on, the object ensures that the output of functions digesting it are also zoo objects with proper, ordered, and row-unique date assignment.

There are natural consequences to the safety of the zoo class. For example, manually adding two elements of a zoo object (with a plus sign) will return an empty numeric value, numeric(0), because it is seen as an illegal operation. We will rarely have to do this, because we will primarily rely on time-series functions to handle our data. In the case that we intend to perform such illegal operations, we can wrap the call to the zoo object in as.numeric() to alleviate this. We will do this frequently in our simulation algorithm in Chapter 7.

CHAPTER 3

■ ■ ■

Data Preparation

In this chapter, we will discuss ways of cleaning data to make analysis faster and more effective. Additionally, we will compute some new data sets we will need in our analysis. For this chapter, you should have the final results of the list DATA and the three directory variables from the previous chapter in your R environment. This list DATA contains 6 zoo objects rather than 500+ stock symbols.

Handling NA Values

There are a handful of specific reasons why a certain stock may have *NA* values on any given day. We want to diagnose and treat these reasons appropriately to ensure the validity of our simulation results.

Note: NA vs. NaN in R

The *NA* value in R means *not applicable*. It is of functional importance because it allows us to denote where data is missing, intentionally or otherwise.

The *NaN* value in R typically arises as a result of failed or impossible computations in R. The value *NaN* stands for *not a number*. It is more related to the native R values Inf and -Inf than to the *NA* value. According to R, for any positive scalar a, $\frac{a}{0} = Inf$, $\frac{0}{0} = NaN$, and $\frac{-a}{0} = -Inf$, and it will output them as such.

This section will concern itself with the *NA* value and not the *NaN* value. We will create solutions for handling accidental impossible calculations in our source code as the need arises.

IPOs and Additions to S&P 500

We need to observe and know our data to determine why *NA*s are present and how to best handle them. Let's start by observing the symbol KORS. Michael Kors is a luxury fashion brand that has gained significant popularity in recent years. It went public in December 2011 and was added to the S&P 500 in November 2013. Our data, and the preview given in Table 3-1, should have *NA* values in all of the days prior to its IPO on December 15, 2011.

© Chris Conlan 2016

C. Conlan, *Automated Trading with R*, DOI 10.1007/978-1-4842-2178-5_3

Table 3-1. *KORS Pre-IPO Data*

Date	Open	High	Low	Close	Volume
2011-12-12	NA	NA	NA	NA	NA
2011-12-13	NA	NA	NA	NA	NA
2011-12-14	NA	NA	NA	NA	NA
2011-12-15	25.00	25.23	23.51	24.20	42259200
2011-12-16	24.45	24.80	23.51	24.10	3998900
2011-12-19	24.50	25.09	24.31	24.88	3245500

It is important to consider that companies are usually included in the S&P 500 many years after their IPOs because they are required to meet many liquidity, domicile, and ownership criteria. Most notably, companies are required to have a $5.3 billion minimum market capitalization. This means that companies often join the S&P 500 as a result of growth and success. Simulating trading strategies with only *current* S&P 500 members biases results by ensuring that, as of the date of simulation, all of the companies have survived enough to maintain their membership in the S&P 500.

Small companies that enjoyed substantial post-IPO growth are likely to have reached the $5.3 billion market capitalization threshold through growth in share value. Including their pre-S&P performance would unfairly bias the simulation by introducing the knowledge that a then-small company will have a market cap greater than $5.3 billion in the future.

To remedy this, we will make sure only to simulate trading on post-inclusion performance. Ideally, we would like to have data on every stock ever in the S&P 500 and include each stock only when active in the index. Unfortunately, many of these old members' data streams are deprecated and incomplete in Yahoo! Finance.

Based on these facts, we have made the calculated decision to adjust for inclusion dates but not pursue historical data for previous members of the S&P 500. The drivers for this decision are index rules and data availability, as discussed. This plan of action makes considerable efforts to reduce bias arising from inclusion of future knowledge but does not fully absolve itself of such bias. If you are using another data source or extending the platform, you are encouraged to research asset indices and grouping criteria used in asset selection to best eliminate bias arising from inclusion of future knowledge.

History on inclusion in the index is scattered and incomplete throughout the Web. My best attempts to compile a useful inclusion history found that many reputable sources have published incomplete and conflicting data for stocks not active in the index or added to the index before the late 1990s. I was able to compile a mostly complete and practically accurate list of "addition dates" for stocks currently in the index. Utilizing this data set will help us eliminate the most bias possible from our simulations.

Listing 3-1 converts all values occurring before addition to the S&P to *NA* values. Missing dates are listed as 1/1/1900 and default to inclusion throughout. Our data reaches as far back as January 1, 2000, so symbols with dates prior to this default to inclusion throughout.

Listing 3-1. Eliminating Pre-S&P Data

```
setwd(rootdir)

if( "SPdates.R" %in% list.files() ){
  source("SPdates.R")
} else {
  url <- "http://trading.chrisconlan.com/SPdates.csv"
  S <- read.csv(url, header = FALSE, stringsAsFactors = FALSE)
```

```
    dump(list = "S", "SPdates.R")
}

names(S) <- c("Symbol", "Date")
S$Date <- strptime(S$Date, "%m/%d/%Y")
for(s in names(DATA[["Close"]])){
  for(i in c("Open", "High", "Low", "Close", "Adj Close", "Volume")){
    Sindex <- which(S[,1] == s)
    if(S[Sindex, "Date"] != "1900-01-01 EST" &
       S[Sindex, "Date"] >= "2000-01-01 EST"){
         DATA[[i]][index(DATA[[i]]) <= S[Sindex, "Date"], s] <- NA
       }
  }
}
```

This process overwrites a lot of data and will take a few minutes. If you want to make sure the process is proceeding, you can insert print(s) into the loop between the last two curly braces. In the final source code, this step will be executed as part of the fetching and updating procedure, significantly speeding it up.

Merging to the Uniform Date Template

In the previous chapter, we made sure to design our data fetching and updating algorithms to be able to handle multiple stocks from multiple countries with different trading schedules. If we had stocks in, say, the United States and Japan, there would be missing values in nonoverlapping trading days. Conventionally, there are a few ways to address this. We will discuss the following:

- Forward replacement

- Linearly smoothed replacement

- Volume-weighted smoothed replacement

- Doing nothing

Forward replacement involves taking each NA value and replacing it with the entry before it, starting at the earliest date and moving forward. Linearly smoothed replacement involves drawing a straight line from the prior nonmissing value to the following. Volume-weighted smoothed replacement takes the two nearest points generated in linearly smoothed replacement and weights them by the volumes of the nearest nonmissing days. We will discuss the case for doing nothing with the missing values.

We will simulate a ten-day period of KORS where we pretend we need to fill in prices on Thanksgiving 2015 and the following Black Friday weekend. Listing 3-2 declares our temporary zoo data frame temp for this discussion.

Listing 3-2. Declaring Temporary Data for Discussion

```
temp <- c(DATA[["Close"]][index(DATA[["Close"]]) %in% c("2015-11-23",
                                                        "2015-11-24",
                                                        "2015-11-25"), "KORS"],
          zoo(NA, order.by = strptime("2015-11-26", "%Y-%m-%d")) ,
          DATA[["Close"]][index(DATA[["Close"]]) %in% c("2015-11-27"), "KORS"],
          zoo(NA, order.by = strptime(c("2015-11-28", "2015-11-29"), "%Y-%m-%d")),
          DATA[["Close"]][index(DATA[["Close"]]) %in% c("2015-11-30",
                                                        "2015-12-01",
                                                        "2015-12-02"), "KORS"])
```

Forward Replacement

The forward replacement function will check whether a missing value is present in the last element of a vector and replace it with the most recent nonmissing value. In Listing 3-3, we will be passing this function to rollapply(), which treats a vector of length n as $n–k$ slices of length k and cycles through them applying the function. We need to specify the variable maxconsec as one plus the maximum number of consecutive NAs we expect in the data. It is generally faster to specify a value a little too high than to compute the maximum number of NAs. Figure 3-1 shows the effects of forward replacement.

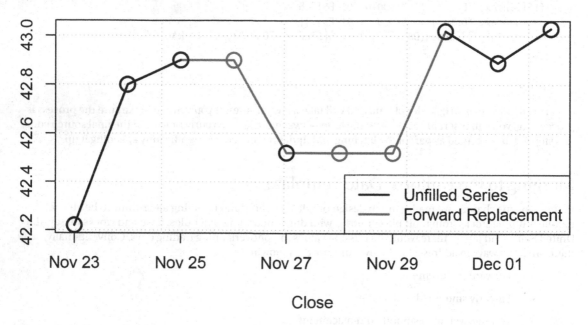

Figure 3-1. *Forward replacement*

We discuss the details of NA handling by rollapply() in later chapters. For now it is worth noting that the first *width*–1=*maxconsec*–1 elements will be missing from the output when we specify align = "right". This means that the full data set desired from the replacement methods we discuss is attained by overlaying the rollapply() output on the NA values of the existing data.

Listing 3-3. Forward Replacement Function

```
# Forward replacement function
forwardfun <- function(v, n) {
  if(is.na(v[n])){
    return(v[max(which(!is.na(v)))])
  } else {
    return(v[n])
  }
}

maxconsec <- 3

# We pass maxconsec to rollapply() in "width = "
# and pass it again to forwardfun() in "n = "
```

```
forwardrep <- rollapply(temp,
            width = maxconsec,
            FUN = forwardfun,
            n = maxconsec,
            by.column = TRUE,
            align = "right")
```

Linearly Smoothed Replacement

For linearly smoothed replacement, maxconsec must be odd and greater than the maximum number of consecutive NAs plus two. In our example, that is five. Listing 3-4 implements linearly smoothed replacement. Figure 3-2 shows the effects of linear and volume-weighted smoothed replacement side by side.

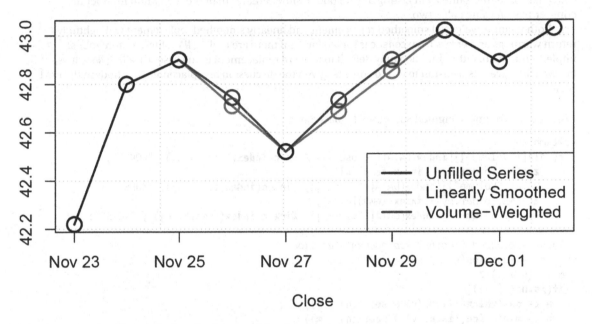

Figure 3-2. *Linearly smoothed and volume-weighted replacement*

Listing 3-4. Linearly Smoothed Replacement

```
# Linearly Smoothed Replacement Function
linearfun <- function(v, n){
  m <- (n + 1)/2
  if(is.na(v[m])){
    a <- max(which(!is.na(v) & seq(1:n) < m))
    b <- min(which(!is.na(v) & seq(1:n) > m))
    return(((b - m)/(b - a)) * v[a] +
           ((m - a)/(b - a)) * v[b])
  } else {
    return(v[m])
  }
}
```

```
maxconsec <- 5
linearrep <- rollapply(temp,
          width = maxconsec,
          FUN = linearfun,
          n = maxconsec,
          by.column = TRUE,
          align = "center")
```

Volume-Weighted Smoothed Replacement

To study volume-weighted smoothing, we will declare a variable containing the KORS volume from the same time period. Listing 3-5 implements volume-weighted smoothed replacement. We specify maxconsec here the same as in Listing 3-4: an odd number greater than the maximum number of consecutive NA values plus two.

Both volume-weighted smoothed replacement and linearly smoothed replacement will rightfully return warnings and errors if maxconsec is set too low or if there are trailing NA values. A more robust implementation of either function may default to forward replacement in the case of trailing NA values, but we will leave this decision to you to consider given the discussion of replacement methods in the next section.

Listing 3-5. Volume-Weighted Smoothed Replacement

```
voltemp <-
  c(DATA[["Volume"]][index(DATA[["Close"]]) %in% c(index(temp)[1:3]), "KORS"],
      zoo(NA, order.by = index(temp)[4]),
      DATA[["Volume"]][index(DATA[["Close"]]) %in% c(index(temp)[5]), "KORS"],
      zoo(NA, order.by = index(temp)[6:7]),
      DATA[["Volume"]][index(DATA[["Close"]]) %in% c(index(temp[8:10])), "KORS"])

# Volume-Weighted Smoothed Replacement Function
volfun <- function(v, n, vol){
  m <- (n + 1)/2
  if(is.na(v[m])){
    a <- max(which(!is.na(v) & seq(1:n) < m))
    b <- min(which(!is.na(v) & seq(1:n) > m))
    return(((v[a] + ((m-a-1)/(b-a)) * (v[b] - v[a])) * vol[a] +
            (v[a] + ((m-a+1)/(b-a)) * (v[b] - v[a])) * vol[b]) /
              (vol[a] + vol[b]))
  } else {
    return(v[m])
  }
}

maxconsec <- 5
volrep <- rollapply(cbind(temp, voltemp),
          width = maxconsec,
          FUN = function(v) volfun(v[,1], n = maxconsec, v[,2]),
          by.column = FALSE,
          align = "center")
```

Discussion of Replacement Methods

Why, in general, might we want to use or avoid certain replacement methods? Which one will help us generate the most accurate simulation results?

Real Time vs. Simulation

Remember that we replace missing values to facilitate comparison between stocks that are traded on different schedules. We want to interpolate price movement in the untraded asset to compare it to the traded asset in both simulation and real-time trading. In this sense, forward replacement is advantageous because it is the only replacement method we discussed that can be computed in both situations.

Running simulations on data that depends on future price movements invalidates simulation results by introducing future information. Even in cases where using future information in simulations does not introduce a drastic bias, the results of the simulation are not reproducible in real time simply because we do not have access to future information in real-time trading.

Forward replacement requires no knowledge of future prices and has practical applications in correcting for certain data anomalies that affect simulation and execution. We will discuss this later in the chapter to correct for symbol deprecation of unknown cause.

Influence on Volatility Metrics

Volatility metrics are generally measured as the mean of a function of changes in asset price. For example, sample variance $\hat{\sigma}^2$ is the mean of squared deviations from the sample mean,

$$\hat{\sigma}^2 = \frac{\sum_{i=1}^{n}(r_i - \overline{r})^2}{n-1} \, ,$$

where r_i represents asset returns and $\overline{r}$ represents the sample mean, typically assumed to be zero for our purposes.

Any smoothing method we use will place a downward bias on volatility metrics by doing the following:

- Increasing the denominator by increasing the number of trading days

- Decreasing the numerator by substituting single larger price changes for many smaller price changes

Linearly smoothed replacement and volume-weighted smoothed replacement will have a strong influence on the numerator because they smooth price changes. Forward replacement will not smooth price changes and therefore will not change the value of the numerator. All of our replacement methods will increase the denominator by adding trading days. This is a case where doing nothing is the best option to preserve the validity of volatility metrics.

Table 3-2 illustrates this concept using our KORS sample. Returns used this example are computed as percentages as opposed to decimals for clarity.

Table 3-2. *Smoothing Effects on Volatility Metrics*

Method	$\sum(r_i - \overline{r})^2$	$n-1$	$\hat{\sigma}^2$
Doing nothing	4.307	5	0.861
Forward replacement	4.307	8	0.538
Linearly smoothed	2.991	8	0.374
Volume-weighted	3.028	8	0.378

Variance metrics are calculated frequently in both indicators and performance metrics. It is easy to see how introducing smoothing bias into variance metrics could corrupt indicators that depend on them like Bollinger Bands and Rolling Sharpe Ratios.

Influence on Trading Decisions

If we smooth prices and simulate trading decisions, we run the risk of triggering trades on days where the asset does not trade, effectively invalidating simulation results. We can programmatically adjust for this, but it will prove to be unnecessarily complicated for our platform. Working this functionality into our platform would require us to keep a parallel data set with Boolean values corresponding to tradable and untradable days. This would be a large memory sacrifice and would add numerous table lookups to our code.

Conclusion

The R language has great facilities for handling NA values. Many important functions have na.rm = TRUE options that allow the user to compute means, medians, standard deviations, and more, with the NA values removed and denominators automatically adjusted. Doing nothing to the NA values will allow R to handle them and serve as a reminder that assets are not to be traded on these days.

In the spirit of maintaining valid data and simulation results, forward replacement and doing nothing are the only correct ways to go. In the spirit of practicality within the R language, we will be *doing nothing* to the NA values discussed in this section.

In the special case where a stock symbol has ceased trading because of a merger, acquisition, or bankruptcy, the data will show NA values from the last trading day until the present. We will use forward replacement to simulate the ability to exit at the final price at any time.

Closing Price and Adjusted Close

It is common in financial literature to use the closing price only when working with discrete-time fixed-frequency data. This holds for indicators, rule sets, and performance metrics. If a reader sees y_t indiscriminately named in financial mathematics, he can safely assume it is referring to the closing price. In the same situation, a reader can safely assume r_t refers to returns or percentage changes of the closing price.

When studying historical stock data, it is often assumed that the reader has adjusted his data for stock splits. It is less often assumed in academic literature that the reader has adjusted for cash dividends. (The famous Black-Scholes model includes dividends as a variable distinct from price.) These are simple and logical transformations of the original closing price series, but they require additional data. In our use case, we study a basket of both dividend-paying and non-dividend-paying stocks, so it is logical for us to adjust for splits and dividends rather than define them separately.

Yahoo! Finance includes an Adj Close variable to handle these adjustments, but it applies only to closing prices. There are no adjusted opens, adjusted highs, or adjusted lows. Interestingly enough, Yahoo! has already adjusted volume to account for splits. The transformation is fairly straightforward. We simply multiply Open, High, and Low of each symbol by the ratio of Adj Close to Close for that stock and then discard Close and use Adj Close in its place. Adj Close more accurately represents the investment value of a stock, rather than its nominal price, as depicted in Figure 3-3.

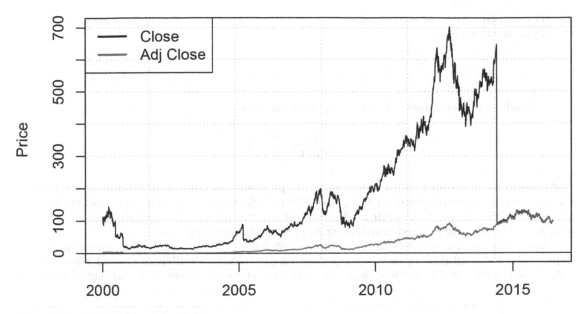

***Figure 3-3.** AAPL close vs. adjusted closee*

Adjusting for Stock Splits

Companies will split their stock for a variety of reasons. It is important to know that, no matter the reason, a stock split does not directly affect the market capitalization of the company or the value of any individual's equity investment in the company.

An $n:m$ split awards shareholders n shares for every m held, increasing the number of outstanding shares by a factor of $\frac{n}{m}$ and fixing the next morning's opening price at $\frac{m}{n}$ of the previous day's closing

price. The financial impact of a stock split is to effectively change nothing but the unit price of the stock.

There are hotly debated corporate motives and psychological impacts of stock splits. The news of a stock split could, in itself, imply or affirm some projections about a company and the state of its stock. For the purposes of simulating portfolios, we want to retroactively adjust prices to give the appearance that splits never happened. In doing this, we differentiate the *numerical* value of a stock price and the *investment* value of a company.

Yahoo! factors splits into Adj Close by multiplying the closing price presplit by $\frac{m}{n}$. We will use the ratio

of Adj Close to Close to find splits, and if a split occurs at time t, we multiply Open, High, and Low by the ratio $\frac{m}{n}$ for $0,...,(t-1)$. Yahoo! has already adjusted volume for splits by multiplying by $\frac{n}{m}$ for $0,...,(t-1)$ to

adjust for the change in total outstanding shares.

We will implement this algorithm in R in conjunction with our dividend adjustment algorithm in Listing 3-6.

Adjusting for Cash Dividends

Companies often give cash dividends on annual or quarterly bases. These companies are typically large and mature, and they believe stocks should represent a proportional claim not only on assets but on earnings. We want to adjust our data to reflect a per-share increase in cash or investable capital without having to keep track of historical cash distributions.

If a company makes a distribution of d dollars per share at time t, Yahoo! has adjusted prices in $0,...,(t-1)$ by a factor of

$$c = 1 - \frac{d}{Close_{t-1}}.$$

In simulation, moving from $(t-1)$ to t, the adjusted data shows

$$r_t = \left(\frac{1}{c} * \frac{Close_t}{Close_{t-1}} \right) - 1$$

on the date of the distribution, where $Close_t$ refers to the price before adjustment. This simulates immediate reinvestment of dividends in the distributing stock. This behavior cannot be guaranteed in real time, but it allows us to account for distributions in a sufficiently realistic manner. We will not adjust volume as we did with stock splits because dividends do not affect the number of outstanding shares.

Accounting for dividends and splits simultaneously produces a stepwise adjustment factor with large steps at splits and small quarterly steps during periods of regular dividend distribution. Figure 3-4 shows the ratio of Close to Adjusted Close, or the inverse of the adjustment factor, for Yahoo!, Ford, and Bank of America.

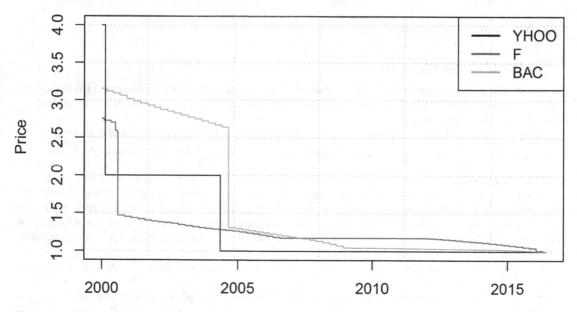

Figure 3-4. *Ratio of Close to Adjusted Close*

Efficient Updating and Adjusted Close

Based on our discussion of Yahoo! Finance adjustments and the purpose of the adjusted close, we know the following:

- The adjusted close at time T, the current time, is equal to the close at time T. In other words, the adjusted close is scaled against the close of T for any t in $0,...,T$.

- A split or dividend at time t affects the value of adjusted close of $0,...,(t-1)$.

This is a problem for our data management system because it makes efficiency gains through incremental downloading and appending within the data directory. If a dividend or split occurs on a stock, the adjusted close values in our data directory become invalid and useless. Simply put, a dividend or split in 2016 propagates through the adjusted close in 2015, 2014, 2013, and so on.

We must make a sacrifice in efficiency to ensure the validity of our data. We will modify our updating procedure in the final source code to download a few extra days of data and check for equality in the adjusted price against the stored data. If a symbol is found to have an unequal adjusted price, we will use a slight modification of Listing 2-6 to download the entire price history from January 1, 2000. Please see the updateStocks.R script in Appendix A to view the changes.

Implementing Adjustments

Some things are extremely easy in R. We will take advantage of R's ability to multiply matrices and data frames with the same dimensionality quickly in straightforward code. In Listing 3-6, we will be processing and writing well over 100MB of new data in about 1.3 seconds on a single computer core. We will be saving the numeric values of Close in a new variable, Price, for use in calculating order sizes in broker communication.

Listing 3-6. Adjusting OHLC Data

```
# Declare new zoo data frame of adjustment factors
MULT <- DATA[["Adj Close"]] / DATA[["Close"]]

# Store Close and Open Prices in new variable "Price" and "OpenPrice"
DATA[["Price"]] <- DATA[["Close"]]
DATA[["OpenPrice"]] <- DATA[["Open"]]

# Adjust Open, High, and Low
DATA[["Open"]] <- DATA[["Open"]] * MULT
DATA[["High"]] <- DATA[["High"]] * MULT
DATA[["Low"]] <- DATA[["Low"]] * MULT

# Copy Adjusted Close to Close
DATA[["Close"]] <- DATA[["Adj Close"]]

# Delete Adjusted Close
DATA[["Adj Close"]] <- NULL
```

We now have seven variables in our DATA list, adjusted Open, adjusted High, adjusted Low, adjusted Close, adjusted Volume, unadjusted Close, and unadjusted Open. We delineate the unadjusted Close and Open by calling Price and OpenPrice, respectively. Unadjusted Close and Open are being kept for use in order execution, account management, and performance assessment in the future.

Test for and Correct Inactive Symbols

For example, we found it beneficial to perform forward replacement on trailing *NA* values resulting from symbol deprecation. Symbol deprecation occurs often in mergers and acquisitions. Forward replacement of trailing *NA* values simulates the shareholder's ability to exit his position at the final closing price, as is the case with mergers and acquisitions.

As mentioned in our discussion of replacement methods, forward replacement has practical applications in correcting for certain data anomalies. We will perform forward replacement on trailing *NA* values, as this represents inactivity of the symbol due to corporate action. This simulates the shareholder's ability to exit his position at the final closing price, as is the case with most corporate action resulting in symbol deprecation. These corporate actions are mainly mergers and acquisitions but can extend to more exotic equity transfers. Listing 3-7 will walk backward in time on each symbol and perform forward replacement if it determines a symbol to be inactive. While transfers of deprecated symbols can still occur privately, setting the volume as zero post-deprecation is the most logically consistent considering the account standards of corporate actions and the effect desired in volume-dependent computations.

Listing 3-7. Forward Replacement on Inactive Symbols

```
for( s in names(DATA[["Close"]]) ){
  if(is.na(DATA[["Close"]][nrow(DATA[["Close"]]), s])){
    maxInd <- max(which(!is.na(DATA[["Close"]][,s])))
    for( i in c("Close", "Open", "High", "Low")){
      DATA[[i]][(maxInd+1):nrow(DATA[["Close"]]),s] <- DATA[["Close"]][maxInd,s]
    }
    for( i in c("Price", "OpenPrice") ){
      DATA[[i]][(maxInd+1):nrow(DATA[["Close"]]),s] <- DATA[["Price"]][maxInd,s]
    }
    DATA[["Volume"]][(maxInd+1):nrow(DATA[["Close"]]),s] <- 0
  }
}
```

Computing the Return Matrix

There are a number of reasons we will need to utilize the return matrix in our simulation and optimization. It is best to compute it in advance and save it for later use.

Note that the return matrix is markedly different (and much simpler) than the return series discussed in Chapter 1. The return matrix will simply be a matrix consisting of every daily return for each stock in our series. We will only compute on the adjusted close for stock prices.

We define the return on asset *j* at time *t* to be

$$r_{t,j} = \frac{y_{t,j} - y_{(t-1),j}}{y_{(t-1),j}} = \frac{y_{t,j}}{y_{(t-1),j}} - 1$$

where $y_{t,j}$ is the price of asset *j* and time *t*.

Listing 3-8 will use the base R functionality lag( ), which moves every element of a time series back *k* spots in a data set. Dividing the original data set by the lagged data and subtracting one gives the return matrix. Be wary of what "back" means. Time-series data sets in some R functions are assumed to be in decreasing-time order. Our data is in increasing-time order, so we will specify the argument *k*=-1 to get the reverse effect.

We will also compute overnight returns to help us simulate purchasing in the morning and selling in the afternoon as a strategy option.

Listing 3-8. Computing Return Matrices

```
# Pad with NAs to preserve dimension equality
NAPAD <- zoo(matrix(NA, nrow = 1, ncol = ncol(DATA[["Close"]])),
             order.by = index(DATA[["Close"]])[1])
names(NAPAD) <- names(DATA[["Close"]])

# Compute Daily Close-to-Close Returns
RETURN <- rbind( NAPAD, ( DATA[["Close"]] / lag(DATA[["Close"]], k = -1) ) - 1 )

# Compute Overnight Returns (Close-to-Open)
OVERNIGHT <- rbind( NAPAD, ( DATA[["Open"]] / lag(DATA[["Close"]], k = -1) ) - 1 )
```

CHAPTER 4

■ ■ ■

Indicators

Indicators are at heart of the trading strategy. They make it unique and profitable. They can be single computations or a long series of analyses.

Many technically focused trading platforms like TradeStation, Metatrader, and Interactive Brokers handle all of the data management and let the user select from a list of common and customizable indicators. These platforms typically emphasize visualization rather than computation. We are handling our own data management because we want to compute indicators over many symbols and assess them numerically rather than visually.

Computing indicators efficiently over batches of symbols in R requires a lot of familiarity with rollapply(). We will give many examples of common indicators implemented this way to make sure you are comfortable using it. Additionally, we will demonstrate how to change indicators outside of the rollapply() function by including function declarations and parameters at the head of documents.

Indicator Types

Indicators have broad classifications related to how they are best visualized and what kinds of rule sets tend to work well with them. We discuss these in this section.

Overlays

Overlays are best characterized by their scale. Overlays typically have the same or similar scale to the underlying asset and are meant to be laid over to chart of price history. Common examples are the simple moving average, Bollinger Bands, and volume-weighted average price. Overlays are commonly computed as the average of something added to a deviation of some form, or the price of the asset added to a curve of some form.

Rule sets often concentrate on the prices interaction with the overlay or the overlay's interaction with components of itself. Here's an example: *If price rises above the simple moving average, buy the stock at market price.*

Oscillators

Oscillators are also best characterized by their scale. Oscillators typically oscillate around zero. Common examples are the MACD, Stochastic Oscillator, and RSI. These are typically plotted below the price history in charts because they do not share scale with it.

Rule sets typically concentrate around the indicator's interaction with the zero line or other components of itself. Here's an example: *If the MACD rises above zero, buy the stock at market price.*

© Chris Conlan 2016
C. Conlan, *Automated Trading with R*, DOI 10.1007/978-1-4842-2178-5_4

Accumulators

Accumulators depend on the value of itself in past periods to calculate future values. This is different from most indicators that depend only on price history, not indicator history. They have the advantage of being window-length independent in that the user does not specify any n periods in the past to be computed. This is an advantage purely on the level of robustness and mathematical elegance. They are very often volume-oriented. Examples are On-Balance Volume, Negative Volume Index, and the Accumulation/Distribution Line.

Rule sets typically concentrate on the relationship between the accumulator and an average or maximum of itself. Here's an example: *If the Negative Volume Index crosses above a moving average of itself, buy the stock at market price.*

Pattern/Binary/Ternary

Pattern indicators are classic technical indicators like the head-and-shoulders. They involve detecting some pattern in the data and triggering a trading signal if found. When we are detecting these patterns with computers, these indicators are often called *binary* or *ternary* because they have two or three possible values, -1 (short), 0 (neutral), and 1 (long).

Rule sets for these indicators are simple because they are essentially built in to the indicator. Practical rule sets including these indicators often combine or index pattern indicators along with other indicators.

Machine Learning/Nonvisual/Black Box

When utilizing machine-learning methods to generate stock signals, the outputs are often multidimensional. These multidimensional outputs easily interact with rule sets optimized to handle them but are most often not worth visualizing. Not surprisingly, these strategies tend to be the most proprietary and have the highest information latency when used correctly.

Example Indicators

We will start by demonstrating how to compute example indicators on a handful of stocks. We will declare a subset of stocks for use in the examples for the sake of speed.

```
exampleset <- c("AAPL", "GOOGL", "YHOO", "HP", "KORS", "COH", "TIF")
```

Simple Moving Average

$$SMA_{t,n} = \frac{1}{n}\sum_{i=0}^{n-1} y_{t-i}.$$

In other words, the *SMA* at time t is the sample average of the n most recent observations. Listing 4-1 computes the SMA using `rollapply()`.

Listing 4-1. Computing SMA with rollapply()

```
n <- 20
meanseries <-
rollapply(DATA[["Close"]][,exampleset],
s          width = n,
           FUN = mean,
           by.column = TRUE,
```

```
          fill = NA,
          align = "right")
```

Moving Average Convergence Divergence Oscillator (MACD)

For $n_1 < n_2$,

$$MACD_{t,n_1,n_2} = SMA_{t,n_1} - SMA_{t,n_2}.$$

Listing 4-2 computes the MACD using rollapply().

Listing 4-2. Computing MACD with rollapply()

```
n1 <- 5
n2 <- 34
MACDseries <-
rollapply(DATA[["Close"]][,exampleset],
          width = n2,
          FUN = function(v) mean(v[(n2 - n1 + 1):n2]) - mean(v),
          by.column = TRUE,
          fill = NA,
          align = "right")
```

Note that we have organized our data as ascending by date. Recognize this direction when specifying functions in rollapply(). Notice how we subset the vector as integers between and including $n_2 - n_1 + 1$ to n_2 to represent the n_1 most recent price points at each time t. Figure 4-1 shows the MACD of GOOGL for the months leading up to June 2016.

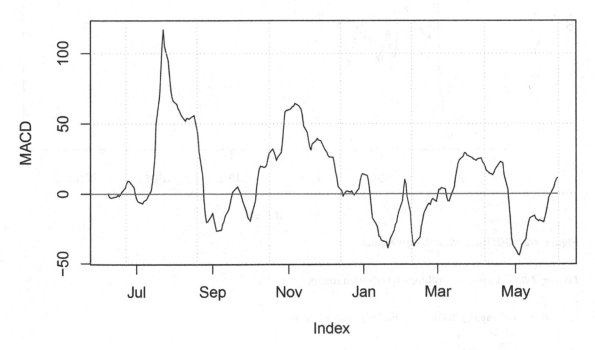

Figure 4-1. *GOOGL MACD*

Bollinger Bands

Bollinger Bands consist of an upper, middle, and lower band. The middle band is a simple moving average, and the upper and lower bands are the middle band plus and minus two rolling sample standard deviations.

$$\sigma_{t,n}^2 = \frac{1}{n-1}\sum_{i=0}^{n-2}\left(y_{t-i} - SMA_{t,n-1}\right)^2.$$

$$Middle_{t,n} = SMA_{t,n}.$$

$$Upper_{t,n} = Middle_{t,n} + 2\sigma_{t,n}.$$

$$Lower_{t,n} = Middle_{t,n} - 2\sigma_{t,n}.$$

Listing 4-3 computes Bollinger Bands using `rollapply()`. Figure 4-2 shows GOOGL plotted with Bollinger Bands for the months leading up to June 2016.

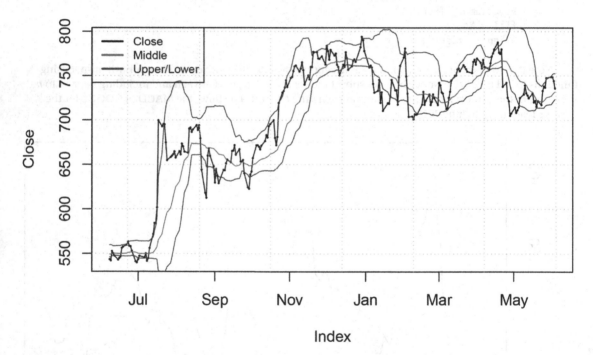

Figure 4-2. *GOOGL with Bollinger Bands*

Listing 4-3. Computing Bollinger Bands with rollapply()

```
n <- 20
rollsd <- rollapply(DATA[["Close"]][,exampleset],
          width = n,
          FUN = sd,
```

```
         by.column = TRUE,
         fill = NA,
         align = "right")

upperseries <- meanseries + 2 * rollsd
lowerseries <- meanseries + 2 - rollsd
```

Custom Indicator Using Correlation and Slope

We will compute a custom indicator by multiplying the rolling R^2 between price and time by the average price change of the period. Listing 4-4 implements this indicator and displays the result in Figure 4-3 for the months leading up to June 2016.

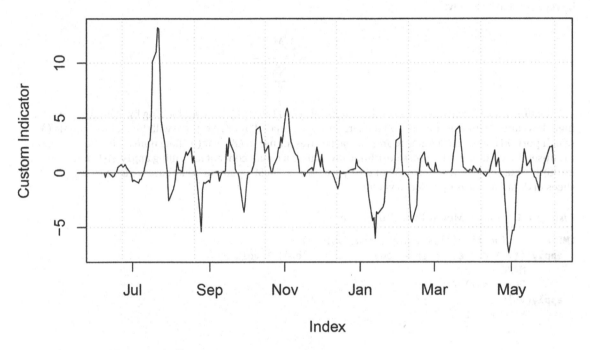

Figure 4-3. *GOOGL custom indicator*

Listing 4-4. Computing Custom Indicator with rollapply()

```
n <- 10
customseries <-
  rollapply(DATA[["Close"]][,exampleset],
         width = n,
         FUN = function(v) cor(v, n:1)^2 * ((v[n] - v[1])/n),
         by.column = TRUE,
         fill = NA,
         align = "right")
```

Indicators Utilizing Multiple Data Sets

Sometimes indicators will utilize information from data sets other than the closing price. Most commonly we will have indicators that use closing price and volume, or indicators that use Open, High, and Low, as well as Close. The rollapply() function takes only one argument to data =, so we will have to manipulate the inputs and functions to accommodate this. The following will illustrate computation of the Chaikin Money Flow with rollapply()

$$MFV_t = \frac{2y_t - h_t - l_t}{h_t - l_t} v_t$$

where $y_t, h_t, l_t,$ and v_t represent the Close, High, Low, and Volume at time t. MFV_t is a component of the Chaikin Money Flow known as the Money-Flow Volume. The Chaikin Money Flow of n periods can then be represented as follows:

$$CMF_{t,n} = \frac{\sum_{i=0}^{n-1} MFV_{t-i}}{\sum_{i=0}^{n-1} v_{t-i}}$$

Listing 4-5 will take advantage of the extensibility rollapply() has over looping by feeding it the close, high, low, and volume as a single zoo data frame concatenated by cbind(). We will then tell rollapply() which portions of the data frame represent each series for use in CMFfunc(). Take note of the method used to subset the combined data set algorithmically. This is a useful concept for calling apply-style functions on multiple data sets. We will make use of the by.column = FALSE option to make sure we feed rollapply() slices of data frames as opposed to vectors.

Listing 4-5. Chaikin Money Flow Using rollapply()

```
CMFfunc <- function(close, high, low, volume){
  apply(((2 * close - high - low) / (high - low)) * volume,
        MARGIN = 2,
        FUN = sum) /
  apply(volume,
        MARGIN = 2,
        FUN = sum)
}


n <- 20
k <- length(exampleset)
CMFseries <-
rollapply(cbind(DATA[["Close"]][,exampleset],
                DATA[["High"]][,exampleset],
                DATA[["Low"]][,exampleset],
                DATA[["Volume"]][,exampleset]),
          FUN = function(v) CMFfunc(v[,(1:k)],
                                    v[,(k+1):(2*k)],
                                    v[,(2*k + 1):(3*k)],
                                    v[,(3*k + 1):(4*k)]),
          by.column = FALSE,
          width = n,
```

```
        fill = NA,
        align = "right")

names(CMFseries) <- exampleset
```

Figure 4-4 plots the result for the months leading up to June 2016.

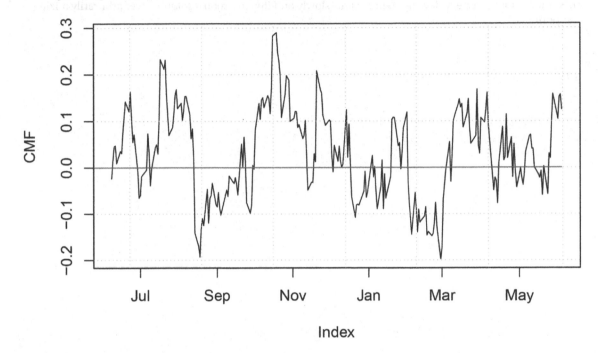

Figure 4-4. *GOOGL Chaikin Money Flow*

Note that we declared CMFfunc() outside of the call to rollapply(). We did this simply because the code is long. We will observe this practice in our source code for functions of all lengths because it will allow us to declare and edit them at the head of our document. For example, placing n <- 20 at the head of the document would allow users to change the lookback value without sifting through code to manually test different values of n in CMFfunc().

Conclusion

What constitutes a good indicator?

Indicators need to be information latent in order to be useful. Information latency is the general ability of an indicator to work with rule sets to produce significantly good trading decisions. We consider random noises and indicators that resemble random noises to be devoid of information. When speaking about information latency, we will assume we are speaking of the indicator when applied to logical and reasonable rule sets.

An indicator devoid of information will have an expected return equal to accumulated expenses for a long/short strategy and the buy-and-hold return less accumulated expenses for a long-only or short-only strategy. A very information-latent indicator will have a simulated return that substantially differs from the expected return of a random noise. Even if a strategy generates extremely negative returns, the indicator will still be considered information-latent because it can generate extremely positive returns if the trading decisions are reversed in the rule set. In other words, if a developer simulates a long-only strategy that generates extremely negative returns, he has likely discovered a very good short-only strategy.

Another possibility is that the rule set is preventing the information contained in the indicator from manifesting itself in a good overall strategy.

Diagnosing which component of the strategy is responsible for a certain behavior as much of an art as it is a science. It requires the developer to have an intimate understanding of the relationship between the data and the strategy. Here's the takeaway: Start with a simple rule set to determine whether a complex indicator is worth pursuing, and start with a simple indicator to determine whether a complicated rule set is worth pursuing. Trading strategy development rewards slowly building to a robust solution over arbitrarily mixing components.

CHAPTER 5

■ ■ ■

Rule Sets

Rule sets link the indicator to the trading decisions. We have given many simple examples in the discussions about indicators, but rule sets tend to get very complex when we include money management elements. It is dangerous to completely decouple the trading decision aspects from the money management aspects of rule sets. In other words, we do not want to decouple the offense from the defense. They should interact and complement each other in an optimal manner discovered through research and optimization. We will discuss common rule sets for making trading decisions as they correspond to certain types of indicators. We will then discuss money management considerations, both integrated and decoupled from generation of trading decisions.

Our Process Flow as Nested Functions

In this chapter, you will notice many calculations performed in the rule sets that can also be performed in the indicators. We will mathematically define our objectives in order to explain why this is expected and acceptable. Our ultimate goal is to find the function F such that

$$F(D_t; A_t) = \Delta P_t$$

In other words, we want a function that transforms stock data, D_t, into portfolio adjustments (trading decisions), ΔP_t, given the account parameters, A_t. Account parameters include account size, commission information, asset holdings, and so on. We have broken down F into components, the indicator function f_i, and the rule set function f_r, such that

$$F(D_t; A_t) = f_r\left(f_i(D_t); A_t\right) = \Delta P_t$$

In the trivial case, f_i could be the identity function, and all of the computational load can be placed on f_r. This discussion is purely to illustrate why it is instructive to separate the two functions and to let you know it is not important how intermediate steps are classified as long as the rule set generates trading decisions.

Terminology

The following terminology will be established for speaking algorithmically about rule sets:

- "If long" is a condition testing whether the current position is net long,

- "If short" is a condition testing whether the current position is net short,

- "If neutral" is a condition testing whether the current position is neither long nor short,

© Chris Conlan 2016
C. Conlan, *Automated Trading with R*, DOI 10.1007/978-1-4842-2178-5_5

- Buy *n* shares.
  - If neutral, establish a long position of *n* shares.
  - If long, add an additional *n* shares to your long position.
  - If short, cover the short position and establish a long position of *n* shares.
- Sell short *n* shares.
  - If neutral, establish a short position of n shares.
  - If long, sell the long position and establish a short position of n shares.
  - If short, add an additional *n* shares to your short position.
- Buy to cover *n* shares.
  - If neutral, the command cannot be executed and is invalid.
  - If long, the command cannot be executed and is invalid.
  - If short, purchase *n* shares to subtract from the short position.
- Sell *n* shares.
  - If neutral, the command cannot be executed and is invalid.
  - If long, sell n shares to subtract from the long position.
  - If short, the command cannot be executed and is invalid.
- Establish long *n* shares.
  - Take necessary steps to establish a net long position of *n* shares.
- Establish short *n* shares.
  - Take the necessary steps to establish a net short position of *n* shares.
- Exit.
  - Take the necessary steps to establish a net zero position.
- "At market,"
  - Execute the command at the current inside ask price for "buy" and "buy to cover" orders.
    * If the order is rejected, attempt to execute again.
  - Execute the command at the current inside bid price for "sell" and "sell to close" orders.
    * If the order is rejected, attempt to execute again.
- "At limit *p*,"
  - Accept no price greater than p for "buy" and "buy to cover" orders.
  - Accept no price less than p for "sell" and "sell to cover" orders.
- "Send stop market *p*."
  - Send stop market order with stop price *p*.
- "Send stop limit p_s, p_l"
  - Send stop limit with stop price p_s and limit price p_l.

More complicated orders are possible and available. These will ultimately be determined by the brokerage, but we will not need these in our platform.

Example Rule Sets

We will give a few example rule sets for various types of indicators. We will focus our attention on the trading decisions rather than the money management in this section.

Overlays

Example #1: Single Stock Simple Moving Average

- If the stock price crosses above the SMA, buy n shares at market.
- If the stock price crosses below the SMA, sell short n shares at market.

Commentary

1. This position is always either long or short, never neutral.
2. The trade size is constant.
3. This trades a single stock and has no portfolio extensibility.

Oscillators

Example #2: Portfolio MACD

1. Calculate the absolute value of a 20-period Rolling Sharpe Ratio for each stock.
2. Calculate the MACD for each stock.
3. This is for ten stocks with the highest absolute value Rolling Sharpe Ratio.
   - Establish long $\frac{n}{10}$ shares at market if the MACD is positive.
   - Establish short $\frac{n}{10}$ shares at market if the MACD is negative.

Commentary

1. This position is always either long or short, never neutral.
2. The trade size is constant.
3. The small trade size enforces some diversification.
4. This works with a portfolio of stocks.

Accumulators

Example #3: Portfolio Accumulation/Distribution Line

1. This is for stocks with an Accumulation/Distribution (A/D) line that had a 200-period minimum in the past 20 periods.
   - Buy $\frac{n}{10}$ shares at market if the 20-period MACD crosses above zero.
   - See rule #3 for the condition.

2. This is for stocks with an A/D line that had a 200-period maximum in the past 20 periods.

- Sell short $\frac{n}{10}$ shares at market if the 20-period MACD crosses above zero.

- See rule #3 for the condition.

3. If buying/selling short in accordance with rule #1 or #2 would require having more than n total shares outstanding,

- Exit position with lowest position-adjusted 10-period rolling Sharpe Ratio at market.

Commentary

1. This position is always either long or short, never neutral.

2. The trade size is constant.

3. The small trade size enforces some diversification.

4. This works with a portfolio of stocks.

Filters, Triggers, and Quantifications of Favor

We see a theme developing with portfolio-based strategies. Components can be classified as a *filter*, *trigger*, or quantification of *favor*. Filter conditions span multiple periods, while trigger conditions span a single period. Filter conditions help select the stocks, and trigger conditions tell the strategy specifically when to enter/exit. For example, *SMA > Close* is a filter condition, while *SMA* crossing above *Close* is a trigger condition. The former is likely to be true or untrue for many periods at a time, while the latter is likely to be true at specific and isolated times and false otherwise.

Quantifications of favor are used to determine which stocks should be exited when the filter and trigger determine the strategy should enter a new trade. Also, quantifications of favor determine which stocks to enter when the filter and trigger determine more positions should be entered than are allowed by the rule set.

Example #1: Single Stock Simple Moving Average

- Filter:

  (a) None

- Trigger:

  (a) SMA crossing zero

- Favor:

  (a) None

Example #2: Portfolio MACD

- Filters:

  (a) Sign of MACD line

  (b) Top 10 absolute-value 20-period rolling Sharpe Ratio

- Trigger:

    (a)   Re-adjust portfolio at every period to reflect filters

- Favor:

    (a)   None

Example #3: Portfolio Accumulation/Distribution Line

- Filters:

    (a)   A/D line had 200-period minimum within last 20 periods

- Triggers:

    (a)   MACD crosses zero

- Favor:

    (a)   10-period rolling Sharpe Ratio

Strategies do not strictly require filters and quantifications of favor to function. Single-stock strategies can perform well with trigger-only strategies. Portfolio strategies find very necessary robustness in the inclusion of filters and quantifications of favor. Thinking about portfolio rule sets in this framework can help simplify development. Developers need to recognize that conventional trigger-only strategies will not work because they provide no way of filtering out undesirable triggers or quantifying the favorability of a stock position at a given time.

CHAPTER 6

High-Performance Computing

In Chapter 7, we will be building our first iteration of a full simulator. We need to cover some high-performance computing concepts so our simulator is not painfully slow. We will begin with a general discussion of high-performance computing in R and then move to implementing different methods in both Windows and UNIX systems. Windows and UNIX systems require different configurations and packages for multicore computing in R.

Hardware Overview

It is important to know the hardware specifications of your machine to configure high-performance computer code. Further, we need to understand how our code interacts with our hardware to minimize compute time. We will discuss important hardware concepts and terminology in this section as a foundation for an in-depth software discussion throughout this chapter.

Processing

Computers have at least one *processor*. A processor is a physical electrical circuit within the computer that performs mathematical computations. Processors typically consist of a logic processing unit (LPU) and a math processing unit (MPU). These are physical electrical circuits that perform logic and math operations like *and*, *or*, addition, subtraction, multiplication, and division. A *scheduler* within a processor cooperates with a computer program to coordinate these tasks.

Multicore Processing

It is rare to find a modern computer without a *multicore* processor. A multicore processor is a single self-contained processing chip with multiple schedulers, logic processing units (LPUs), and math processing units (MPUs), effectively having *n* processors within itself. An inexpensive laptop nowadays is at minimum dual-core. Home desktops can be four- or six-core. Servers can have in extreme cases 12- or 18-core processors, with many *sockets* for supporting many multicore processors at a time.

A socket is an electrical interface between a processor and the motherboard. One socket holds one processor, regardless of the internal configuration and type of processor. Theoretically, a single motherboard could house infinitely many sockets, which provides the potential to craft an extremely powerful computer on a single motherboard. For this reason, commercial software intended for use on commercial servers is typically priced on a per-socket rather than per-server basis.

© Chris Conlan 2016
C. Conlan, *Automated Trading with R*, DOI 10.1007/978-1-4842-2178-5_6

Hyperthreading

Modern processors all have some form of *hyperthreading* built in. This is a concept invented by Intel that allows a single processing core to run multiple *threads* at the same time. A single program will usually run a single thread. For example, if a computer is running four programs, such as an Internet browser, a photo editor, a music player, and a text editor, all at the same time, a dual-core machine will hyperthread two threads (one for each program) on each core. Hyperthreading allows the computer to simulate a virtually infinite number of threads on a single core, rather than restricting one core to one thread.

Generally, hyperthreading produces the most speed gains when running multiple different programs simultaneously rather than multiple threads of the same program. This is important to be aware of, because R will allow us to run any k threads on an n-core machine by hyperthreading $\frac{n}{k}$ threads on each core. In the theoretical case, where a computer is doing nothing but running R, it is best to run one thread per core to minimize thread management overhead. Realistically, your computer has a sophisticated operating system with many background and security tasks running constantly. Because your operating system will prevent every core on your computer from running simultaneously without interruption, we will find that it is best to optimize the number of threads to a value greater than the number of computer cores but not unduly large.

Figure 6-1 shows a functional diagram of the processing components of a computer. Ellipses show how processing can be nested at the socket level, the CPU core level, and the hyperthreading level indefinitely within any single computer.

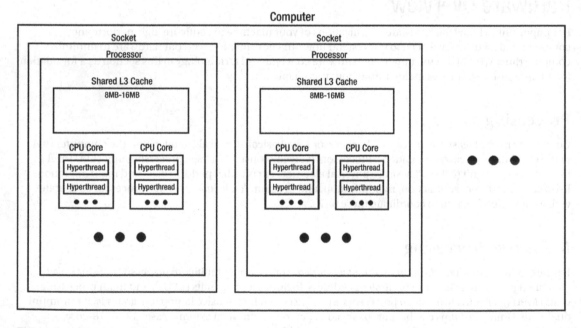

Figure 6-1. *Functional diagram of processing components*

Figure 6-2 zooms in on the CPU core to show its functional components. You may see MPU and LPU identified as *integer arithmetic unit* and *floating-point arithmetic unit* elsewhere. Note that hyperthreading has not been identified in this figure because it is actually a software functionality of the scheduler.

CPU Core

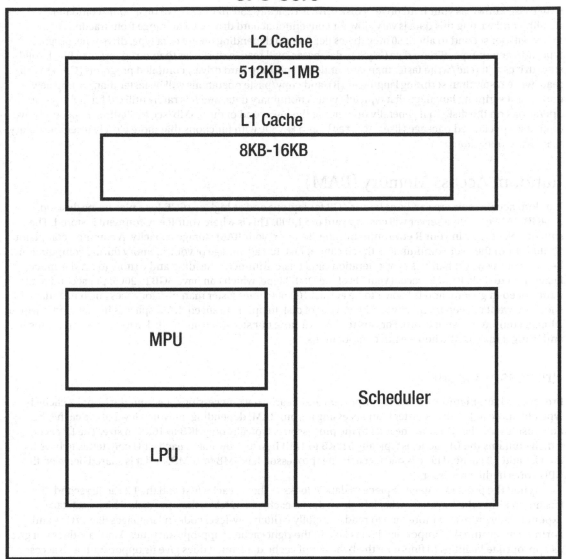

Figure 6-2. *Functional diagram of CPU core*

Memory

Processors access and manipulate memory to make computations. They can access the following hardware modules.

The Disk

Otherwise known as your hard drive, a disk drive is typically 250GB to 1,000GB on a home computer. Reading and writing this data is very slow for conventional hard drives. It can range from fractions of a megabyte per second to about 50 megabytes per second depending on the data type, drive type, program type, and action type. Binary data (MySQL databases) will read/write faster than text data (.csv files), solid-state drives will read/write faster than conventional spinning hard drives, compiled programs (C/C++) will read/write faster than scripting languages (R), and copy/paste operations will be faster than writing new data. R is a scripting language that typically writes nonbinary data, and it is rarely utilized for copy/paste operations on the disk, so it generally operates at the lower end of the 0.5Mb/sec to 50Mb/sec spectrum. We often use specialized packages like data.table and RMySQL with functions that more closely resemble binary read/write operation.

Random Access Memory (RAM)

Random access memory can be as low as 4GB for laptops and as high as 16GB for a nice home desktop. A 64GB RAM card on a server will cost upward of $1,000. This is where your R environment is stored. The sum of object sizes in your R environment cannot exceed your RAM storage capacity. A common complaint about R from the user community is that it cannot take full advantage of your memory during computation because of the way it handles copy operations and basic arithmetic. Reading and writing to RAM is much faster than to disk. RAM in recent years is of the DDR3 type, which can have 5GB to 20GB per second read/write speed in general and is known to be at least 100,000 times faster than disk for accessing binary data. In short, we want to keep memory in RAM and out of disk to optimize speed. RAM space is limited and is wiped when a computer is shut down. For this reason, we store our stock data in the disk when we are not using it and bring it into RAM when we run computations.

Processor Cache

Processors have memory caches for important and nearby data. Accessing data from the L1 or L2 cache is typically three to ten times faster than accessing it from RAM, depending on which level of the cache the data resides in. The L1 cache, nearest to the processor, is typically only 8KB to 16KB in size. The L2 cache, which contains the L1 cache, is typically 512KB to 1MB in size. Nowadays, each CPU core tends to have its own L1 and L2 cache. There is one L3 cache per processor. It is 8MB to 16MB, and it is shared between the CPU cores in the processor.

When the processor needs a piece of data, it looks in the L1 cache first and the L2 cache second. If it is not in either the L1 or L2 cache, it looks in the L3 cache, then RAM, then the disk, which each take exponentially more and more time to read. Carefully written low-level code in languages like C/C++ and Fortran can ensure that important data is kept in the right cache at appropriate times. Vanilla R does not give us appropriate facilities to fine-tune the behavior of cache data, but it does give us opportunities to access cache-optimized binary programs.

Swap Space

When your machine runs out of RAM, memory spills onto the disk, but the program treats that overflowing data just like it would treat RAM. Your operating system has defined space on the disk called *swap space* that acts as *virtual random access memory*, otherwise shortened to *virtual memory* or *virtual RAM*. The amount of swap space on the disk is specified during installation of the operating system and is usually equal to anywhere from half to a little more (about 2GB more) than the RAM space on the machine. This memory is extremely slow to access on computers with traditional spinning hard disk drives (HDDs) because it is stored directly on the disk. Laptops and specialized hardware with solid-state drives (SSDs) will suffer less of a penalty when accessing swap memory, but it slows your program to a crawl nonetheless.

When testing R programs, it is helpful to open your system's performance monitor and observe your RAM and swap memory as your program runs. You should aim to store nothing in swap memory. It is worth noting that, depending on your R distribution and OS, R itself may not be able to store memory on swap space. If this is the case, R will either crash or notify you if it runs out of RAM. Regardless of whether R is capable of storing data on your specific swap space, it is capable of prioritizing memory for itself, running other critical programs onto swap space. If other programs are occupying swap space, your program will suffer the same slowdowns as the programs fight for memory access and manipulate swap data in the background.

Software Overview

R is a unique and complex scripting language. It is important to know where R lives within the world of software to better understand its strengths and weaknesses. We will use this knowledge to write faster code.

Compiled vs. Interpreted

In native compiled languages, like C/C++, Fortran, and Visual Basic, a developer's workflow involves programming, compiling, and running the program. Before code in these languages can be executed, a compiler must read through it and convert it to *machine code* (also called *binaries*). Machine code is a binary executable of optimized CPU directives. Compiled languages are considered *low level* because the compiler translates them directly into CPU directives. The word *low* refers to the proximity of the programming language to the core of the computer. Compiled code can be fine-tuned and optimized to make very efficient decisions with various levels of memory and compute resources.

Strictly interpreted languages, like R, PHP, and MATLAB, involve sequentially executing precompiled binaries. A single command in any of these languages will run some sequence of compiled subroutines. For example, the mean() function depends on subroutines like vector summation, element counting, dimension checking, NA filtering, and floating-point division. The term *subroutine* is used loosely because, without investigation, we do not know at what level these subroutines are being run. Vector summation may occur at the R level by calling the R function sum(), or it may occur at the compiled level by calling a binary specifically for mean(). In the end, every instruction and computation must be completed in a compiled binary along the way. If mean() does not have its own binary, then it depends on sum(), is.na(), length(), and the division operator, which all have their own binaries.

Since the binaries of interpreted languages are precompiled, they can originate from any compiled language. In 2016, a study by BlackDuck|OpenHub showed that, counting by lines, base R is about 40.0 percent C/C++, 27.3 percent Fortran, and 20.7 percent R. It is interesting to mention that, looking through the source code, R's plotting functions are almost pure Fortran. In addition, R packages can be built from any compiled or interpreted language as long as the end user has the appropriate binaries on his machine. A handful of important packages have been written in Java and Perl.

Many important programming languages are hybrids. These languages include Java, Python, and the .NET framework. They are interpreted languages that either require or give the option to compile to *bytecode*. Bytecode is a set of platform-independent low-level directives to machine code. A *run-time environment* is responsible for mapping the bytecode to machine code. These environments include the Java Runtime Environment (for Java) and the Common Language Runtime (for .NET).

Figure 6-3 shows the process flow of different programming languages with common examples languages, compilers, and run-time environments. Note the R run-time environment lists RRO/MRO (Revolution/Microsoft R Open) as an example. This is a modified run-time environment developed by Revolution Analytics and later purchased by Microsoft.

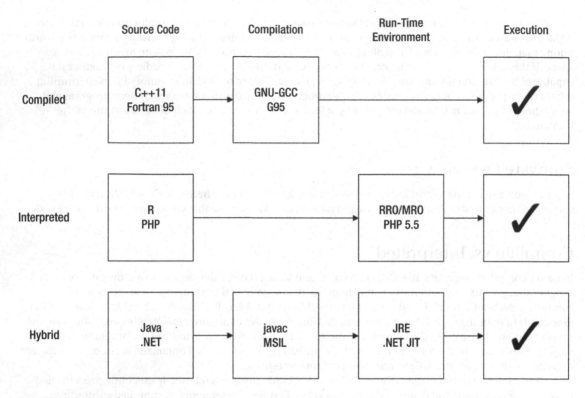

Figure 6-3. Compiled vs. Interpreted Programming Languages

Scripting Languages

Scripting languages are programming languages built for fast writing or "scripting" of code in domain-specific applications. R is a scripting language for statistical computing, and PHP is a scripting language for programming the Web. Scripting languages are almost always interpreted languages. So, when people refer to R as a scripting language, they are typically pointing out that it is domain-specific to statistical computing and an interpreted language.

The term *scripting* is usually used to delineate a language from a general-purpose programming language, where the goal is broad, dense, full-system applicability. C/C++, Java, and most compiled languages are considered programming languages, while languages like R, Python, and PHP are considered scripting languages.

Speed vs. Safety

Further distinguishing scripting languages from interpreted languages is the concept of *safety*. Before we begin discussing, note that safety is only typical of scripting languages, not required. Also note that more safety for interpreted languages can be implemented at the compiler level.

Safety is the broad concept of disallowing unintended memory access at execution time. In R, objects know their own size. In other words, the size and dimensions of an object are stored in memory as attributes of the object. When a user accesses an element or some elements of an object, R makes sure that the user is not attempting to access something outside the dimensions of the object. If R detects this error, it stops the program and reports an error message. The next logical question is "What if I write a flawless program that never requests out-of-bounds elements?" The answer: R will still waste a lot of time checking every time a user accesses an object.

The flip side to safety is speed. For example, if a user is processing a picture of a cat and a picture of a dog in C++ and unintentionally accesses indices outside the dimensions of the picture of the cat, he might end up with the right side of a cat and the left side of a dog in one picture. C and C++ do not check whether the indices are within the dimensions of the object being accessed. If a user accesses element 101 in a vector of length 100, unsafe languages will move one space to the right of the position of element 100 in your memory and attempt to process the value. The user will not get any error messages and is expected to diagnose and treat these problems himself. Obviously, when the program *does* work at expected, it is very fast because it is does not waste time checking the indices.

This is another reason why we want to call fewer powerful binaries as opposed to many more general binaries. Once R ships the job off to the binaries, most safety checks are done. We want to perform fewer safety checks to minimize computation time.

Takeaways

R is an interpreted scripting language. Compiled binaries run much faster than sequences of compiled binaries. We will minimize computation time of our R scripts by minimizing the time spent *calling* the binaries and maximizing the time spent *in* the binaries.

Listing 6-1 illustrates this point.

Listing 6-1. Binaries vs. for Loops

```
# Declare 10mil random numbers in a data frame
df <- data.frame(matrix(nrow = 10000, ncol = 1000, runif(n = 10000 * 1000)))

# Compute the sum of each row with a for loop
# Completes in 96.692 seconds
v1 <- rep(NA, 10000)
for( i in 1:10000 ) {
  v1[i] <- sum(df[i,])
}

# Use rowSums() binary
# Completes in 0.053 seconds
v2 <- rowSums(df)

# Results are exactly the same
# Expression evaluates to TRUE
all.equal(v1, v2)
```

We will discuss the nuances of this concept throughout the chapter. There are many ways to invoke single binaries that may seem unintuitive or hidden. Additionally, there are a lot of functions that look like calls to single binaries but are really just wrappers for slow R loops.

for Loops vs. apply Functions

In R, many programming problems give us the choice to use either for loops or an apply-style function. To illustrate this point, we will recompute the RETURN variable from Listing 3-8 using various for loops and apply methods.

for Loops and Memory Allocation

As discussed, we want to avoid for loops when possible because they sequentially call binaries rather than use a single precompiled binary. We will illustrate the use of for loops to compute the return matrix and benchmark them against other methods.

Listing 6-2 will touch on another important point. Memory allocation in R is slow. Expressions like this

```
x <- 1:10
y <- x[1] * 2
for( i in 2:10 ) y <- c(y, x[i] * 2)
```

where c() can be any concatenation operator like c(), cbind(), or rbind() can slow down a program substantially if called many times because it changes the size of the variable y. Every time this is called, R must create a temporary variable corresponding to c(x,y), re-declare (or re-allocate) y as a larger variable with new dimensions, and then assign the variable to the new y. Remember, this is fine in general, but expressions like these are often placed inside loops when building larger data sets. A program will always run faster if expressed like this:

```
z <- rep(numeric(), 10)
x <- 1:10
for( i in 1:10 ) z[i] <- x[i] * 2
```

The vector z at the end of the second snippet is the same as y at the end of the first snippet. The vector z was declared (or pre-allocated) at the beginning to have ten numeric elements, allowing R to make only one memory allocation but ten equivalent assignments.

Listing 6-2 illustrates this point with the RETURN matrix calculated in Listing 3-7. There is a very significant time difference between pre-allocating and re-allocating.

Note that we will be calculating and re-calculating the return matrix many times throughout this chapter. We will concentrate on the computation rather than formatting and post-processing for the sake of brevity. This means that all.equal() can output confusing results because of differences in dimension, object type, and attributes. All the versions of RETURN we compute will contain the same data but in varying formats. The original computation of the return matrix in Listing 3-8 both computes the fastest and outputs RETURN in the intended format.

Listing 6-2. Pre-allocation vs. Re-allocation

```
# Sequentially re-allocating space in a for loop
RETURN <- NULL
for(i in 2:nrow(DATA[["Close"]])){
  RETURN <- rbind(RETURN, t((matrix(DATA[["Close"]][i, ]) /
                            matrix(DATA[["Close"]][i-1, ])) - 1))
}
RETURN <- zoo( RETURN, order.by = index(DATA[["Close"]])[-1])
# 99.68 seconds

# Pre-allocating space and computing in a for loop
RETURN <- zoo(matrix(ncol = ncol(DATA[["Close"]]),
                     nrow = nrow(DATA[["Close"]])),
          order.by = index(DATA[["Close"]]))

for(i in 2:nrow(DATA[["Close"]])){
  RETURN[i,] <- t((matrix(DATA[["Close"]][i, ]) / matrix(DATA[["Close"]][i-1, ])) - 1)
}
#54.34 seconds
```

apply-Style Functions

apply-style functions are a staple in the R language. They include apply(), lapply(), sapply(), and vapply(), in the base R. Contributed packages, like zoo, have domain-specific implementations like rollapply() for time series. apply-style functions are extremely useful because of their extensibility. Many multicore packages will readily accept apply-style functions, and the applied function can be cleanly modified outside of the apply implementation. We will make heavy use of these functions in this chapter.

apply-style functions are often confused as being necessarily faster than for loops. They can be faster in some scenarios but are not generally. The counterargument to the assertion that apply-style functions are faster is that they actually depend on R-level for loops to run. This has given rise to the term *loop hiding*, highlighting the idea that apply-style functions look and generalize nicer than for loops but are really just a clever and flexible wrapper.

apply-style functions pre-allocate memory to the assigned variable by default but contain a lot of internal constructs for safety and generality that can slow them down. An efficiently written apply-style function will be slightly slower but more generalizable than an efficiently written for loop. Listing 6-3 computes the RETURN matrix in two different ways using rollapply(). Giving consideration to how apply-style functions work internally can help speed them up.

Listing 6-3. Writing Efficient apply-Style Functions

```
# Using rollapply() element-by-element
RETURN <- rollapply(DATA[["Close"]],
            width = 2,
            FUN = function(v) (v[2]/v[1]) - 1,
            align = "right",
            by.column = TRUE,
            fill = NA)
# 105.77 seconds

# Using rollapply() row-by-row
RETURN <- rollapply(DATA[["Close"]],
            width = 2,
            FUN = function(v) (v[2,]/v[1,]) - 1,
            align = "right",
            by.column = FALSE,
            fill = NA)
# 65.37 seconds
```

Use Binaries Creatively

This section exists to drive home that binaries are faster. Sometimes there is no clear way to utilize an existing binary, as in Listing 6-1 with rowSums(), so you will have to search for a more creative method to keep the loop inside the binary. Dissecting Listing 6-4, we see the division operator, the lag() function, and the subtraction operator. All of these operators loop the specified operation inside the binary after checking for equal dimension and class. This line of code works well over 100 times faster than our next best solution in this chapter.

Listing 6-4. Calculating the Return Matrix with Binaries

```
# Using the "lag" method introduced in Listing 3.8
RETURN <- ( DATA[["Close"]] / lag(DATA[["Close"]], k = -1) ) - 1
# 0.459 seconds
```

Table 6-1 organizes the compute times we have observed thus far in this chapter. The "Re-allocated" column is empty for functions where it is not logical to ever execute a re-allocated variation because of the structure of the function. We will expand on this table for more functions and their multicore variations later in this chapter.

Table 6-1. *Compute Times of the Return Matrix (Seconds)*

Function	Granularity	Pre-allocated	Re-allocated
for()	Row	54.34	99.68
rollapply()	Element	105.77	NA
rollapply()	Row	65.37	NA
x/lag(x) - 1	Data frame	0.459	NA

Note on Measuring Compute Time

There are lots of ways to measure compute time in R. The most straightforward method is the function proc. time(). Save the output of the function in a variable, execute your function, and then print the difference of the current value of proc.time() to the previous. There are three values in proc.time(), and users need only the third.

proc.time()

```
##   user  system  elapsed
##  1.793   0.154    2.299
```

User time is an approximate number generated by your operating system that represents the CPU time in seconds devoted to executing user instructions at the process level. System time represents the CPU time in seconds devoted to executing user instructions at the system level. This is unnecessarily confusing, and a proper discussion of the nuances of CPU clocks is not necessary to optimize code in R. We only care about the third value, elapsed time, that represents the actual time in seconds elapsed between assigning and differencing proc.time(). See Listing 6-5 for a practical wrapper for measuring the compute time of any amount of code. This method was used to generate time measurements in this chapter.

When using this method, make sure to highlight and send the entire chunk of code to the console at the same time, or use the source function or Run button to run the entire script. We do not want our typing speed to affect the results of the time measurement.

Listing 6-5. Measuring Compute Time

```
timeLapse <- proc.time()[3]
for( i in 1:1000000) v <- runif(1)
proc.time()[3] - timeLapse

## elapsed
##   1.826
```

Multicore Computing in R

This section will explore multicore computing in R for UNIX and Windows systems. We will cover the most flexible packages for multicore CPU computing. We will distinguish between parallel back ends for UNIX and Windows but focus on multicore packages that work on any operating system that supports a parallel back end. We will introduce integer mapping concepts that extend to multicore computing in every language. We will discuss how multicore computing in R compares to other languages in flexibility and memory efficiency.

Embarrassingly Parallel Processes

The phrase *embarrassingly parallel* was coined by veteran programmers that observed their peers neglecting to parallelize simple processes. It was considered criminal (in jest) not to parallelize an embarrassingly parallel process if using a low-level language because the program would waste a lot of time that can be saved by little programming effort. These are examples of embarrassingly parallel processes:

- Converting hundreds of images from color to grayscale
- Serving files to many users on a web server
- Simple brute-force searches
- Summing millions of floating-point numbers
- Generating bootstrap estimates
- Generating Monte Carlo simulations

Algorithms can be hard to parallelize when processes need to communicate with each other during computation. If an algorithm can be executed by splitting up the data, handing a piece to each process, and aggregating the results, it is simple to parallelize. Computation of the RETURN matrix is an embarrassingly parallel process. We will study it to determine whether it nets significant speed gains from parallelization.

Remember that *embarrassingly parallel* is a technical phrase with no actual negative connotation. An embarrassingly parallel process is not necessarily easy to program. R gives us limited facilities for communicating between processes in multicore computations, so most of our implementations will be embarrassingly parallel. Most importantly, remember that R is an interpreted language, so speed gains from utilizing purely binaries will almost always exceed speed gains from parallelizing for loops or other loop-hiding functions.

doMC and doParallel

The package doMC provides an interface between the foreach packages and the parallel package using the UNIX system call fork to replicate the R run-time environment n times for execution as independent processes on k cores.

According to the documentation, the processes should share memory in most cases but will replicate the data in the parent environment if it determines the processes are modifying it. We will generally assume the parallel back end replicates memory for every process because this behavior is OS-specific and poorly documented. This is an important reason to keep an eye on your memory, swap memory, and CPU utilization when testing multicore code. If a process spills into swap memory or throws an out-of-memory error because it is replicating the parent environment, you may want to consider reducing the number of processes or computing the algorithm on a single core.

Listings 6-6 and 6-7 show how to register a parallel back end in UNIX and Windows systems, respectively. The workers variable should be declared with the number of processes you would like to run. Your computer will dole out processes in a round-robin fashion to your available CPU cores, so setting workers to a value higher than the number of physical CPU cores in your machine will trigger hyperthreading. As mentioned previously in this text, this may be advantageous on machines that will run other non-R processes concurrently with the trading platform. We will study this behavior later in the chapter.

Listing 6-6. Registering Parallel Back End in UNIX

```
library(doMC)
workers <- 4
registerDoMC( cores = workers )
```

The parallel backend in Windows relies on the base R function system() to spin up multiple independent R run-time environments. This is possible in UNIX but avoided because of the clear memory-sharing advantages of R working with fork. Running system(command = "Rscript scriptname.R ...") in R is equivalent to running "Rscript scriptname.R ..." in a UNIX or Windows terminal. The Rscript terminal command takes the path to an R script and a list of parameters and runs the R script with no GUI. The parallel back end for Windows manipulates this functionality to attempt to simulate UNIX's fork. In reality, it operates very differently from fork. Instead of sharing memory, each R instance is given its own global environment, which is intended to mimic the function-level environment from which foreach() is called. This opens the door to a number of coding inconsistencies and memory inefficiencies that can complicate development for Windows users. We will continue to discuss and expand on these issues throughout Chapter 6 and in Appendix B.

Listing 6-7. Registering Parallel Back End in Windows

```
library(doParallel)
workers <- 4
registerDoParallel( cores = workers )
```

The foreach Package

Now that we have registered a parallel backend, we can use the foreach package to parallelize our computations. The package provides an intuitive and flexible interface for dispatching jobs to separate R processes. It works just like a typical R for loop, but with a few caveats. Given an iterator variable, *i*, it will dispatch one process per value in the looping range of *i*. If multiple iterators are supplied, *i* and *j*, it will dispatch a number of processes equal to the number of elements in the smaller of the two ranges of *i* and *j*. This means there is no recycling. There is not a technical need to ever supply multiple iterators, so we will always be supplying only one iterator. The results are returned in a list by default. We will usually specify the .combine argument with the function c(), rbind(), or cbind() to let the function know we want the results returned in a concatenated vector or data frame of the results. Listing 6-8 gives you an idea of how foreach() returns results.

Listing 6-8. Examples with foreach Package

```
library(foreach)

# Returns a list
foreach( i = 1:4 ) %dopar% {
  j <- i + 1
  sqrt(j)
}

# Returns a vector
foreach( i = 1:4, .combine = c ) %dopar% {
  j <- i + 1
  sqrt(j)
}
```

```
# Returns a matrix
foreach( i = 1:4, .combine = rbind ) %dopar% {
  j <- i + 1
  matrix(c(i, j, sqrt(j)), nrow = 1)
}

# Returns a data frame
foreach( i = 1:4, .combine = rbind ) %dopar% {
  j <- i + 1
  data.frame( i = i, j = j, sqrt.j = sqrt(j))
}
```

Obviously these examples are too small to gain efficiency from multicore processing. They are almost certainly slower because the workload of the process communication overhead is greater than that of the mathematics. In the next section, we will use the software we have set up to speed up calculations of indicators.

The foreach Package in Practice

There are a handful of interesting mathematical challenges we face when parallelizing even the simplest processes. We will discuss integer mapping, output aggregation, and load balancing.

Integer Mapping

Integer mapping involves breaking up a numerical problem into equally sized pieces. For simple problems, like computing the sum of each row, the integer mapping process is straightforward. For 100 rows in 4 processes, we dispatch rows 1 through 25 to process 1, rows 26 through 50 to process 2, and so on. For more complicated processes, like moving averages, the window size complicates integer mapping. A moving average of length $k=5$ on $n=100$ rows of data would return 96 rows. To make sure each process computes 24 rows and has sufficient data available, we would dispatch rows 1 through 28 to process 1, rows 25 through 52 to process 2, rows 49 through 76 to process 3, and rows 73 to 100 to process 4.

The problem becomes even more complex when the number of rows is not divisible by the number of processes. We will talk through building an algorithm for integer mapping right-aligned time-series computations under the assumption that each row takes equal time to compute.

Here are some facts to consider:

- A right-aligned time series computation with window size k on n rows of input returns $n_o = n - k + 1$ rows of output.

- A properly dispatched set of p processes will compute a maximum of $\left\lceil \dfrac{n_o}{p} \right\rceil$ rows of output per process and a minimum of $\left\lceil \dfrac{n_o}{p} \right\rceil - p + 1$ rows of output per process.

- For the output to have the same number of rows as the input, we must mimic rollapply(... , fill = NA) by appending k-1 rows of NA values to the beginning of the output.

Listing 6-9 declares the function delegate() that returns the indices of rows required for process i given n rows of data, a window size of k, and p total processes.

Listing 6-9. Integer Mapping for Multicore Time-Series Computations

```
delegate <- function( i = i, n = n, k = k, p = workers ){
  nOut <- n - k + 1
  nProc <- ceiling( nOut / p )
  return( (( i - 1 ) * nProc + 1) : min(i * nProc + k - 1, n) )
}

# Test i as 1 through 4 to verify it matches our example
lapply(1:4, function(i) delegate(i, n = 100, k = 5, p = 4))
```

We will use this function throughout the chapter and our platform to make easy use of foreach.

Computing the Return Matrix with foreach

Listing 6-10 will show how to use for loops inside foreach() to compute the return matrix. Listing 6-11 will use rollapply(). We will benchmark performance against examples in Table 6-1 as we progress.

Listing 6-10. Computing the Return Matrix with foreach and for Loops

```
k <- 2

# Using for a for loop, pre-allocated
RETURN <- foreach( i = 1:workers, .combine = rbind,
                   .packages = "zoo" ) %dopar% {

  CLOSE <- as.matrix(DATA[["Close"]])

  jRange <- delegate( i = i, n = nrow(DATA[["Close"]]), k = k, p = workers)

  subRETURN <- zoo(
    matrix(numeric(),
         ncol = ncol(DATA[["Close"]]),
         nrow = length(jRange) - k + 1),
    order.by = (index(DATA[["Close"]])[jRange])[-(1:(k-1))])

  names(subRETURN) <- names(DATA[["Close"]])

  for( j in jRange[-1] ){
    jmod <- j - jRange[1]
    subRETURN[jmod, ] <- (CLOSE[j,] / CLOSE[j-1,]) - 1
  }
  subRETURN

}
#Completes in 6.99 seconds
```

These results are admittedly confusing. In theory, breaking up an algorithm into p parallel processes should increase its speed by no more than p times. Here, we see a speed increase of almost eight times using four processes. This only serves to prove that we should test everything in R, because we cannot anticipate every behavior and quirk of the language and its packages.

It should be said that this code was run on Red Hat Linux Enterprise Server 7.1 with 12 CPU cores and 64GB of RAM. The efficiency of memory sharing through the `fork` system call in Red Hat might exceed that of other operating systems and is certainly not replicable in Windows where no `fork` call exists. Additionally, R processes do not dedicate themselves to specific cores; rather, they drift between cores, even at full load where the number of processes equals the number of cores. Running a 4-process test on a 12-core machine may increase cache efficiency in unanticipated ways.

Listing 6-11. Computing the Return Matrix with rollapply()

```
# Using rollapply(), automatically pre-allocated
RETURN <- foreach( i = 1:workers, .combine = rbind,
                   .packages = "zoo") %dopar% {

  jRange <- delegate( i = i, n = nrow(DATA[["Close"]]), k = k, p = workers)

  rollapply(DATA[["Close"]][jRange,],
      width = k,
      FUN = function(v) (v[2,]/v[1,]) - 1,
      align = "right",
      by.column = FALSE,
      na.pad = FALSE)

}
# Completes in 22.58 seconds
```

These results make more sense at first glance. We have a speed increase of about 2.9 from distributing to 4 processes. As a cursory explanation, we can say that the speed increase is attributed to distribution to 4 processes, and the discrepancy between 2.9 and 4 is due to communication overhead between the processes. As we can see from Listing 6-10, this explanation probably fails to cover all of the bases. We simply do not know everything that goes on under the hood.

In my opinion, sizable treatments of compute-time dynamics in R are hard to come by because they require researchers and readers to embrace unknown behaviors. This text invites users to embrace unknown behaviors and exploit them for speed gains.

Keep in mind that computing the return matrix is somewhat of a trivial example because we already have a very fast method for computing it using binaries that keep the loop in C/C++. The following sections will cover nontrivial examples of computing indicators and rule sets with foreach().

Computing Indicators with foreach

We will make the most use of foreach() when computing indicators. It becomes harder to build solutions with R binaries as indicators get more complex and customized. We will cover computation of the indicators introduced in Chapter 4. Listing 6-12 computes the simple moving average with a few methods using foreach().

Listing 6-12. Wrapper Function for Multicore Time-Series Computations

```
mcTimeSeries <- function( data, tsfunc, byColumn, windowSize, workers, ... ){

  # For Windows compatability
  args <- names(mget(ls()))
  export <- ls(.GlobalEnv)
```

```r
export <- export[!export %in% args]

# foreach powerhouse
SERIES <- foreach( i = 1:workers, .combine = rbind,
                   .packages = loadedNamespaces(), .export = export) %dopar% {

  jRange <- delegate( i = i, n = nrow(data), k = windowSize, p = workers)

  rollapply(data[jRange,],
    width = windowSize,
    FUN = tsfunc,
    align = "right",
    by.column = byColumn)

}

# Correct formatting of column names and dimensions
names(SERIES) <- gsub("\\..+", "", names(SERIES))

if( windowSize > 1){
  PAD <- zoo(matrix(nrow = windowSize-1, ncol = ncol(SERIES), NA),
             order.by = index(data)[1:(windowSize-1)])
  names(PAD) <- names(SERIES)
  SERIES <- rbind(PAD, SERIES)
}
if(is.null(names(SERIES))){
  names(SERIES) <- gsub("\\..+", "", names(data)[1:ncol(SERIES)])
}

# Return results
return(SERIES)

}
```

You will notice this is only a slight modification of our first multicore `rollapply()` implementation in Listing 6-11. This makes it remarkably easy to compute indicators and rule sets for time series by swapping out the function declaration, window size, and byColumn parameters. We will very quickly illustrate in Listing 6-13 how to compute indicators from Chapter 4 with very little code. All of the outputs from this function have the same number of rows, same `order.by` attribute, and same column names as your original input data. You can even use `cbind()` to bind OHLC data together, and you will still get the correct number of columns with the correct names.

Listing 6-13. Computing Indicators with Our Multicore Wrapper

```r
# Computing the return matrix
tsfunc <- function(v) (v[2,] / v[1,]) - 1
RETURN <- mcTimeSeries( DATA[["Close"]], tsfunc, FALSE, 2, workers )

# Computing a simple moving average
SMA <- mcTimeSeries( DATA[["Close"]], mean, TRUE, 20, workers )
```

```
# Computing an MACD, n1 = 5, n2 = 34
tsfunc <- function(v) mean(v[(length(v) - 4):length(v)]) - mean(v)
MACD <- mcTimeSeries( DATA[["Close"]], tsfunc, TRUE, 34, workers )

# Computing Bollinger Bands, n = 20, scale = 2
SDSeries <- mcTimeSeries(DATA[["Close"]], function(v) sd(v), TRUE, 20, workers)
upperBand <- SMA + 2 * SDSeries
lowerBand <- SMA - 2 * SDSeries

# Computing custom indicator as in Listing 4.3
tsfunc <- function(v) cor(v, length(v):1)^2 * ((v[length(v)] - v[1])/length(v))
customIndicator <- mcTimeSeries( DATA[["Close"]], tsfunc, TRUE, 10, workers )

# Computing Chaikin Money Flow, n = 20, (Using CMFfunc() function from Listing 4.5)
cols <- ncol(DATA[["Close"]])
CMFseries <- mcTimeSeries( cbind(DATA[["Close"]],
                                 DATA[["High"]],
                                 DATA[["Low"]],
                                 DATA[["Volume"]]),
                    function(v) CMFfunc(v[,(1:cols)],
                                        v[,(cols+1):(2*cols)],
                                        v[,(2*cols + 1):(3*cols)],
                                        v[,(3*cols + 1):(4*cols)]),
                    FALSE, 20, workers)
```

With our wrapper function, the average time-series computation takes about two lines of code and is just shy of p times as fast. Additionally, declaring all the arguments to the wrapper function outside of the function call allows us to modify them from anywhere in our code. The most useful application for you would be to place the function declaration for the indicator at the top of your code for easy adjustment. Our growing code base is really only worthy of the title "platform" because it offers extended functionalities of other commercial trading platforms (for example, TradeStation, Metatrader) by allowing users to change the indicator and more from the head of the document with a single line of code. We will make heavy use of our multicore wrapper in Chapter 7 as we build our first backtester. We will clean up the R environment to prepare.

```
rm(list = setdiff(ls(), c("datadir", "functiondir", "rootdir",
                          "DATA", "OVERNIGHT", "RETURN",
                          "delegate", "mcTimeSeries", "workers")))
gc()

##            used (Mb) gc trigger (Mb) max used (Mb)
## Ncells 538982 28.8     1168576 62.5  1168576 62.5
## Vcells 869518  6.7     3090461 23.6  3087872 23.6
```

CHAPTER 7

■ ■ ■

Simulation and Backtesting

In this chapter, we will use the data and functions established thus far to build a backtester to simulate the results of trading with a given strategy. We will run our simulator with a few example strategies. We will introduce many practical trading considerations as we construct sample strategies.

Recall in Chapter 5 we established the indicator and rule set for a strategy from a composite function accepting stock data, D_t, and account variables, A_t, to output portfolio adjustments, ΔP_t, as follows

$$f_r\big(f_i(D_t); A_t\big) = P_t$$

where f_r and f_i are the rule set and indicator functions, respectively. We will use multicore functions from Chapter 6 to compute the proper inputs to reach ΔP_t from stock data and account variables by *walking through* time in a loop.

Example Strategies

Example #1: Long-Only Portfolio MACD

1. Calculate the 20-period Rolling Sharpe Ratio for each stock.

2. Calculate the MACD for each stock with n_1=5 and n_2=34.

3. Define k to be the number of positions held and K=10 to be the maximum number of positions held. Define C to be uninvested cash.

4. For stocks with a Rolling Sharpe Ratio higher than the 80th percentile for the period,

   - If MACD crosses above 0,

     - If K positions are held, exit the position with the lowest Rolling Sharpe Ratio at market.

     - Establish long $\dfrac{C}{(K-k)}$ dollars at market of triggering stock.

Example #2: Portfolio Bollinger Bands

1. Calculate the 20-period Rolling Standard Deviation for each stock.

2. Calculate the 20-period and 100-period Simple Moving Averages for each stock.

3. Define k to be the number of positions held and K=20 to be the maximum amount of positions held. Define C to be uninvested cash.

© Chris Conlan 2016
C. Conlan, *Automated Trading with R*, DOI 10.1007/978-1-4842-2178-5_7

4. Define $b_t = \dfrac{Close - SMA_{t,20}}{\sigma_{t,20}}$ and $B_t = \dfrac{SMA_{t,20} - SMA_{t,100}}{\sigma_{t,20}}$.

5. For stocks where $1 \le B_t < 3$,

   - Establish long $\dfrac{C}{(K-k)}$ dollars at market if b_t crosses below -2.

6. For stocks where $-3 < B_t \le -1$,

   - Establish short $\dfrac{C}{(K-k)}$ dollars at market if bt crosses above 2.

7. For stocks where $B_t \ge 3$,

   - Establish short $\dfrac{C}{(K-k)}$ dollars at market if b_t crosses above 2.

8. For stocks where $B_t \le -3$,

   - Establish long $\dfrac{C}{(K-k)}$ dollars at market if b_t crosses below -2.

9. For all positions,

   - Exit the position at market if B_t crosses 0.

10. For all long positions,

    - Exit the position at market if b_t crosses above 2.

11. For all short positions,

    - Exit the position at market if b_t crosses below -2.

12. If entering a position requires holdings more than $K=20$ stocks,

    - Enter the new position after exiting the position with the lowest mean return.

Example #3: Portfolio RSI Reversal

1. Calculate the 20-period Average True Range as $ATR_{t,20}$ for each stock.

2. Calculate the 20-period Relative Strength Index as $RSI_{t,20}$ for each stock.

3. Calculate the 100-period Rolling Minimum as $MIN_{t,100}$ and 100-period Rolling Maximum as $MAX_{t,100}$ for each stock.

4. Define k to be the number of positions held and $K=20$ to be the maximum amount of positions held. Define C to be uninvested cash.

5. Define $m_t^+ = \dfrac{MAX_{t,100} - Close_t}{ATR_{t,20}}$ and $m_t^- = \dfrac{Close_t - MIN_{t,100}}{ATR_{t,20}}$.

6. For stocks where $m_t^+ \le 2$,

   - Establish short $\dfrac{C}{(K-k)}$ dollars at market if $RSI_{t,20}$ crosses below 70.

7. For stocks where $m_t^- \le 2$,

   - Establish long $\dfrac{C}{(K-k)}$ dollars at market if $RSI_{t,20}$ crosses above 30.

8. For all long positions,

   - Exit the position at market if $RSI_{t,20}$ crosses above 70.

   - Exit the position at market if $RSI_{t,20}$ crosses below 15.

9. For all short positions,

   - Exit the position at market if $RSI_{t,20}$ crosses below 30.

   - Exit the position at market if $RSI_{t,20}$ crosses above 85.

10. If entering a position requires holdings more than $K=20$ stocks,

   - Enter the new position after exiting the position with the lowest mean return.

Our Simulation Workflow

Listing 7-1 is a large function for simulating the performance of portfolio strategies. It aims to balance speed and flexibility by taking minimal inputs computed outside of the function and specifying many of the most important features of portfolio strategies. Reading the code may not be productive for all readers, so we will discuss the steps of the algorithm in pseudocode, making sure to mark in the code the corresponding sections of the pseudocode.

Listing 7-1: Pseudocode

1. Check that ENTRY, EXIT, and FAVOR match in dimensionality with DATA[["Close"]], throwing an error if nonmatching.

2. Assign account variables based on function inputs. Allocate space for share count matrix P, entry price matrix p, equity curve vector equity, and cash vector C. Note that the share count matrix accounts for shorts with negative share counts.

3. The walk-through optimization begins. Repeat steps 4 through 12 for each trading day.

4. Carry over cash and positions from the last period.

5. Determine which stocks to enter based on ENTRY. If in excess of K, eliminate extras by favorability based on FAVOR.

6. Determine which stocks to exit by trigger based on EXIT.

7. Determine whether more stocks must be exited to respect K, the maximum number of assets held at any given time. Determine which of these stocks to exit by favorability based on FAVOR. Stocks that have been marked for exit by the trigger in the previous step cannot also be marked for exit based on favorability.

8. Finalize the vector of stocks to exit.

9. Exit all stocks marked for exit.

10. Enter all stocks marked for entry.

11. Loop through active positions to determine equity for the period.

12. If verbose = TRUE, output optimization diagnostics every 21 trading days (about monthly).

13. Return the equity curve, cash vector, share count matrix, and entry price matrix.

Listing 7-1: Explanation of Inputs and User Guide

- OPEN will most often be DATA[["Open"]]. This is given as a nontrivial input for cross validation and optimization purposes in Chapter 8. Remember that we trade at the open because of the nature of our data. We gain access to a given day's closing price at least 15 minutes after the market closes, so the next opportunity we have to trade is the open of the following day.

- CLOSE will most often be DATA[["Close"]]. Similarly to OPEN, this will be an important input in Chapter 8.

- ENTRY is a zoo object with the same dimensions as DATA[["Close"]] that specifies which stocks to enter when. A 0 corresponds to no action, a 1 corresponds to long, and a -1 corresponds to short. A stock triggered by ENTRY will have $\dfrac{C}{(K-k)}$ dollars allocated to either the long or short position. If ENTRY denotes more than K stocks should be entered that period, it will pick K stocks according to favorability.

- EXIT is a zoo object with the same dimensions as DATA[["Close"]] that specifies when to deliberately exit a stock. A 0 corresponds to no action, a 1 corresponds to exiting a long position, a -1 corresponds to exiting a short position, and a 999 corresponds to exiting any position. In every case, the entire position is liquidated. For strategies that only require ENTRY and FAVOR, EXIT can be set to all zeros.

- FAVOR is a zoo object with the same dimensions as DATA[["Close"]] that specifies the favorability of a given stock at any given time. This is required when ENTRY indicates more than K stocks to enter, and when ENTRY requires some, existing positions must be liquidated in order to avoid owning more than K stocks. A higher value of FAVOR indicates a desirable long position and an undesirable short position. A lower or more negative value of FAVOR indicates a desirable short position or an undesirable long position. Good defaults are mean return and Rolling Sharpe Ratio. It may be of theoretical interest in certain strategies to fill FAVOR with random numbers. Any NA values in FAVOR will be replaced with zeros at the initiation of the simulator. This object is sorted and ordered frequently in the course of simulation, and NA values cannot be handled via default R behavior.

- maxLookback is the greatest number of periods any indicator looks back in time plus one. This is necessary to ensure matrices are not being processed when they contain all NA values or incomplete computations due to na.rm=TRUE. We typically want to use na.rm=TRUE to allow for maintenance of NA values in our uniform date template data, but we do not want to abuse it to allow computations of $SMA_{t,100}$ at $t=2$.

- maxAssets is equal to K, which specifies the greatest number of stocks or unique assets to be held at any given time. Our simulator allows portfolio management with equal allocation of cash between K stocks. It will distribute startingCash among K stocks and then distribute on-hand cash equally between new stocks as the money compounds.

- startingCash is simply the amount invested initially. It is important to specify a realistic value to each individual to study the interaction between account sizes and commission structures.

- slipFactor is a percentage of slippage to be added to each trade. Slippage is defined as the difference between the price in data and the price in execution not accounting for spreads. Realistically, slippage can work for or against you, but it is necessary to account for a small amount to simulate realistic trading results. We will discuss the degree of slippage that is appropriate for our sample strategies, which will highlight the importance of automation. For this input, 0.001 corresponds to a 0.1 percent handicap in each entry and exit. This will increase the prices when buying and decrease them when selling.

- spreadAdjust is the dollar value to handicap each trade. It works as the dollar-value analog to slipFactor but is most commonly used to adjust for paying the spread in market orders. A value of 0.01 corresponds to a one-cent handicap and is realistic when trading small-dollar volumes on liquid stocks during nonvolatile trading.

- flatCommission is the dollar value of a commission for a single trade of any size. It is incorporated at both entry and exit. If your brokerage offers a $7 flat commission on each trade, 7.00 is the appropriate value. If your brokerage offers a $7 flat commission at only the entry, a value of 3.50 will simulate this properly.

- perShareCommission is the dollar value to handicap the price of each share to simulate the effects of commissions charged on a per-share basis. If the per-share commission is one-half of a cent each way, the proper value is 0.005. At the time of writing, I am unaware of any scenario where the per-share commission is charged on entry only, so one-way per-share commissions are not supported in this function but can be approximated by entering half of the value as in flat commissions.

- verbose is a logical flag indicating whether to output performance information as the function walks through time. We will not use this when running the function through multicore algorithms because the console output is discarded. Some time can be saved reaching the final results by setting this to FALSE.

- failThresh is the dollar value of the equity curve at which to halt the process, returning the incomplete equity curve and a warning message. When testing strategies manually, in a sequential loop, multicore loop, or otherwise, halting failing strategies without throwing errors may help the user save time. It defaults to 0, which is hard to breach because of the geometric nature of compounding, but it is well utilized when set to some fraction of starting cash. There are situations, like during gradient optimization or early exploratory research, where it would be unwise to set this value to something other than zero.

- initP and initp are used during cross validation to pass position and account information across strategy simulations. We will not touch these until the end of Chapter 8.

- equNA is a function used in the data preparation that dynamically enforced maxLookback on stocks that start their S&P tenure in the middle of OPEN and CLOSE.

Listing 7-1. Simulating Performance

```
equNA <- function(v){
  o <- which(!is.na(v))[1]
  return(ifelse(is.na(o), length(v)+1, o))
}
```

```
simulate <- function(OPEN, CLOSE,
                      ENTRY, EXIT, FAVOR,
                      maxLookback, maxAssets, startingCash,
                      slipFactor, spreadAdjust, flatCommission, perShareCommission,
                      verbose = FALSE, failThresh = 0,
                      initP = NULL, initp = NULL){

# Step 1
if( any( dim(ENTRY) != dim(EXIT) ) |
    any( dim(EXIT) != dim(FAVOR) ) |
    any( dim(FAVOR) != dim(CLOSE) ) |
    any( dim(CLOSE) != dim(OPEN)) )
  stop( "Mismatching dimensions in ENTRY, EXIT, FAVOR, CLOSE, or OPEN.")

if( any( names(ENTRY) != names(EXIT)) |
  any( names(EXIT) != names(FAVOR) ) |
  any( names(FAVOR) != names(CLOSE) ) |
  any( names(CLOSE) != names(OPEN) ) |
  is.null(names(ENTRY)) | is.null(names(EXIT)) |
  is.null(names(FAVOR)) | is.null(names(CLOSE)) |
  is.null(names(OPEN)) )
  stop( "Mismatching or missing column names in ENTRY, EXIT, FAVOR, CLOSE, or OPEN.")

FAVOR <- zoo(t(apply(FAVOR, 1, function(v) ifelse(is.nan(v) | is.na(v), 0, v) )),
             order.by = index(CLOSE))

# Step 2
K <- maxAssets
k <- 0
C <- rep(startingCash, times = nrow(CLOSE))
S <- names(CLOSE)

P <- p <- zoo( matrix(0, ncol=ncol(CLOSE), nrow=nrow(CLOSE)),
               order.by = index(CLOSE) )

if( !is.null( initP ) & !is.null( initp ) ){
  P[1:maxLookback,] <-
    matrix(initP, ncol=length(initP), nrow=maxLookback, byrow = TRUE)
  p[1:maxLookback,] <-
    matrix(initp, ncol=length(initp), nrow=maxLookback, byrow = TRUE)
}
names(P) <- names(p) <- S

equity <- rep(NA, nrow(CLOSE))

rmNA <- pmax(unlist(lapply(FAVOR, equNA)),
      unlist(lapply(ENTRY, equNA)),
      unlist(lapply(EXIT, equNA)))

for( j in 1:ncol(ENTRY) ){
  toRm <- rmNA[j]
```

```
  if( toRm > (maxLookback + 1) &
      toRm < nrow(ENTRY) ){
    FAVOR[1:(toRm-1),j] <- NA
    ENTRY[1:(toRm-1),j] <- NA
    EXIT[1:(toRm-1),j] <- NA
  }
}

# Step 3
for( i in maxLookback:(nrow(CLOSE)-1) ){

  # Step 4
  C[i+1] <- C[i]
  P[i+1,] <- as.numeric(P[i,])
  p[i+1,] <- as.numeric(p[i,])

  longS <- S[which(P[i,] > 0)]
  shortS <- S[which(P[i,] < 0)]
  k <- length(longS) + length(shortS)

  # Step 5
  longTrigger <- setdiff(S[which(ENTRY[i,] == 1)], longS)
  shortTrigger <- setdiff(S[which(ENTRY[i,] == -1)], shortS)
  trigger <- c(longTrigger, shortTrigger)

  if( length(trigger) > K ) {

    keepTrigger <- trigger[order(c(as.numeric(FAVOR[i,longTrigger]),
                                 -as.numeric(FAVOR[i,shortTrigger])),
                            decreasing = TRUE)][1:K]

    longTrigger <- longTrigger[longTrigger %in% keepTrigger]
    shortTrigger <- shortTrigger[shortTrigger %in% keepTrigger]
    trigger <- c(longTrigger, shortTrigger)

  }

  triggerType <- c(rep(1, length(longTrigger)), rep(-1, length(shortTrigger)))

  # Step 6
  longExitTrigger <- longS[longS %in%
                        S[which(EXIT[i,] == 1 | EXIT[i,] == 999)]]

  shortExitTrigger <- shortS[shortS %in%
                          S[which(EXIT[i,] == -1 | EXIT[i,] == 999)]]

  exitTrigger <- c(longExitTrigger, shortExitTrigger)

  # Step 7
  needToExit <- max( (length(trigger) - length(exitTrigger)) - (K - k), 0)
```

```
if( needToExit > 0 ){

  toExitLongS <- setdiff(longS, exitTrigger)
  toExitShortS <- setdiff(shortS, exitTrigger)

  toExit <- character(0)

  for( counter in 1:needToExit ){
    if( length(toExitLongS) > 0 & length(toExitShortS) > 0 ){
      if( min(FAVOR[i,toExitLongS]) < min(-FAVOR[i,toExitShortS]) ){
        pullMin <- which.min(FAVOR[i,toExitLongS])
        toExit <- c(toExit, toExitLongS[pullMin])
        toExitLongS <- toExitLongS[-pullMin]
      } else {
        pullMin <- which.min(-FAVOR[i,toExitShortS])
        toExit <- c(toExit, toExitShortS[pullMin])
        toExitShortS <- toExitShortS[-pullMin]
      }
    } else if( length(toExitLongS) > 0 & length(toExitShortS) == 0 ){
      pullMin <- which.min(FAVOR[i,toExitLongS])
      toExit <- c(toExit, toExitLongS[pullMin])
      toExitLongS <- toExitLongS[-pullMin]
    } else if( length(toExitLongS) == 0 & length(toExitShortS) > 0 ){
      pullMin <- which.min(-FAVOR[i,toExitShortS])
      toExit <- c(toExit, toExitShortS[pullMin])
      toExitShortS <- toExitShortS[-pullMin]
    }
  }

  longExitTrigger <- c(longExitTrigger, longS[longS %in% toExit])
  shortExitTrigger <- c(shortExitTrigger, shortS[shortS %in% toExit])

}

# Step 8
exitTrigger <- c(longExitTrigger, shortExitTrigger)
exitTriggerType <- c(rep(1, length(longExitTrigger)),
                     rep(-1, length(shortExitTrigger)))

# Step 9
if( length(exitTrigger) > 0 ){
  for( j in 1:length(exitTrigger) ) {

    exitPrice <- as.numeric(OPEN[i+1,exitTrigger[j]])

    effectivePrice <- exitPrice * (1 - exitTriggerType[j] * slipFactor) -
      exitTriggerType[j] * (perShareCommission + spreadAdjust)

    if( exitTriggerType[j] == 1 ){

      C[i+1] <- C[i+1] +
```

```
      ( as.numeric( P[i,exitTrigger[j]] ) * effectivePrice )
      - flatCommission

    } else {

      C[i+1] <- C[i+1] -
        ( as.numeric( P[i,exitTrigger[j]] ) *
            ( 2 * as.numeric(p[i, exitTrigger[j]]) - effectivePrice ) )
      - flatCommission
    }

    P[i+1, exitTrigger[j]] <- 0
    p[i+1, exitTrigger[j]] <- 0

    k <- k - 1
  }
}

# Step 10
if( length(trigger) > 0 ){
  for( j in 1:length(trigger) ){

    entryPrice <- as.numeric(OPEN[i+1,trigger[j]])

    effectivePrice <- entryPrice * (1 + triggerType[j] * slipFactor) +
      triggerType[j] * (perShareCommission + spreadAdjust)

    P[i+1,trigger[j]] <- triggerType[j] *
      floor( ( (C[i+1] - flatCommission) / (K - k) ) / effectivePrice )

    p[i+1,trigger[j]] <- effectivePrice

    C[i+1] <- C[i+1] -
      ( triggerType[j] * as.numeric(P[i+1,trigger[j]]) * effectivePrice )
      - flatCommission

    k <- k + 1

  }
}

# Step 11
equity[i] <- C[i+1]
for( s in S[which(P[i+1,] > 0)] ){
  equity[i] <- equity[i] +
    as.numeric(P[i+1,s]) *
    as.numeric(OPEN[i+1,s])
}

for( s in S[which(P[i+1,] < 0)] ){
  equity[i] <- equity[i] -
```

```r
    as.numeric(P[i+1,s]) *
    ( 2 * as.numeric(p[i+1,s]) - as.numeric(OPEN[i+1,s]) )
  }

  if( equity[i] < failThresh ){
    warning("\n*** Failure Threshold Breached ***\n")
    break
  }

  # Step 12
  if( verbose ){
    if( i %% 21 == 0 ){
      cat(paste0("############################### ",
              round(100 * (i - maxLookback) /
                    (nrow(CLOSE) - 1 - maxLookback), 1), "%",
              " ###############################\n"))
      cat(paste("Date:\t",as.character(index(CLOSE)[i])), "\n")
      cat(paste0("Equity:\t", " $", signif(equity[i], 5), "\n"))
      cat(paste0("CAGR:\t ",
              round(100 * ((equity[i] / (equity[maxLookback]))^
                      (252/(i - maxLookback + 1)) - 1), 2),
              "%"))
      cat("\n")
      cat("Assets:\t", S[P[i+1,] != 0])
      cat("\n\n")
    }
  }

}

# Step 13
return(list(equity = equity, C = C, P = P, p = p))

}
```

Discussion

It is important to consider that this simulator is built around the limitations of our platform and data. We only have access to prices after the market close, so the simulator will simulate making decisions the night before and entering the position in the morning. Opening prices often differ from closing prices, which is not ideal. This is a drawback we will have to live with when using Yahoo! Finance data to make trading decisions.

We have assumed and only allowed for fixed-proportion compounding in our simulator. Simulators and strategies can be arbitrarily complex, and users are invited to modify the simulator as they see the need. Speed is the biggest motivator to build case-specific simulators. In arriving at the simulator presented in this text, many faster simulators were built with fewer points of flexibility. For example, ignoring the need for the EXIT matrix, neglecting to support shorts, and returning less output removes logic gates and subprocesses that slow down the simulator. Many users will want to build long-only simulators if trading only large-cap U.S. equities.

This simulator views portfolios as unlevered. This means that a long or short position is assumed to be fully purchased in cash or fully collateralized in cash, respectively. In other words, the leverage multiple is one or the margin ratio is 100 percent. The motivation for this comes from the idea that leveraged accounts can almost always utilize their leverage in either direction, long or short, if leverage is available at all. In effect, this is equivalent to trading with a large account size with limitations on how much can be lost. The simulator views portfolios as unlevered but can be parameterized to simulate levered accounts. Additionally, there is a comparability advantage in handling leverage in this manner.

Simulation of levered has greater comparability when we consider startingCash to be the total available dollar value for trading given the leverage multiple and consider failThresh to be the dollar value at which the account is automatically liquidated by the brokerage. For example, if a trader placed $2,000 of cash into an account with the leverage multiple 50, he would have $100,000 to trade, but the brokerage would liquidate his positions if the equity value of his assets fell below $98,000, the point where he can no longer collateralize loss. We can achieve this behavior in our simulator by setting startingCash to $100,000 and failThresh to $98,000. Thus, we can fully accommodate for simulation of leveraged portfolios if we view leverage as loaned cash. Traders can further adjust slipFactor, spreadAdjust, flatCommission, and perShareCommission to account for higher trading costs accrued in the course of leveraging.

To build a simulator that supports shorts, we need to be able calculate the equity value of a short position at any given time. The equity value of a position expresses the cash value of any position at a given time. The formulation for the value of a long position is simple. The equity of a long position at time t is equal to the number of shares n multiplied by the price y_t. For shorts, the equity value of the position depends on the entry price. For entry price y_e, an unlevered short involves fully collateralizing ny_e dollars at initiation and buying back the stock at time t for a profit of $n(y_e - y_t)$ dollars. When the trade is exited, the cash is freed (no longer required as collateral) and the trader receives the profit. Therefore, the equity value of a short at time t is $ny_e + n(y_e - y_t) = n(2y_e - y_t)$. This logic is reflected in steps 9 and 11 in our simulator.

Implementing Example Strategies

We will compute the required matrices to simulate the example strategies outlined earlier in this chapter with our simulator function. Listings 7-2, 7-3, and 7-4 will compute inputs and simulate trading for example strategies #1, #2, and #3, respectively.

Listing 7-5 in the following section will compute summary statistics and performance metrics for example strategy #1. We have removed the first 3,500 rows of our data for discussion in this section.

Using the formulas and listings from Chapter 1 should allow you to explore and study strategies thoroughly. Chapter 8 will build on this ability by automating the research process further.

Listing 7-2. Long-Only Portfolio MACD

```
SUBDATA <- lapply(DATA, function(v) v[-(1:3500),])
SUBRETURN <- RETURN[-(1:3500),]

n1 <- 5
n2 <- 34
nSharpe <- 20
shThresh <- 0.80

INDIC <- mcTimeSeries(SUBDATA[["Close"]],
                      function(v) mean(v[(n2 - n1 + 1):n2]) - mean(v),
                      TRUE, n2, workers)

entryfunc <- function(v){
  cols <- ncol(v) / 2
  as.numeric(v[1,1:cols] <= 0 &
             v[2,1:cols] > 0 &
```

```
                    v[2,(cols+1):(2*cols)] >
                    quantile(v[2,(cols+1):(2*cols)], shThresh, na.rm = TRUE)
            )
}

FAVOR <- mcTimeSeries(SUBRETURN,
                    function(v) mean(v, na.rm = TRUE)/sd(v, na.rm = TRUE),
                    TRUE, nSharpe, workers)

ENTRY <- mcTimeSeries(cbind(INDIC, FAVOR),
                    entryfunc,
                    FALSE, 2, workers)

EXIT <- zoo(matrix(0, ncol=ncol(SUBDATA[["Close"]]), nrow=nrow(SUBDATA[["Close"]])),
            order.by = index(SUBDATA[["Close"]]))
names(EXIT) <- names(SUBDATA[["Close"]])

K <- 10

maxLookback <- max(n1, n2, nSharpe) + 1

RESULTS <- simulate(SUBDATA[["Open"]], SUBDATA[["Close"]],
                    ENTRY, EXIT, FAVOR,
                    maxLookback, K, 100000,
                    0.0005, 0.01, 3.5, 0,
                    TRUE, 0)
## Attaching package: 'tools'
##
## The following object is masked from 'package:XML':
##
##      toHTML
```

Listing 7-3. Portfolio Bollinger Bands

```
SUBDATA <- lapply(DATA, function(v) v[-(1:3500),])
SUBRETURN <- RETURN[-(1:3500),]

n1 <- 20
n2 <- 100
maxLookback <- max(n2, n1) + 1

SD <- mcTimeSeries(SUBDATA[["Close"]],
                    function(v) sd(v, na.rm = TRUE),
                    TRUE, n1, workers)

MOVAVG <- mcTimeSeries(SUBDATA[["Close"]],
                    function(v) mean(v, na.rm = TRUE),
                    TRUE, n1, workers)

LONGMOVAVG <- mcTimeSeries(SUBDATA[["Close"]],
                    function(v) mean(v, na.rm = TRUE),
                    TRUE, n2, workers)
```

```r
bt <- (SUBDATA[["Close"]] - MOVAVG) / SD
Bt <- (MOVAVG - LONGMOVAVG) / SD

triggerfunc <- function(v, columns) {

  goLong <- as.numeric(
    ((v[2,1:columns] >= 1 & v[2,1:columns] < 3) | v[2,1:columns] <= -3) &
    (v[1,(columns+1):(2*columns)] >= -2 & v[2,(columns+1):(2*columns)] < -2)
  )

  goShort <- as.numeric(
    ((v[2,1:columns] > -3 & v[2,1:columns] <= -1) | v[2,1:columns] >= 3) &
    (v[1,(columns+1):(2*columns)] <= 2 & v[2,(columns+1):(2*columns)] > 2)
  )

  return( goLong - goShort )

}

exitfunc <- function(v, columns){

  exitLong <- as.numeric(v[2,(columns+1):(2*columns)] >= 2 &
                         v[1,(columns+1):(2*columns)] < 2)

  exitShort <- -as.numeric(v[1,(columns+1):(2*columns)] >= -2 &
                           v[2,(columns+1):(2*columns)] < -2)

  exitAll <- 999 * as.numeric( (v[1,1:columns] >= 0 & v[2,1:columns] < 0) |
                   (v[1,1:columns] <= 0 & v[2,1:columns] > 0) )

  out <- exitLong + exitShort + exitAll

  out[out > 1] <- 999
  out[!out %in% c(-1,0,1,999)] <- 0

  return( out )

}

columns <- ncol(SUBDATA[["Close"]])

ENTRY <- mcTimeSeries(cbind(Bt, bt), function(v) triggerfunc(v, columns),
                   FALSE, 2, workers)

FAVOR <- mcTimeSeries(SUBRETURN, mean, TRUE, n1, workers)

EXIT <- mcTimeSeries(cbind(Bt, bt), function(v) exitfunc(v, columns),
                   FALSE, 2, workers)

K <- 20
```

```
RESULTS <- simulate(SUBDATA[["Open"]], SUBDATA[["Close"]],
                    ENTRY, EXIT, FAVOR,
                    maxLookback, K, 100000,
                    0.0005, 0.01, 3.5, 0,
                    TRUE, 0)
```

Listing 7-4. Portfolio RSI Reversal

```
SUBDATA <- lapply(DATA, function(v) v[-(1:3500),])
SUBRETURN <- RETURN[-(1:3500),]

truerangefunc <- function(v, cols){
  pmax(v[2, (cols+1):(2*cols)] - v[2,1:cols],
    abs(v[2, 1:cols]-v[1, (2*cols + 1):(3*cols)]),
    abs(v[1, (cols+1):(2*cols)]-v[2, (2*cols + 1):(3*cols)]))
}

cols <- ncol(SUBDATA[["Close"]])
TR <- mcTimeSeries(cbind(SUBDATA[["Low"]], SUBDATA[["High"]], SUBDATA[["Close"]]),
                   function(v) truerangefunc(v, cols), FALSE, 2, workers)

# Calculate ATR with SMA method
ATR <- mcTimeSeries(TR, mean, TRUE, 20, workers)

ROLLMIN <- mcTimeSeries(SUBDATA[["Close"]], min, TRUE, 100, workers)
ROLLMAX <- mcTimeSeries(SUBDATA[["Close"]], max, TRUE, 100, workers)

m_plus <- (ROLLMAX - SUBDATA[["Close"]]) / ATR
m_minus <- (SUBDATA[["Close"]] - ROLLMIN) / ATR

RS <- mcTimeSeries(SUBRETURN,
                   function(v) mean(v[v>0], na.rm = T) / mean(v[v<0], na.rm = T),
                   TRUE, 20, workers)

RSI <- mcTimeSeries( RS, function(v) 100 - (100 / (1 + v)), FALSE, 1, workers)

entryfunc <- function(v, cols){

  goshort <- v[2,1:cols] <= 2 &
    (v[1,(2*cols+1):(3*cols)] > 70 &
      v[2,(2*cols+1):(3*cols)] <= 70 )

  golong <- v[2,(cols+1):(2*cols)] <= 2 &
  (v[1,(2*cols+1):(3*cols)] < 30 &
    v[2,(2*cols+1):(3*cols)] >= 30 )

  return( as.numeric(golong) - as.numeric(goshort) )

}

ENTRY <- mcTimeSeries(cbind(m_plus, m_minus, RSI),
                      function(v) entryfunc(v, cols), FALSE, 2, workers)
```

```
FAVOR <- mcTimeSeries(SUBRETURN, mean, TRUE, 20, workers)

exitfunc <- function(v){
  cols <- ncol(SUBDATA[["Close"]])
  exitlong <- as.numeric(v > 70 | v < 15)
  exitshort <- as.numeric(v < 30 | v > 85)
  return( exitlong - exitshort )
}

EXIT <- mcTimeSeries(RSI, exitfunc, FALSE, 1, workers)

K <- 20

RESULTS <- simulate(SUBDATA[["Open"]], SUBDATA[["Close"]],
                    ENTRY, EXIT, FAVOR,
                    maxLookback, K, 100000,
                    0.0005, 0.01, 3.5, 0,
                    TRUE, 0)
```

Summary Statistics and Performance Metrics

Listing 7-5 computes summary statistics and performance metrics given the list() results of a run with the simulator function. The outputs of the simulator function are sufficient to compute performance metrics as described in Table 1-1. Figures 7-1 and 7-2 plot the return series and equity curve for the abbreviated data running the MACD long-only strategy.

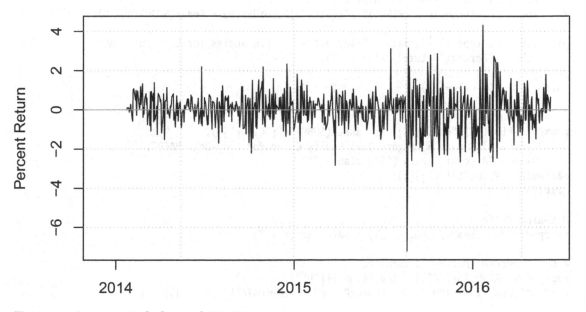

Figure 7-1. *Return series for long-only MACD*

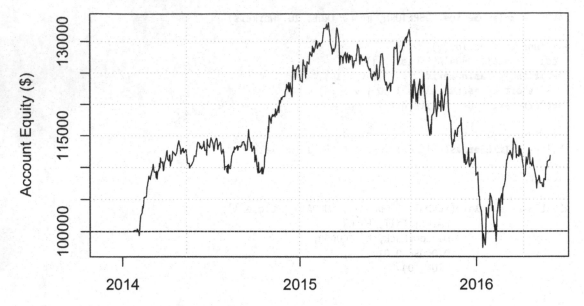

Figure 7-2. *Equity curve for long-only MACD*

Listing 7-5. Summary Statistics and Performance Metrics

```
changeInEquity <- c(NA, RESULTS[["equity"]][-1] -
                    RESULTS[["equity"]][-length(RESULTS[["equity"]])])

# Return Series as defined in Chapter 1
R <- zoo(changeInEquity / (RESULTS[["equity"]]), order.by = index(SUBDATA[["Close"]]))

plot(100 * R, type = "l", main = "Figure 7.1: Return Series for Long-Only MACD",
     ylab = "Percent Return", xlab = "")
grid()
abline( h = 0, col = 8 )

# Equity Curve
plot(y = RESULTS[["equity"]], x = index(SUBDATA[["Close"]]),
     type = "l", main = "Figure 7.2: Equity Curve for Long-Only MACD",
     ylab = "Account Equity ($)", xlab = "")
abline(h = RESULTS[["C"]][1])
grid()

# Sharpe Ratio
sharpeRatio <- mean(R, na.rm = T) / sd(R, na.rm = T)

# Daily percent portfolio turnover
changeP <- RESULTS[["P"]] - lag(RESULTS[["P"]], k = -1)
percentTurnover <- 100 * (sum(changeP > 0) / nrow(DATA[["Close"]])) / K
```

Conclusion

In this chapter, we built a simulator that balances flexibility and speed. Depending on complexity of the strategy and volume of data used in simulation, the simulation process can take anywhere from 30 seconds to a few hours to run. This is extremely useful for manual exploration and research into the effectiveness of certain trading strategies, but we eventually want to settle on a specific strategy and test a range of parameters for it. In Chapter 8, we will place the simulator function inside a for loop to search for optimal parameters on our behalf. Depending on the objectives of the developer, we may use a handful of different methods to accomplish this.

CHAPTER 8

■ ■ ■

Optimization

Optimization is more than finding the best simulation results. It is itself a complex and evolving field that, subject to certain information constraints, allows data scientists, statisticians, engineers, and traders alike to perform reality checks on modeling results. We will discuss common ideological pitfalls and how to avoid them. We will talk about cross validation and its specific application to time series, and we will use our simulator from Chapter 7 to project trading performance with confidence and validity.

We will discuss the best optimization methods and performance metrics. Our simulator takes a considerable amount of time to run, so it is in our best interest to condense parameters and minimize calls to the function within an optimizer.

Cross Validation in Time Series

In Chapter 7, we built a simulator. The simulator tells us how a given strategy with certain account constraints performs over a period of time. Developers can manually test and reconfigure strategies to learn which strategies and configurations perform best over a certain period of time. Developers will be tempted to assume that a configuration that performs well in one period will perform similarly in another. As a basic principle of statistics, we know that good performance in the past does not guarantee good performance in the future. The vast majority of people will avoid this ideological pitfall.

There are less obvious ideological pitfalls we need to avoid. A developer may feel some sense of accomplishment when he discovers a strategy and configuration that performs well over a long period of time. Naturally, there is reason to get excited about a strategy that makes solid returns over years or decades and avoids catastrophic losses during recessions. Unfortunately, this is a substantial ideological pitfall.

The developer has tinkered with the strategy and parameters to optimize performance over a long period of time. He assumes that this strategy will perform well in the future because it weathered many business cycles and made consistent gains. He is excited to put the strategy into production and start generating profits, but important logistics questions remain. How will he determine the best strategy a year from now? Will he keep using the current strategy? Or will he repeat the process of optimizing over all available data and use the best new strategy in the following year? Important projection questions remain. If the strategy made 30 percent in 2016, how much can the developer expect to make 2017?

Any performance projections of a strategy optimized in this manner are invalid because of the use of information in the future to adjust parameters in the past. In classical statistics, optimization in this manner is called *curve fitting* and is solved by *cross validation*.

In statistics, the concepts of tests and models correspond to the concepts of simulations and strategies in trading. The motivating idea behind cross validation is that test results are not valid unless there is (at minimum) a weakly deterministic process for arriving at the parameterization of the model using information outside and independent of the test data set.

In trading terms, simulation performance is not valid unless there is (at minimum) a weakly deterministic process for arriving at the parameterization of the trading strategy using only data available before data in the test data set.

A weakly deterministic process is one that relies on strictly deterministic processes and constrained randomness. A strictly deterministic process is a deliberate and repeatable functional mapping of one set of information to another. Constrained randomness is the generation of random numbers per a strictly deterministic probability distribution. The inclusion of weak determinism in addition to strict determinism exists to allow optimization procedures to declare search points and initial values at random.

Notice in our definition how "outside and independent" in statistics terms equates to "available before" in trading terms. This is a translation from the more general statistical definition of cross validation to the application-specific time-series definition. In most statistical applications, observations are assumed independent, so we can separate training and testing data by randomly sampling observations. In time series, if we want to simulate performance starting at time t, all data before t is our training data and all data after t is our testing data.

In short, simulation results for data occurring any time after t are trivial acts of curve fitting unless they use only information both occurring and available before t to determine the strategy. To generate performance simulations for the duration of our data, we will move through time, generating a given year's performance simulation with a strategy determined by data available prior to it. This will necessarily exclude the performance simulation for the first year of our data, the year 2000, and include everything up to the present.

Numerical vs. Analytical Optimization

In general, the goal of an optimization problem for objective function $f(\cdot)$ is to find the parameter vector θ such that

$$\theta = \underset{\theta}{argmin}\left[f(\theta)\right].$$

Ultimately, we may find the actual value of θ, or we might find an estimate $\hat{\theta}$ because of natural constraints of the problem. We touched on the difference between analytical and numerical optimization in the introduction of this text. We will delineate further here.

In analytical optimization, we know the form and gradient of the objective function. Note that a gradient is a vector of derivatives in each dimension of the candidate parameter vector. To find the minimum of a function in analytical optimization, we solve for the points where the derivative is equal to zero and test them, keeping the arguments of the minimum value as the global minimum of the function. In almost every case, analytical optimization will find θ rather than $\hat{\theta}$. Analytical optimization is a problem commonly found in calculus and other advanced mathematics that is seldom seen again by practitioners in data science, statistics, and algorithmic trading.

Numerical optimization involves algorithmically searching for the minimum of a function with a known form but an unknown gradient. Claiming to *know* the form of the objective function is a mathematical technicality. We may know how to compute the objective function but find it too computationally expensive to examine its form comprehensively. We not only aim to find the minimum of a function with an undefined gradient but minimize the steps and time taken to find a reasonable estimate for a minimum.

We will only be dealing with numerical optimization in this text. The output of our objective function is a performance metric computed from the results of a simulation, and our simulations are very computationally expensive to run. We will cover a handful of optimization algorithms including Exhaustive, Genetic, Pattern Search, Nelder-Mead, and BFGS. Numerous functions and packages exist to run these algorithms given data and an objective function, but they typically assume near-instantaneous computation of the objective function and strictly continuous inputs. There is a clear necessity to program our own optimizers and adapt them to handle common problems and constraints of trading strategy optimization.

Note that we seek the minimum as opposed to the maximum of the objective function purely as convention. Most performance metrics in finance are designed to be maximized, so we minimize the negative of the performance metric in practice.

Numerical Optimization Overview

We will outline major concepts in numerical optimization and explain their uses.

Gradient optimization involves approximating the gradient of the objective function with respect to its parameters to point the algorithm in the direction of a minimum value. These procedures perform best finding the minima of smooth functions with a medium to large number of parameters (ten or more). The algorithm generally takes steps in the parameter space proportional to the negative gradient in search of minima. Gradient optimization requires the objective function be relatively smooth. Substantial research efforts have sought to generalize gradient optimization to work with nonsmooth objective functions.

While it is possible to implement gradient procedures in trading strategy optimization, we will generally avoid them. Sophisticated gradient optimization algorithms are capable of efficiently locating minima of nonsmooth objective functions, but our objective function has the added challenge of taking integer parameters. Search methods are typically designed to find the minima of objective functions with continuous inputs, so integer inputs must be rounded after declaration to give the objective function a real-valued domain. This is a problem for gradient optimization because the objective function becomes stepwise with respect to integer-valued parameters. Gradients are computed to estimate the magnitude of parameter changes required to find the minimum. Numerical gradient estimates throw unwieldy and misleading values in stepwise functions because the gradient is technically undefined at every step. If we are rounding integer inputs before simulation, the true gradient is undefined at every point $x+0.5$ where x is any integer. Particularly unwieldy and misleading behavior occurs when calculating the gradient near or within steps, leading to unrealistically large or zero-valued gradients, respectively. Figure 8-1 illustrates this phenomenon for a one-dimensional parameter vector θ and the objective function $f(\cdot)$.

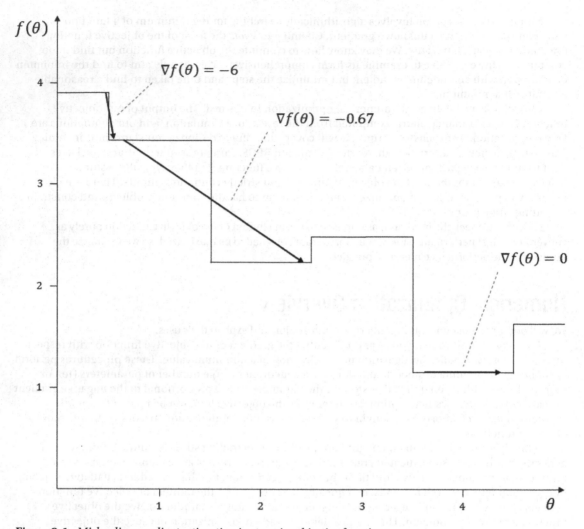

Figure 8-1. *Misleading gradient estimation in stepwise objective functions*

We will avoid gradient search methods in favor of *direct search* methods. Direct search methods use searching algorithms to iteratively discover minima in the objective function. Direct search methods typically take an intuitive search procedure in a one- or two-dimensional parameter space and generalize them to *n*-dimensional parameter vectors. We will cover exhaustive search, generalized pattern search, and Nelder-Mead optimization. We will make preparations to run these algorithms in the next sections.

Parameter Transform for Unbounded Search Algorithms

The generalized pattern search and Nelder-Mead algorithms assume continuous real-valued parameters on the domain of $(-\infty, \infty)$. We will take the logistic transform of the parameters when optimizing with these algorithms. Even in algorithms that do not strictly require continuous unbounded inputs, transforming the parameters improves search robustness in general. Where x represents the input to the logistic function and p represents the logistic transform,

$$p = \frac{1}{1+e^x}$$

with the inverse

$$x = \ln\left(\frac{p}{1-p}\right).$$

The output of the logistic function is bounded by $(0,1)$. In practice, the optimizer will generate candidate vectors that are continuous on the domain $(-\infty,\infty)$. The purpose of the logistic transform is clearer from the manner in which we compute inputs into the simulator. Where θ_{sim} is the candidate parameter vector of logically bounded inputs to the simulator, θ_{min} is a vector of logical minima of the parameter vector, θ_{max} is a vector of logical maxima of the parameter vector, and θ_{opt} is the unbounded candidate vector generated by the optimization algorithm that exists on the domain $(-\infty,\infty)$,

$$\theta_{sim} = \theta_{min} + (\theta_{max} - \theta_{min})\frac{1}{1+e^{-\theta_{opt}}}.$$

This process maps the unbounded candidate vectors generated by optimizers to logically bounded domains specific to each parameter.

Declaring an Evaluator

Optimization algorithms are fairly plug-and-play given a compact evaluator function. An optimization algorithm needs to be able to evaluate the objective function given any valid candidate parameter vector. For our use case, we will declare an evaluator that takes a named parameter vector, transforms the inputs based on rectangular bounds (two constant named vectors) on the parameter vector, subsets our data for a given year, and returns a performance metric for the strategy.

The evaluator function, declared in Listing 8-1, will look sloppier than much of the code we have written up to this point. Any given evaluator function is not part of our code base, but it is a flexible outline of a specific strategy of interest. This function and declaration of inputs to the simulator, which will look strikingly similar, are the most fluid pieces of code presented in this text. They will be changed frequently while researching strategies.

■ **Note:** The code for generating inputs to the long-only MACD has been optimized for speed within the evaluator. It does not match Listing 7-2. In this case, it was found that the `runmean()` function from the caTools package computes means faster than `mcTimeSeries()` because of internal algorithmic improvements. This sacrifices the ability to fine-tune NA-handling at the indicator level, but this is not an issue given the structure of our stock data as established in this text. Users with alternate data containing periodic or regular NA values should explore the ability of `mcTimeSeries()` and `rollapply()` to handle NA values at the indicator level.

Listing 8-1: Pseudocode

1. If requested, transform unbounded parameters to their original domains bounded between minVal and maxVal. This allows optimizers that require continuous unbounded inputs to communicate with our simulator that requires bounded and often integer-only values. If transformOnly = TRUE is specified,

exit the function by returning the bounded parameters after transformation. This is a helpful shortcut for transforming unbounded parameters back into their practical domains without going through the lengthy simulation step.

2.   Regardless of whether the supplied parameters underwent transformation in the first step, this step enforces numeric type and bounding rules as to not break the simulator. For example, we enforce that n1 is an integer greater than or equal to 2. Then we enforce that n2 is an integer greater than or equal to both n1 and 3. This code should be modified as new strategies are built into the evaluator. Incorrect bounding conditions during optimization is a large source of run-time errors.

3.   We subset the data according to the argument y. This can be a range of years or a single year. The simulator will run over the range of years supplied.

4.   The subset requires elements of the DATA object according to the previous step.

5.   Compute the ENTRY, EXIT, and FAVOR matrix according to the strategy specified. This and step 2 are the most variable sections of code. They will change often as you research and develop new strategies.

6.   Simulate the strategy and store the results in a list. If account parameters are passed to the evaluator, supply them to the simulator.

7.   Compute the performance metric and return it. By default, we have supplied the High-Frequency Sharpe Ratio. This will change frequently as users explore new performance metrics. Return the negative of the performance metric if requested. Return the data from simulation rather than the performance metric if requested.

Listing 8-1: Explanation of Inputs and User Guide

- PARAM is a named vector of inputs. These can be bounded according to minVal and maxVal or unbounded on the domain $(-\infty,\infty)$ depending on the value of

  transform. PARAM must have names matching minVal and maxVal if they are supplied.

- minVal and maxVal are named vectors of logical bounds on the values of parameters inputted to the strategy. They need to be supplied if transform or transformOnly is set to TRUE.

- y is a single number, pair of numbers, or range of numbers corresponding to the years to evaluate over. y = 2016 will evaluate performance in 2016. y = 2011:2016 and y = c(2011,2016) will both evaluate performance from 2011 up to and through 2016.

- transform specifies if PARAM is supplied as unbounded parameters subject to our domain transformation based on the logistic transform. If transform = TRUE, minVal and maxVal are required inputs. An example of PARAM input when transform = TRUE could be c(n1 = -0.23, nFact = 3.6, nSharpe = -2.5, shThresh = 3.1). An example of PARAM input with transform = FALSE could be c(n1 = 21, nFact = 3, nSharpe = 43, shThresh = 0.80).

- verbose is the same as in Listing 7-1. This parameter is passed to the simulator if the user desires run-time diagnostics.

- negative specified whether to return the negative value of the performance metric. This assumes that all performance metrics are coded such that greater values correspond to a better assessment of performance. This is useful for extending the evaluator to algorithms that perform minimization as opposed to algorithms that perform maximization.

- transformOnly is set to TRUE if the user desires to use the evaluator as a shortcut to transform to unbounded parameters back to their logically bounded domains. It simply performs the transformation and halts the function early to return the logically bounded parameters.

- returnData is set to TRUE if the user desires to bypass computation of the performance metric and return the list of account variables normally output from the simulator.

- accountParams is set if the user desires to pass positions and cash data of the account across evaluations. This will come into play in Listing 8-6 when we cross validate using the optimization algorithms discussed in the chapter. The list provided to this argument must contain the final row of P, the final row of p, and the final element of C as defined in the Listing 7-1 pseudo-code and as seen in the output of Listing 7-1. See Listing 8-6 for an implementation example.

Listing 8-1. Declaring the Evaluator Function

```
y <- 2014

minVal <- c(n1 = 1, nFact = 1, nSharpe = 1, shThresh = .01)
maxVal <- c(n1 = 150, nFact = 5, nSharpe = 200, shThresh = .99)

PARAM <- c(n1 = -2, nFact = -2, nSharpe = -2, shThresh = 0)

# Declare entry function for use inside evaluator
entryfunc <- function(v, shThresh){
  cols <- ncol(v)/2
  as.numeric(v[1,1:cols] <= 0 &
             v[2,1:cols] > 0 &
             v[2,(cols+1):(2*cols)] >
             quantile(v[2,(cols+1):(2*cols)],
                      shThresh, na.rm = TRUE)
          )
}

evaluate <- function(PARAM, minVal = NA, maxVal = NA, y = 2014,
                     transform = FALSE, verbose = FALSE,
                     negative = FALSE, transformOnly = FALSE,
                     returnData = FALSE, accountParams = NULL){

  # Step 1
  # Convert and declare parameters if they exist on unbounded (-inf,inf) domain
  if( transform | transformOnly ){
    PARAM <- minVal +
    (maxVal - minVal) * unlist(lapply( PARAM, function(v) (1 + exp(-v))^(-1) ))
    if( transformOnly ){
    return(PARAM)
```

```r
    }
}

# Step 2
# Declare n1 as itself, n2 as a multiple of n1 defined by nFact,
# and declare the length and threshold in sharpe ratio for FAVOR.
# This section should handle rounding and logical bounding
# in moving
n1 <- max(round(PARAM[["n1"]]), 2)
n2 <- max(round(PARAM[["nFact"]] * PARAM[["n1"]]), 3, n1+1)
nSharpe <- max(round(PARAM[["nSharpe"]]), 2)
shThresh <- max(0, min(PARAM[["shThresh"]], .99))
maxLookback <- max(n1, n2, nSharpe) + 1


# Step 3
# Subset data according to range of years y
period <-
  index(DATA[["Close"]]) >= strptime(paste0("01-01-", y[1]), "%d-%m-%Y") &
  index(DATA[["Close"]]) < strptime(paste0("01-01-", y[length(y)]+1), "%d-%m-%Y")

period <- period |
  ((1:nrow(DATA[["Close"]]) > (which(period)[1] - maxLookback)) &
  (1:nrow(DATA[["Close"]]) <= (which(period)[sum(period)]) + 1))

# Step 4
CLOSE <- DATA[["Close"]][period,]
OPEN <- DATA[["Open"]][period,]
SUBRETURN <- RETURN[period,]

# Step 5
# Compute inputs for long-only MACD as in Listing 7.2
# Code is optimized for speed using functions from caTools and zoo
require(caTools)
INDIC <- zoo(runmean(CLOSE, n1, endrule = "NA", align = "right") -
                runmean(CLOSE, n2, endrule = "NA", align = "right"),
             order.by = index(CLOSE))
names(INDIC) <- names(CLOSE)

RMEAN <- zoo(runmean(SUBRETURN, n1, endrule = "NA", align = "right"),
             order.by = index(SUBRETURN))

FAVOR <- RMEAN / runmean( (SUBRETURN - RMEAN)^2, nSharpe,
                          endrule = "NA", align = "right" )
names(FAVOR) <- names(CLOSE)

ENTRY <- rollapply(cbind(INDIC, FAVOR),
                   FUN = function(v) entryfunc(v, shThresh),
                   width = 2,
                   fill = NA,
                   align = "right",
                   by.column = FALSE)
names(ENTRY) <- names(CLOSE)
```

```
EXIT <- zoo(matrix(0, ncol=ncol(CLOSE), nrow=nrow(CLOSE)),
            order.by = index(CLOSE))
names(EXIT) <- names(CLOSE)

# Step 6
# Max shares to hold
K <- 10

# Simulate and store results
if( is.null(accountParams) ){
  RESULTS <- simulate(OPEN, CLOSE,
          ENTRY, EXIT, FAVOR,
          maxLookback, K, 100000,
          0.001, 0.01, 3.5, 0,
          verbose, 0)
} else {
  RESULTS <- simulate(OPEN, CLOSE,
      ENTRY, EXIT, FAVOR,
      maxLookback, K, accountParams[["C"]],
      0.001, 0.01, 3.5, 0,
      verbose, 0,
      initP = accountParams[["P"]], initp = accountParams[["p"]])
}

# Step 7
if(!returnData){

  # Compute and return sharpe ratio
  v <- RESULTS[["equity"]]
  returns <- ( v[-1] / v[-length(v)] ) - 1
  out <- mean(returns, na.rm = T) / sd(returns, na.rm = T)
  if(!is.nan(out)){
    if( negative ){
      return( -out )
    } else {
      return( out )
    }
  } else {
    return(0)
  }

} else {
  return(RESULTS)
}
}

# To test value of objective function
objective <- evaluate(PARAM, minVal, maxVal, y)
```

Exhaustive Search Optimization

It is wise to start your research on a new strategy with a wide-spanning exhaustive search. Exhaustive searches involve scanning an n-dimensional grid of parameters, where n is the number of parameters tested. Exhaustive testing is computationally expensive. If testing k_i points for each parameter $i \in 1,2,...,n$, the number of calls to the evaluate() function required to complete the optimization is

$$\prod_{i=1}^{n} k_i.$$

Exhaustive searches are helpful because they allow us to view surface plots of the objective function, informing more detailed exhaustive searches or initial values for other search methods. Listing 8-2 performs an exhaustive search by declaring every possible combination of the test points in the OPTIM data frame. Throughout this chapter, the OPTIM data frame will make a point of storing the inputs and results of every call to the evaluate function made by an algorithm, even when the algorithm does not call for or depend on this data.

Listing 8-2 includes a simple clock for estimating time to completion. It assumes the average completion time is constant throughout the optimization process, which is not necessarily true when parameters increase the maximum lookback and computational complexity as the search progresses. Nonetheless, it will give a rough estimate of time to completion for an optimization. Careless declaration of bounds and step sizes can initialize an optimization process that takes weeks or years.

Notice in Listing 8-2 that we declare equal lower and upper bounds onnFact and nSharpe. This is intentional in order to declare these values in the optimization but prevent the search procedure from scanning through different values of nFact and nSharpe.

We will declare transform = FALSE in our evaluator function to let it know we are not giving it transformed inputs. In Listing 8-2, we optimize with constant step size. You may want to specify transform = TRUE to test with a nonconstant step size in an unbounded parameter space. You can step into the beginning of this code and replace the elements of the POINTS list with any desired sequence of test points without disrupting the rest of the code.

Listing 8-2. Exhaustive Optimization

```
# Declare bounds and step size for optimization
lowerBound <- c(n1 = 5, nFact = 3, nSharpe = 22, shThresh = 0.05)
upperBound <- c(n1 = 80, nFact = 3, nSharpe = 22, shThresh = 0.95)
stepSize <- c(n1 = 5, nFact = 1, nSharpe = 1, shThresh = 0.05)

pnames <- names(stepSize)
np <- length(pnames)

# Declare list of all test points
POINTS <- list()
for( p in pnames ){
  POINTS[[p]] <- seq(lowerBound[[p]], upperBound[[p]], stepSize[[p]])
}
```

```
OPTIM <- data.frame(matrix(NA, nrow = prod(unlist(lapply(POINTS, length))),
                           ncol = np + 1))
names(OPTIM)[1:np] <- names(POINTS)
names(OPTIM)[np+1] <- "obj"

# Store all possible combinations of parameters
for( i in 1:np ){
  each <- prod(unlist(lapply(POINTS, length))[-(1:i)])
  times <- prod(unlist(lapply(POINTS, length))[-(i:length(pnames))])
  OPTIM[,i] <- rep(POINTS[[pnames[i]]], each = each, times = times)
}

# Test each row of OPTIM
timeLapse <- proc.time()[3]
for( i in 1:nrow(OPTIM) ){
  OPTIM[i,np+1] <- evaluate(OPTIM[i,1:np], transform = FALSE, y = 2014)
  cat(paste0("## ", floor( 100 * i / nrow(OPTIM)), "% complete\n"))
  cat(paste0("## ",
             round( ((proc.time()[3] - timeLapse) *
                     ((nrow(OPTIM) - i)/ i))/60, 2),
         " minutes remaining\n\n"))
}
```

Listing 8-3 gives examples of useful visualizations of exhaustive search results. There are many 3D visualization packages in R. The lattice package typically comes with base-R and is lightweight and easy to use. For wireframes, users will have to play with the visualization axes to view the surface plot properly. I suggest keeping x negative and y unchanged so that the plot is oriented with the objective function pointing upward. Adjust the z access to rotate the plot clockwise and counterclockwise to get the best angle.

I suggest the rgl package in R for manually rotating and viewing 3D plots in an interactive GUI.

Listing 8-3. Surface Plots and Level Plots for Exhaustive Optimization

```
library(lattice)
wireframe(obj ~ n1*shThresh, data = OPTIM,
          xlab = "n1", ylab = "shThresh",
          main = "Long-Only MACD Exhaustive Optimization",
          drape = TRUE,
          colorkey = TRUE,
          screen = list(z = 15, x = -60)
)

levelplot(obj ~ n1*shThresh, data = OPTIM,
          xlab = "n1", ylab = "shThresh",
          main = "Long-Only MACD Exhaustive Optimization"
)
```

Figures 8-2 and 8-3 show surface and level plots of the same optimization. In these figures, nFact and nSharpe were held constant at 3 and 22, respectively.

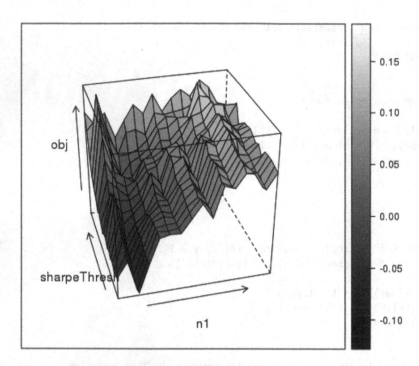

Figure 8-2. *Long-only MACD surface plot*

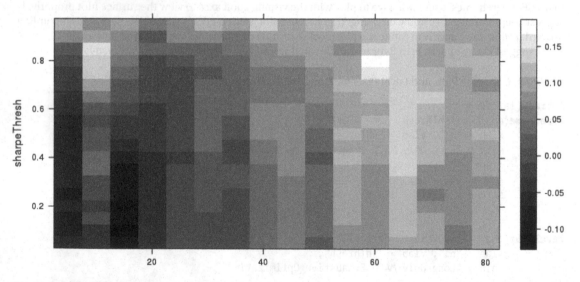

Figure 8-3. *Long-only MACD level plot*

Figures 8-4 and 8-5 show surface and level plots of the same optimization. In these figures, nSharpe and shThresh were held constant at 22 and 0.8, respectively.

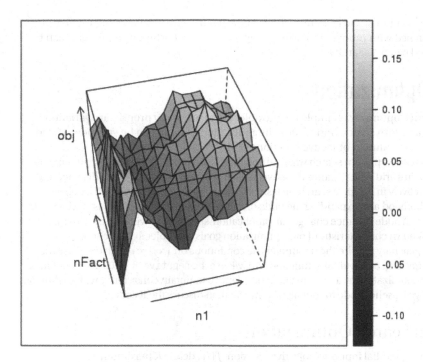

Figure 8-4. *Long-only MACD Sharpe Ratio: surface*

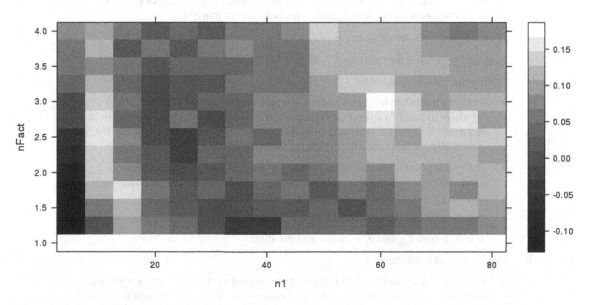

Figure 8-5. *Long-Only MACD Sharpe Ratio: level*

The two optimizations shown in Figures 8-2 through 8-5 took 304 and 208 calls to the evaluator function and found the maxima of the objective function to be about 1.77 and 1.74, respectively. After this lengthy analysis, we have left much of the parameter space unsearched because time constraints forced us to search only two parameter spaces at a time, while fixing the remaining two. A solution to this problem may be to

113

perform many small exhaustive optimizations where sections of the parameter space with high values of the objective function are searched with more granularity for higher maxima. Fortunately, this logic can be automated through generalized pattern search algorithms.

Pattern Search Optimization

The concept of the pattern search optimizer is simple and flexible. There are many proprietary variations to pattern searches. Tailoring a pattern search optimizer to its application domain can be very powerful for discovering the minima of highly nonlinear objective functions.

Similarly to exhausting searches, a pattern search will go through a maximum of K iterations searching the vicinity of the candidate point θ_k in a grid with distance Δ_k between each adjacent node. The node distance and candidate point will change iteratively in a logical searching fashion, shrinking the node distance if it believes the minima is within the neighborhood and expanding the node distance if it believes it should cast a wider net. The details of point movement and node distance changes are application-specific. We will discuss generalized pattern search and tailor it to a known characteristic of our optimization goals and objective function.

Pattern search algorithms generally require the parameters be continuous on $(\infty, -\infty)$, so we will use the default `transform = TRUE` argument in our evaluator function. We will use the `negative = TRUE` argument in our evaluator function, treating the optimization as a minimization problem, to maintain consistency with traditional optimization literature. We will give pseudocode for our algorithm and then discuss the R code.

Generalized Pattern Search Optimization

1. Given range-bound sigmodial inputs to objective function $f(\cdot)$, define K maximum iterations, iteration k, n-dimensional candidate parameter vector θ_k, the i-th element of the k-th candidate parameter vector $\theta_{k,i}$, initial step size $_0 > 0$, iterative step size vector Δ_k, completion threshold Δ_T, and scale factor σ such that $\sigma > 1$.

2. Set $k = 0$. Set $\theta_{0,i} = 0$ for all $i \in 1,...,n$.

3. Evaluate $f(\theta_k)$. Store the result as f_{min}. Start SEARCH subroutine.

4. Define the SEARCH subroutine:

   - Perform n random searches at dual test points $\theta_k \pm \left(2B(.5)-1\right)U\left(\Delta_k, \sigma\Delta_k\right)$ where $B(p)$ and $U(a,b)$ represent two n-dimensional vectors of n independent Bernoulli distributed and uniformly distributed random numbers, respectively. The evaluator function will be called a total of $2n$ times.

   - If any test points evaluate to less than f_{min}, store the new minimum value as f_{min}, store the responsible parameter vector as θ_{k+1}, and increase the step size such that $\Delta_{k+1} = \sigma\Delta_k$. Set $k=k+1$ and repeat the SEARCH subroutine.

   - If no test points evaluate to less than f_{min}, begin the POLL subroutine.

   - If $k=K$, return f_{min} and θ_k, end the optimization.

5. Define the POLL subroutine:

   - For $i \in 1,...,n$, search at dual test points generated as $\theta_k \pm v_i\sigma$, where v_i is an n-dimensional vector with 1 in position i and 0s elsewhere. The evaluator function will be called a total of $2n$ times.

   - If any test points evaluate to less than f_{min}, store the new minimum value as f_{min}, store the responsible parameter vector as θ_{k+1}, and increase the step size such that $\Delta_{k+1} = \sigma\Delta_k$. Set $k=k+1$ and run the SEARCH subroutine.

- If no test points evaluate to less than f_{min}, decrease the step size such that $\Delta_{k+1} = \dfrac{\Delta_k}{\sigma}$. Set $k=k+1$.

  - If $k = K$, return *fmin* and θk, end the optimization.

  - If $\Delta_k < \Delta_T$, set $\Delta_k = \Delta_0$, $\theta_k = U(-\sigma\Delta_k, \sigma\Delta_k)$, and $f_{min} = f(\theta_k)$. Run the SEARCH subroutine.

  - Else run the SEARCH subroutine.

We will define a box to be the n-dimensional analog to a square or cube in this discussion. The algorithm will begin with the SEARCH subroutine, which will test n randomly selected points inside a box with side length $2_\sigma\Delta_k$ but outside a box with side length $2\Delta_k$, both centered at θ_k. This region will be referred to as the *search region* given θ_k, Δ_k, and σ. The SEARCH subroutine also tests the reflections of the n randomly selected points about θk, which will naturally also lie in the search region. This process is exemplified in Figure 8-6. Figures 8-6 and 8-7 plot θk as a hollow circular point and test points as triangles. The gray-shaded area represents the random search region.

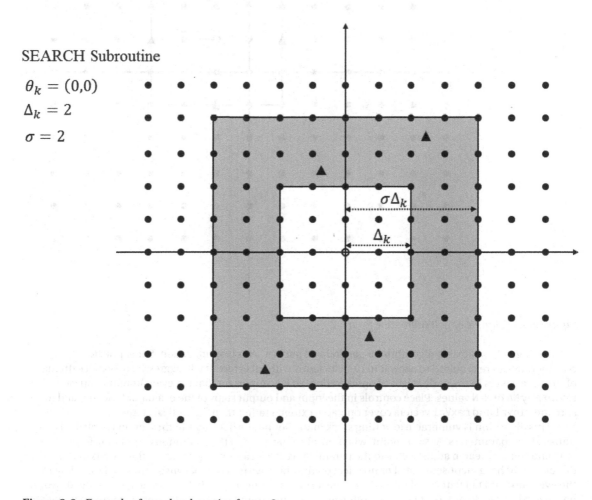

Figure 8-6. *Example of search subroutine for n = 2*

The SEARCH subroutine either will establish a better θ_k, grow the search region, and repeat, or will trigger the POLL subroutine. The POLL subroutine will search adjacent points by picking a parameter $\theta_{k,i}$ and adjusting it by Δ_k in both the positive and negative directions. The POLL subroutine will either establish a better θ_k, grow the search region, and trigger the SEARCH subroutine, or will shrink the search region and trigger the SEARCH subroutine. This process is exemplified in Figure 8-7.

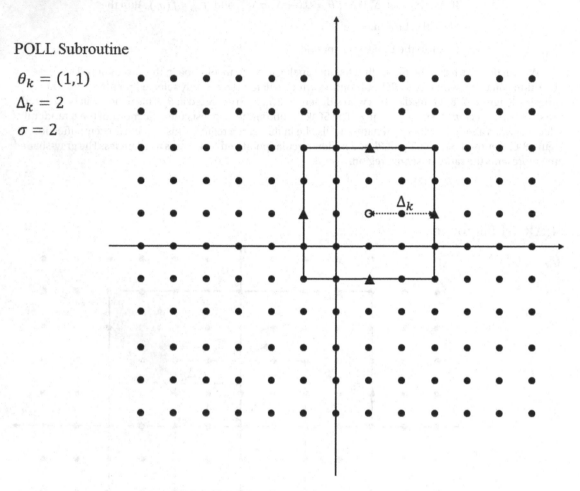

POLL Subroutine

$$\theta_k = (1,1)$$

$$\Delta_k = 2$$

$$\sigma = 2$$

Figure 8-7. *Example of poll subroutine for n = 2*

Listing 8-4 is a flexible algorithm for generalized pattern search optimization. Some practical considerations are required to allow it to run efficiently without errors. It will aggressively search extrema of the parameters in the early stages of optimization, so it is important that the evaluator function cannot return any NA or NaN values. Place controls in the input and output steps of the evaluator function, and make sure the minVal and maxVal vectors cover operable extrema rather than theoretical extrema.

This algorithm is vulnerable to getting stuck in the boundless flat zones in the extrema of the logistic-transformed parameters. At some point, when the absolute value of the continuous input transform is around ten or greater, adjustments to the parameter vector of around up to two or three units in any direction will have inconsequential or no effect on the objective function because of internal rounding in the evaluator and tail flatness of the logistic transform. Adjusting for this behavior is a double-edged sword, because while we do not like to see the optimizer puttering around near-equal extrema, it arrives at that area of the parameter space because there is evidence of global minima and nontrivial local minima.

We will exploit the randomness of the SEARCH subroutine and restart the algorithm with a randomly generated initial parameter vector. This will move the initial search box of the SEARCH algorithm, ideally introducing a new path to local minimization. Whether the path is superior and results in a better minima is trivial, because the information will be stored in the OPTIM data frame along with the previous optimization.

If studying the search path of the optimization repeatedly shows parameters butting up against their extrema, the user should expand the bounds of minVal and maxVal such that they are still functionally logical but allow the optimization to settle somewhere other their extrema. This will make time-consuming calls to the evaluator function more efficient.

It is important to note that pattern search optimizers in general are guaranteed to converge to a local minima but not necessarily guaranteed to converge to a global minimum of the objective function. We randomly initialize new starting points after detecting convergence by the size of Δ_k for this reason. Even where we have successfully avoided allowing the parameters to drift into similar maxima, the algorithm promises to find us only local minima. It is important that we are aware of this so that we can correctly interpret the results of our research.

In any numerical optimization problem, we are only guaranteed to locate a local minimum. We study many optimization problems with a goal of finding the most significant local minima quickly.

Listing 8-4. Generalized Pattern Search Optimization

```
# Maximum iterations
# Max possible calls to evaluator is K * (4 * n + 1)
K <- 100

# Restart with random init when delta is below threshold
deltaThresh <- 0.05

# Set initial delta
delta <- deltaNaught <- 1

# Scale factor
sigma <- 2

# Vector theta_0
PARAM <- PARAMNaught <- c(n1 = 0, nFact = 0, nSharpe = 0, shThresh = 0)

# bounds
minVal <- c(n1 = 1, nFact = 1, nSharpe = 1, shThresh = 0.01)
maxVal <- c(n1 = 250, nFact = 10, nSharpe = 250, shThresh = .99)

np <- length(PARAM)

OPTIM <- data.frame(matrix(NA, nrow = K * (4 * np + 1), ncol = np + 1))
names(OPTIM) <- c(names(PARAM), "obj"); o <- 1

fmin <- fminNaught <- evaluate(PARAM, minVal, maxVal, negative = TRUE, y = y)
OPTIM[o,] <- c(PARAM, fmin); o <- o + 1

# Print function for reporting progress in loop
printUpdate <- function(step){
  if(step == "search"){
    cat(paste0("Search step: ", k,"|",l,"|",m, "\n"))
  } else if (step == "poll"){
```

```
      cat(paste0("Poll step: ", k,"|",l,"|",m, "\n"))
   }
  names(OPTIM)
  cat("\t", paste0(strtrim(names(OPTIM), 6), "\t"), "\n")
  cat("Best:\t",
      paste0(round(unlist(OPTIM[which.min(OPTIM$obj),]),3), "\t"), "\n")
  cat("Theta:\t",
      paste0(round(unlist(c(PARAM, fmin)),3), "\t"), "\n")
  cat("Trial:\t",
      paste0(round(as.numeric(OPTIM[o-1,]), 3), "\t"), "\n")
  cat(paste0("Delta: ", round(delta,3) , "\t"), "\n\n")
}

for( k in 1:K ){

  # SEARCH subroutine
  for( l in 1:np ){
    net <- (2 * rbinom(np, 1, .5) - 1) * runif(np, delta, sigma * delta)
    for( m in c(-1,1) ){

      testpoint <- PARAM + m * net
      ftest <- evaluate(testpoint, minVal, maxVal, negative = TRUE, y = y)
      OPTIM[o,] <- c(testpoint, ftest); o <- o + 1
      printUpdate("search")

    }
  }

  if( any(OPTIM$obj[(o-(2*np)):(o-1)] < fmin ) ){

    minPos <- which.min(OPTIM$obj[(o-(2*np)):(o-1)])
    PARAM <- (OPTIM[(o-(2*np)):(o-1),1:np])[minPos,]
    fmin <- (OPTIM[(o-(2*np)):(o-1),np+1])[minPos]
    delta <- sigma * delta

  } else {

    # POLL Subroutine
    for( l in 1:np ){
      net <- delta * as.numeric(1:np == l)
      for( m in c(-1,1) ){
        testpoint <- PARAM + m * net
        ftest <- evaluate(testpoint, minVal, maxVal, negative = TRUE, y = y)
        OPTIM[o,] <- c(testpoint, ftest); o <- o + 1
        printUpdate("poll")

      }
    }
```

```
    if( any(OPTIM$obj[(o-(2*np)):(o-1)] < fmin ) ){

      minPos <- which.min(OPTIM$obj[(o-(2*np)):(o-1)])
      PARAM <- (OPTIM[(o-(2*np)):(o-1),1:np])[minPos,]
      fmin <- (OPTIM[(o-(2*np)):(o-1),np+1])[minPos]
      delta <- sigma * delta

    } else {

      delta <- delta / sigma

    }

  }

  cat(paste0("\nCompleted Full Iteration: ", k, "\n\n"))

  # Restart with random initiate
  if( delta < deltaThresh ) {

    delta <- deltaNaught
    fmin <- fminNaught
    PARAM <- PARAMNaught + runif(n = np, min = -delta * sigma,
                                 max = delta * sigma)

    ftest <- evaluate(PARAM, minVal, maxVal,
                      negative = TRUE, y = y)
    OPTIM[o,] <- c(PARAM, ftest); o <- o + 1

    cat("\nDelta Threshold Breached, Restarting with Random Initiate\n\n")

  }

}

# Return the best optimization in untransformed parameters
evaluate(OPTIM[which.min(OPTIM$obj),1:np], minVal, maxVal, transformOnly = TRUE)
```

The pattern search in Listing 8-4 is much more effective than exhaustive optimization at locating meaningful minima of the objective function. In about 475 calls to the evaluator, at iteration 31, it located a point with a Sharpe Ratio of 0.227. This is far superior to our exhaustive optimization where we made 512 calls to the evaluator over two separate optimizations to find a maximum Sharpe Ratio of 0.177. Both of these optimizations will take between one and two hours on a home computer. Figure 8-8 shows the running minimum of the negative Sharpe Ratio in a run of the pattern search optimizer. Note that the x-axis represents the number of calls to the evaluator (equivalently row number in OPTIM) rather than iteration number k. A single iteration can make between $2n$ and $4n+1$ calls to the evaluator.

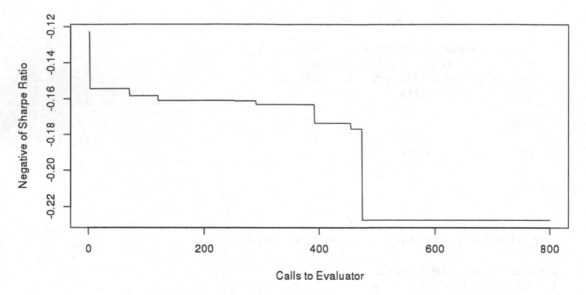

Figure 8-8. *Running minimum of objective function for pattern search*

Notice how we manually set up two separate runs of the exhaustive optimizer, but we simply let the pattern search optimizer run with no user input. A good approach to using the pattern search optimizer in Listing 8-4 is to set *K* extremely high and let the optimizer run over the night, day, or week. Plan on manually stopping the optimizer when the output is showing no improvements for a significant amount of time.

Nelder-Mead Optimization

The final optimization method we will discuss is Nelder-Mead. This algorithm is a direct search process in a class of optimizers called *simplex methods*. Simplex methods iteratively transform an *n*-dimensional simplex to locate minima of the objective function. In the same way we defined a box to be an *n*-dimensional analog to a square or cube, the term *simplex* is a more formal one that defines the *n*-dimensional analog of a triangle or triangular pyramid. It can be simply defined as a set of *n*+1 points that form a polyhedron with finite nonzero *n*-volume in an *n*-dimensional space.

Nelder-Mead with Random Initialization

1. Given range-bound sigmodial inputs to objective function $f(\cdot)$, define *K* maximum iterations, iteration *k*, *n*+1 vertices of an *n*-dimensional simplex that represents candidate parameter vectors θ_i for $i \in 1,...,n+1$. The *j*-th element of the *i*-th simplex point as $\theta_{i,j}$ for $j \in 1,...,n$.

2. Define reflection factor α such that $\alpha > 0$, expansion factor γ such that $\gamma > 0$, contraction factor ρ such that $0 < \rho < 1$, and shrink factor σ such that $0 < \sigma < 1$, initial simplex size Δ such that $\Delta > 0$, and convergence threshold δ such that $\delta > 0$.

3. Set $\theta_{i,j} = -\dfrac{\Delta}{2} + \Delta v_{j-1}$ for all $i \in 1,...,n+1$ and all $j \in 1,...,n$, where v_j represents an *n*-dimensional vector with 1 in the *j*-th position and 0 elsewhere. v_0 is a zero vector.

4. Set $k=0$. Define θ_0 to be centroid of the vertices θ_i for $i \in 1,...,n$ computed as the mean of each dimension such that

$$\theta_{0,j} = \frac{\sum_{i=1}^{n} \theta_{i,j}}{n}.$$

5. Evaluate $f(\theta_i)$ and store as f_i for all $i \in 1,...,n+1$.

6. Define the ORDER subroutine:

    - Set $k = k + 1$.
    - Order the evaluations f_i. Reassign indices to θ_i and f_i for $i \in 1,...,n+1$ such that $f_1 \le f_2 \le ... \le f_{n+1}$.
    - Run the CONVERGENCE subroutine.
    - Compute the updated centroid θ_0.
    - Start the REFLECT subroutine.

7. Define the REFLECTION subroutine:

    - Compute the reflected point $\theta_r = \theta_0 + \alpha(\theta_0 - \theta_{n+1})$. Evaluate $f_r = f(\theta_r)$.
    - If $f_1 \le f_r < f_n$, set $\theta_{n+1} = \theta_r$ and $f_{n+1} = f_r$. Start the ORDER subroutine.
    - If $f_r < f_1$, start the EXPAND subroutine.

8. Define the EXPAND subroutine:

    - Compute the expansion point $\theta_e = \theta_0 + \gamma(\theta_r - \theta_0)$. Evaluate $f_e = f(\theta_e)$.
    - If $f_e < f_r$, set $\theta_{n+1} = \theta_e$ and $f_{n+1} = f_e$. Start the ORDER subroutine.
    - If $f_r < f_e$, set $\theta_{n+1} = \theta_r$ and $f_{n+1} = f_r$. Start the ORDER subroutine.

9. Define the CONTRACT subroutine:

    - Compute contraction point $\theta_c = \theta_0 + \rho(\theta_{n+1} - \theta_0)$. Evaluate $f_c = f(\theta_c)$.
    - If $f_c < f_{n+1}$, set $\theta_{n+1} = \theta_c$ and $f_{n+1} = f_c$. Start the ORDER subroutine.
    - If $f_r < f_e$, set $\theta_{n+1} = \theta_r$ and $f_{n+1} = f_r$. Start the ORDER subroutine.

10. Define the SHRINK subroutine:

    - Set $\theta_i = \theta_1 + \sigma(\theta_i - \theta_1)$ and compute $f_i = f(\theta_i)$ for $i \in 2,...,n+1$.
    - Start the ORDER subroutine.

11. Define the CONVERGENCE subroutine:

    - Define s, a proxy for the size of a simplex, to be the maximum of a scaled 1-norm distance from θ_i to θ_0 for all $i \in 1,...,n+1$ such that

$$s = \max_i \left[\frac{1}{n} \sum_{j=1}^{n} |\theta_{i,j} - \theta_{0,j}| \right].$$

- If $s<\delta$, declare the new simplex as $\theta_i = U(-\Delta,\Delta)$ where $U(a,b)$ represents an independent pull from a uniform distribution and compute $f_i = f(\theta_i)$ for all $i \in 1,...,n+1$.

- If $k=K$, end the optimization. Return f_i and θ_1.

The motivations behind the steps taken in this algorithm are very intuitive. The original Nelder-Mead algorithm was created in 1965 when researchers had far less computing power to work with. Naturally, the test functions for numerical optimization algorithms were generally more theoretical and smooth. The prevailing logic for direct search minimization in this context was that it is better to move directly away from maxima than directly toward a minima. This logic provides a robust framework for direct search minimization.

The motivation behind the REFLECT subroutine is to take the point with the highest value θ_{n+1} and test a value opposite to it, or to reflect away from it. The motivation behind the EXPAND subroutine is that if reflecting produced a new minimum in the simplex, there are likely interesting points further in the same direction. If the reflection produced a very poor value, there are likely interesting points within the simplex, so we run CONTRACT and move away from θ_{n+1} toward the centroid. If none of these subroutines produces values better than f_{n+1}, we push for convergence with the SHRINK subroutine by moving all other θ_i toward θ_1. Figures 8-9 and 8-10 give visual representations of the subroutines in a two-dimensional space.

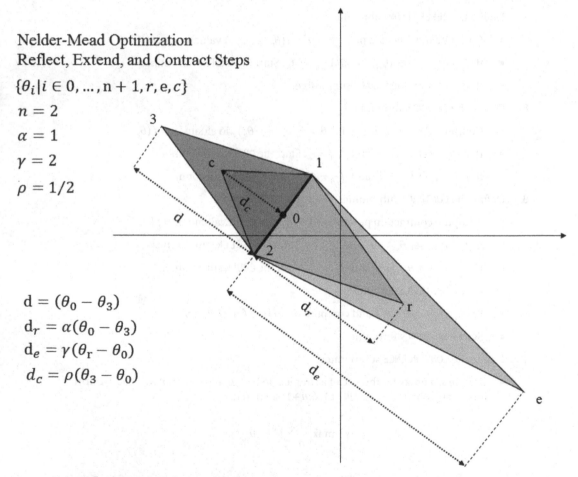

Nelder-Mead Optimization
Reflect, Extend, and Contract Steps
$\{\theta_i | i \in 0, ..., n + 1, r, e, c\}$
$n = 2$
$\alpha = 1$
$\gamma = 2$
$\rho = 1/2$

$d = (\theta_0 - \theta_3)$
$d_r = \alpha(\theta_0 - \theta_3)$
$d_e = \gamma(\theta_r - \theta_0)$
$d_c = \rho(\theta_3 - \theta_0)$

Figure 8-9. *Reflect, extend, and contract steps*

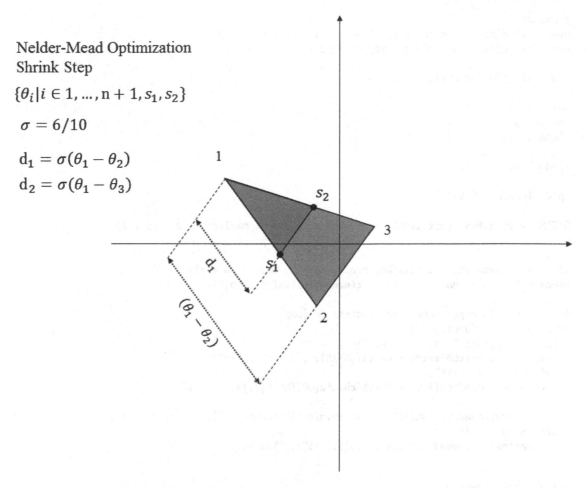

Nelder-Mead Optimization
Shrink Step

$$\{\theta_i | i \in 1, \dots, n+1, s_1, s_2\}$$

$$\sigma = 6/10$$

$$d_1 = \sigma(\theta_1 - \theta_2)$$
$$d_2 = \sigma(\theta_1 - \theta_3)$$

Figure 8-10. *Shrink step*

Nelder-Mead is effective at discovering local minima but is guaranteed only to converge to a local minimum under certain conditions. For this reason, as with the pattern search algorithm, we make heuristic improvements to the algorithm such as testing for convergence by simplex size and random initialization after first restart. Random initialization helps substantially in quickly discovering unique and important local minima but makes the optimization weakly deterministic. Listing 8-5 is a lightweight algorithm for Nelder-Mead optimization as outlined at the beginning of this section. Similarly to the pattern search algorithm, the Nelder-Mead optimizer is best utilized by setting *K* very high and stopping manually later.

Listing 8-5. Nelder-Mead Optimization

```
K <- maxIter <- 200

# Vector theta_0
initDelta <- 6
deltaThresh <- 0.05
PARAM <- PARAMNaught <-
  c(n1 = 0, nFact = 0, nSharpe = 0, shThresh = 0) - initDelta/2
```

```r
# bounds
minVal <- c(n1 = 1, nFact = 1, nSharpe = 1, shThresh = 0.01)
maxVal <- c(n1 = 250, nFact = 10, nSharpe = 250, shThresh = .99)

# Optimization parameters
alpha <- 1
gamma <- 2
rho <- .5
sigma <- .5

randomInit <- FALSE

np <- length(initVals)

OPTIM <- data.frame(matrix(NA, ncol = np + 1, nrow = maxIter * (2 * np + 2)))
o <- 1

SIMPLEX <- data.frame(matrix(NA, ncol = np + 1, nrow = np + 1))
names(SIMPLEX) <- names(OPTIM) <- c(names(initVals), "obj")

# Print function for reporting progress in loop
printUpdate <- function(){
  cat("Iteration: ", k, "of", K, "\n")
  cat("\t\t", paste0(strtrim(names(OPTIM), 6), "\t"), "\n")
  cat("Global Best:\t",
      paste0(round(unlist(OPTIM[which.min(OPTIM$obj),]),3), "\t"), "\n")
  cat("Simplex Best:\t",
      paste0(round(unlist(SIMPLEX[which.min(SIMPLEX$obj),]),3), "\t"), "\n")
  cat("Simplex Size:\t",
      paste0(max(round(simplexSize,3)), "\t"), "\n\n\n")
}

# Initialize SIMPLEX
for( i in 1:(np+1) ) {

  SIMPLEX[i,1:np] <- PARAMNaught + initDelta * as.numeric(1:np == (i-1))
  SIMPLEX[i,np+1] <- evaluate(SIMPLEX[i,1:np], minVal, maxVal, negative = TRUE,
                             y = y)
  OPTIM[o,] <- SIMPLEX[i,]
  o <- o + 1

}

# Optimization loop
for( k in 1:K ){

  SIMPLEX <- SIMPLEX[order(SIMPLEX[,np+1]),]
  centroid <- colMeans(SIMPLEX[-(np+1),-(np+1)])
```

```
cat("Computing Reflection...\n")
reflection <- centroid + alpha * (centroid - SIMPLEX[np+1,-(np+1)])

reflectResult <- evaluate(reflection, minVal, maxVal, negative = TRUE, y = y)
OPTIM[o,] <- c(reflection, obj = reflectResult)
o <- o + 1

if( reflectResult > SIMPLEX[1,np+1] &
    reflectResult < SIMPLEX[np, np+1] ){

  SIMPLEX[np+1,] <- c(reflection, obj = reflectResult)

} else if( reflectResult < SIMPLEX[1,np+1] ) {

  cat("Computing Expansion...\n")
  expansion <- centroid + gamma * (reflection - centroid)
  expansionResult <- evaluate(expansion,
                  minVal, maxVal, negative = TRUE, y = y)

  OPTIM[o,] <- c(expansion, obj = expansionResult)
  o <- o + 1

  if( expansionResult < reflectResult ){
    SIMPLEX[np+1,] <- c(expansion, obj = expansionResult)
  } else {
    SIMPLEX[np+1,] <- c(reflection, obj = reflectResult)
  }

} else if( reflectResult > SIMPLEX[np, np+1] ) {

  cat("Computing Contraction...\n")
  contract <- centroid + rho * (SIMPLEX[np+1,-(np+1)] - centroid)
  contractResult <- evaluate(contract, minVal, maxVal, negative = TRUE, y = y)

  OPTIM[o,] <- c(contract, obj = contractResult)
  o <- o + 1

  if( contractResult < SIMPLEX[np+1, np+1] ){

    SIMPLEX[np+1,] <- c(contract, obj = contractResult)

  } else {
    cat("Computing Shrink...\n")
    for( i in 2:(np+1) ){
      SIMPLEX[i,1:np] <- SIMPLEX[1,-(np+1)] +
        sigma * (SIMPLEX[i,1:np] - SIMPLEX[1,-(np+1)])
      SIMPLEX[i,np+1] <- c(obj = evaluate(SIMPLEX[i,1:np],
                                       minVal, maxVal,
                                       negative = TRUE, y = y))
    }
```

```
        OPTIM[o:(o+np-1),] <- SIMPLEX[2:(np+1),]
        o <- o + np

    }

}

    centroid <- colMeans(SIMPLEX[-(np+1),-(np+1)])
    simplexSize <- rowMeans(t(apply(SIMPLEX[,1:np], 1,
                                    function(v) abs(v - centroid))))

    if( max(simplexSize) < deltaThresh ){

      cat("Size Threshold Breached: Restarting with Random Initiate\n\n")

      for( i in 1:(np+1) ) {

      SIMPLEX[i,1:np] <- (PARAMNaught * o) +
        runif(n = np, min = -initDelta, max = initDelta)

      SIMPLEX[i,np+1] <- evaluate(SIMPLEX[i,1:np],
                                  minVal, maxVal, negative = TRUE, y = y)
      OPTIM[o,] <- SIMPLEX[i,]
      o <- o + 1

      SIMPLEX <- SIMPLEX[order(SIMPLEX[,np+1]),]
      centroid <- colMeans(SIMPLEX[-(np+1),-(np+1)])
      simplexSize <- rowMeans(t(apply(SIMPLEX[,1:np], 1, function(v) abs(v - centroid))))

      }
    }

    printUpdate()

}

# Return the best optimization in untransformed parameters
evaluate(OPTIM[which.min(OPTIM$obj),1:np], minVal, maxVal, transformOnly = TRUE)
```

The optimization performs worse than the pattern search optimizer for our Sharpe Ratio test on the long-only MACD. Figure 8-11 shows the running minimum against calls to the evaluator. Intuitively, this algorithm should perform better with smoother objective functions like many of those discussed in Chapter 1. You are encouraged to try to compare.

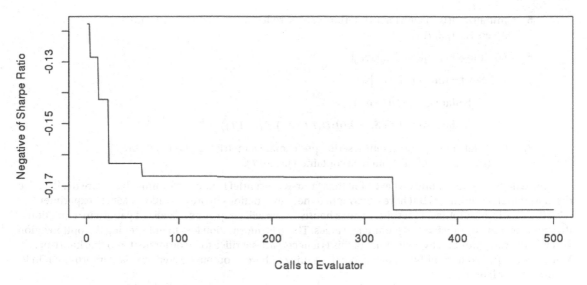

Figure 8-11. *Running minimum of objective function for Nelder-Mead*

Projecting Trading Performance

Now that we have a sturdy optimization toolbox, we can start using our optimized parameters to simulate real trading performance. The beginning of this chapter discussed the difference between cross validation and curve fitting. If we were to use our optimization algorithms to generate the best parameters for a given time period and then claim we could replicate that performance in production trading, we would be falling victim to curve fitting logic. To project valid and honest results of a strategy, we need to generate optimal parameters in one period and then evaluate them in the following period. The performance of the strategy from the following period is what can be validly and honestly expected in production trading because the means to arriving at such performance figures are replicable in real time. This does not mean we are forced to test purely the optimal parameters in the previous period on the following period. We are allowed to create arbitrarily complex rules for establishing the parameters used in simulation as long as they adhere to the principles of cross validation.

We will define a heuristic using the language of this text for generating valid performance projections.

1. Define time t where $t \in 1,...,T$, where 1 represents the beginning of the data and T the last time period in the data.

2. Define $D(a,b)$ as all data and $A(a,b)$ as all account variables such that $a < t \leq b$. Define $f(\theta; D(a, b))$ to be the objective function that takes parameter vector θ and data as arguments. Define the optimizer $g(\cdot)$ such that

$$g\big(D(a,b)\big) = \underset{\theta}{argmin}\Big[f\big(\theta; D(a,b)\big)\Big].$$

3. Define the simulator $h(\cdot)$ that returns account variables such that

$$A(a+1,b) = h\big(\theta; D(a,b), A(a-1,a)\big).$$

4. Define longitudinal step values for optimization and projection as δ_O and δ_P, respectively, such that $0 < \delta_O, \delta_P < T$.

5. Initialize $A(0,T)$ with logical starting values, reflecting holding all cash and no assets for $1,...,T$.

6. For integers $i \in [\delta_O/\delta_p],...,[T/\delta_p]$

    - Set $t = \min[i\delta_p, T - \delta_p]$.

    - Calculate $\theta = g(D(t - \delta_O, t))$.

    - Calculate $A(t+1, t+\delta_p) = h(\theta; D(t, t+\delta_p), A(t-1, t))$.

7. Calculate equity curve, return series, performance metrics, and other desired metrics for $t \in 0,...,T$ from data contained in $A(0,T)$.

We will use the functions we have built thus far to write a brief listing performing this heuristic. We have discussed many optimizers but have not wrapped them in functions in order to allow users to experiment with their various outputs and results. For this heuristic, we will wrap our generalized pattern in a function that returns only untransformed parameter values. There is information loss in not keeping the optimization variables in the parent R environment, but this is a necessary sacrifice to incorporate it into this heuristic. You are encouraged to modify any of the functions utilized here to output desired auxiliary information in R list objects for later use.

We will not repeat code here for declaration of the *optimize()* function. You should wrap any of the three optimization algorithms covered in this chapter in a function and pass parameters y,minVal, and maxVal to it. Add the following return line to end of the function call to evaluate $g(\cdot)$ as defined in our heuristic.

```
optimize(y, minVal, maxVal){

  # Insert Listing 8.2, 8.4, or 8.5
  # passing y, minval, and maxval
  # as parameters.

  # Make sure y, minVal, and maxVal are not
  # overwritten anywhere inside the function.
  # They should remain unaltered from their
  # supplied values.

  # Finally, return the named vector of
  # optimal parameters. This return() statement
  # will work for any listing you include.
  return(
  evaluate(OPTIM[which.min(OPTIM$obj),1:np],
          minVal, maxVal, transformOnly = TRUE)
  )
}
```

Additionally, when wrapping the optimization, it is suggested users lower the maximum iterations value of K to something more manageable.

Listing 8-6 executes the heuristic with $\delta_O = \delta_p = 1year$. The equity curve assembled from this process is a valid cross validation for time series that validly and responsibly estimates the performance of your strategy in the future.

This is a key step often ignored in commercial trading platforms. It is usually possible but strenuous to implement this type of cross validation in a commercial platform.

This heuristic is best left to run overnight. It is the final version of many nested functions and loops developed throughout the book. The final output is a list object of the portfolio, cash, and equity curve information for each year. We have added code at the end to consolidate the equity curve information for quick analysis. Otherwise, this is where post-optimization analysis can get arbitrarily complex based on users' desire to study trade frequency, recession performance, effects of drawdown schedules, and so on.

Note that we started our simulation in 2004 because our parameters can reach as far back as 150*5 days according to the minVal and maxVal in Listing 8-6.

Listing 8-6. Generating Valid Performance Projections with Cross Validation

```
minVal <- c(n1 = 1, nFact = 1, nSharpe = 1, shThresh = .01)
maxVal <- c(n1 = 150, nFact = 5, nSharpe = 200, shThresh = .99)

RESULTS <- list()
accountParams <- list ()
testRange <- 2004:2015

# As defined in heuristic with delta_O = delta_P = 1 year
for( y in testRange ){

  PARAM <- optimize(y = y, minVal = minVal, maxVal = maxVal)

  if( y == testRange[1] ){

    RESULTS[[as.character(y+1)]] <-
      evaluate(PARAM, y = y + 1, minVal = minVal, maxVal = maxVal,
               transform = TRUE, returnData = TRUE, verbose = TRUE )

  } else {

    # Pass account parameters to next simulation after first year
    strYear <- as.character(y)
    aLength <- length(RESULTS[[strYear]][["C"]])
    accountParams[["C"]] <-(RESULTS[[strYear]][["C"]])[aLength]
    accountParams[["P"]] <- (RESULTS[[strYear]][["P"]])[aLength]
    accountParams[["p"]] <- (RESULTS[[strYear]][["p"]])[aLength]

    RESULTS[[as.character(y+1)]] <-
      evaluate(PARAM, y = y + 1, minVal = minVal, maxVal = maxVal,
               transform = TRUE, returnData = TRUE, verbose = TRUE,
               accountParams = accountParams)

  }

}

# extract equity curve
for( y in (testRange + 1) ){

  strYear <- as.character(y)
  inYear <- substr(index(RESULTS[[strYear]][["P"]]), 1, 4) == strYear
```

```
equity <- (RESULTS[[strYear]][["equity"]])[inYear]
date <- (index(RESULTS[[strYear]][["P"]]))[inYear]

if( y == (testRange[1] + 1) ){
  equitySeries <- zoo(equity, order.by = date)
} else {
  equitySeries <- rbind(equitySeries, zoo(equity, order.by = date))
}
}
```

Figure 8-12 shows the equity curve for our cross-validated trading simulation. The strategy suffered going into 2008, perhaps because it was long-only and had no exit criteria. It is likely the Sharpe Ratio is not a robust enough performance metric for generating optimal parameters at $t+1$ from information in t.

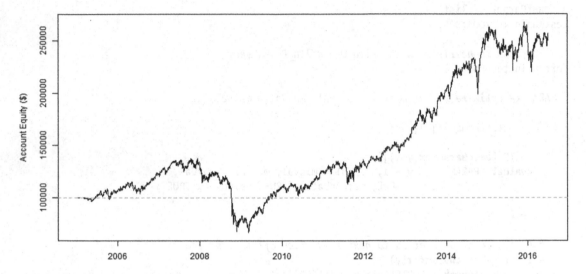

Figure 8-12. *Cross-validated equity curve for long-only MACD*

Most importantly, this is an accurate representation of how the strategy would have performed if running from 2005 through 2016 in real time. Fitting a successful strategy to all the data at once simply proves existence of a solution. Discovering an optimization process and a strategy framework that work together to generate consistently good results in cross validation is a significant feat of financial engineering.

Conclusion

Optimization can be a daunting field. We have presented large volumes of code in this chapter that will make up the most flexible and research-centered parts of the code base. Before we move to production trading, Chapter 9 will discuss APIs for sending trades to brokerages. Chapter 10 and on will focus on practical considerations for running your platform daily.

CHAPTER 9

■ ■ ■

Networking Part II

In this chapter, we will discuss the available APIs for automating your trading strategies. The structure of commercially available APIs varies widely with each requiring a specific set of skills and software considerations. We will survey the most popular and accessible APIs to help traders determine the optimal system to pursue or how to best integrate with an existing brokerage. See Chapter 2, Networking Part I, for a general introduction to APIs.

Most brokerages will restrict access to API documentation to developers they have vetted and approved. These brokerages will restrict the developer's ability to share and distribute the code and documentation associated with the API thereafter. This chapter will give you the tools and direction you need to utilize a variety of retail brokerage APIs.

Market Overview: Brokerage APIs

The quantity and variety of commercially available APIs can be daunting. They generally market themselves as accommodating to all developers of all programming backgrounds, but this is rarely the case. For regulatory reasons, we will discuss APIs that allow retail traders access to U.S. equities and that require a secure connection established by a lower-level programming language, typically C++, .NET, or Java. The R language is great at calling certain low-level languages to handle such connections, so it is important to know what programming languages an API supports before committing to a brokerage.

Table 9-1 gives software specifications for a handful of APIs as of June 2016. There may be a lot of new terminology in this table if you are unfamiliar with advanced networking concepts. This chapter will cover these terms so that traders have an accurate idea of the considerations required to trade using these APIs. The APIs have mixed feasibility for integration with R, which we will discuss at length.

© Chris Conlan 2016
C. Conlan, *Automated Trading with R*, DOI 10.1007/978-1-4842-2178-5_9

Table 9-1. Software Specifications for Common APIs

Brokerage	Communication Method	Response Format	Documentation	Languages	Assets
Interactive Brokers	SSL via SDK	Unique	Public	C++, Java, .NET, DDE, ActiveX	Equities, futures, forex
E*Trade	SSL via SDK	XML/JSON	Private	VC++, PHP, Java,	Equities, futures
Pinnacle	SSL via SDK	FIX	Private	C++, .NET, Java Visual Basic, Win32, FIX Engine	Equities, futures, forex
TradeKing	HTTPS and OAuth 1.0a	JSON and FIXML	Public	Any	Equities, futures, forex
Lightspeed	SSL via SDK	Unknown	Private	C++ (DLLs only)	Equities, futures, forex
OptionsXpress	Unknown	XML	Private	Unknown	Equities, futures
TDAmeritrade	Unknown	Unknown	Private	Unknown	Equities, futures
OANDA REST	HTTPS and OAuth 2.0	JSON	Public	Any	Forex

Secure Connections

Every brokerage has some security measures to authenticate users and pass messages through a secure connection. At the highest level, brokerages use some form of the Secure Sockets Layer (SSL) protocol, which uses private and public keys to encrypt messages before they are sent to be decrypted by the receiving party. SSL is used over TCP/IP ports specified by the brokerage. TCP/IP refers to a high-level concept of client-server communications that includes specific application protocols such as HTTP/HTTPS, SMTP, and FTP. Brokerages differ in how they implement SSL by which authentication and application protocols they utilize to connect and communicate.

The majority of brokerages listed in Table 9-1 communicate via specific SSL implementations given to clients in a software developer kit (SDK). An SDK can be either a collection of source code or a dynamic loading library (DLL) that allows users to code the API in supported languages. DLLs are simply the precompiled counterparts of APIs distributed in source code. They are unique to C++. It is worth noting that brokerages listed with unknown communication methods likely utilize SSL via SDKs rather than HTTPS.

Brokerages listed with HTTPS as a communication method have APIs similar to the Yahoo! Finance and YQL APIs covered in Chapter 2. They first verify identity through OAuth, and then they use HTTPS to communicate with the program.

Establishing SSL Connections

SSL is used generally to refer to the original SSL and its functional successor, Transport Layer Security (TLS). Through cryptographic software suites, two parties can negotiate an algorithm for transmitting encrypted data such that an eavesdropper is unable to decrypt the messages.

Flavors of SSL vary widely. The process of establishing a connection can become complicated, especially on the Web where single servers intend to establish secure connections with many anonymous users. The process becomes more straightforward when a host communicates with a known client, as is the case with broker-client communications. Broker-client communications on proprietary SSL programs (as in SDKs) will typically use a predetermined secret key, while secure connections between a server and an anonymous client (HTTPS) will typically rely on a signing authority.

In cases where the server does not need to identify the user, from a networking rather than a personal identity standpoint, only the server is required to have a private key. This is typically the case when shopping online over HTTPS. In more secure applications, like those in the SDKs listed in Table 9-1, both parties can be required to have a private key. The private keys help both parties come to an agreement on a public key without communicating the public key over the connection. This private key allows the parties to communicate by repeatedly encrypting and decrypting messages with symmetric cryptography algorithms.

We will give a very general outline for the steps SSL takes in both single private key and dual private key instances.

1. Negotiation Phase

    • The client server generates a random number, lists its supported encryption algorithms and SSL versions, and sends them to the host server.

    • The host server and client server agree on an encryption algorithm and SSL version supported by each party.

- The servers verify that the proper parties own the proper private keys. This is verified through encrypted signatures on the keys. These private keys, as the name would imply, are never communicated explicitly by the servers. To verify ownership, the servers combine an explicitly communicated random number and encryption process with the privately held keys. Ownership is verified by the equality of a signature generated by a combination of the aforementioned elements.

- At this point, the servers both have the public key in hand without having ever communicated it. The combination of the publicly communicated random number and the encryption algorithm with the private key allow the public key to be generated at each server without ever being communicated explicitly. This is of course dependent on the joint ownership of the private key, which is verified in the previous step. By this step, the servers have established a unique encryption process for transferring data over the SSL connection.

2. The host server communicates that all communications are now encrypted. The host server sends an encrypted message communicating the connection has been established. The client server checks that the initial encrypted message is valid.

3. The client server communicates that all communications are now encrypted. The client server sends an encrypted message communicating the connection has been established. The host server checks that the initial encrypted message is valid.

4. The connection is established, and application communications between the host and client are encrypted.

Proprietary SSL Connections

HTTP/HTTPS communication is very straightforward, so it may seem strange that a brokerage would opt to use its own version of an SSL protocol. We will discuss some reasons that this benefits the brokerage.

Brokerages build their own SSL protocols and release their own SDKs to make trading safer. Note that brokerages trade in exchanges on our behalf and face a lot of regulation from governmental organizations and exchanges themselves. When brokerages require that we trade through their SDKs, they seek to pass some or most of these regulations on to the trader.

The most important regulation the brokerage seeks to enforce is the *heartbeat* requirement. The system must check in at regular intervals to be considered active and connected. If a heartbeat check-in fails and further attempts to contact the system by the server are unsuccessful, the system will be considered disconnected. Certain orders are canceled automatically, and special rules kick in to ensure orders are not executed when owners of the system are unable to monitor performance.

Brokerages reserve the *right to refuse* on any order a trader sends their way. This is a right not often exercised by brokerages, as it would damage the reputation of a brokerage that overused it. Increased security requirements mostly serve to broaden the scope of justifiable uses of right to refuse in the brokerage's favor. Exchanges also hold the right to refuse, but they exercise it in a more well-defined manner. Brokerages seek to minimize their risk by extending the reach of these exchange restrictions and are not required to explicitly define these restrictions. While an exchange might implement a minimum heartbeat (check-in) frequency of once per 0.5 seconds, a brokerage trading in that exchange might enforce a heartbeat requirement on its client of once per 0.2 seconds. Brokerages shoulder considerable risk in executing trades on behalf their clients, so they will act in a variety ways to increase security for clients running automated systems.

HTTPS with or without OAuth cannot enforce heartbeat requirements with low enough latency to be practical in most cases, so it is generally not enforced by brokerages allowing HTTPS access. HTTP may have low enough latency to support heartbeat requirements but is unsecured and therefore not used. A *heartbeat* is a check-in message verifying that a network connection is live and stable.

Brokerages often specify specific ports on which their SSL connections communicate such that they do not interfere with commonly used ports devoted to other activities.

HTTP/HTTPS

HTTP and HTTPS are TCP/IP protocols that communicate on ports 80 and 443, respectively, by default. HTTP is not secure and therefore not used for trading communication. HTTPS uses a form of SSL that does not require the host and client to agree on a private key in advance. It enables the server to connect with anonymous clients securely by relying on a server-side private key and independent verification by a predetermined signing authority.

Since HTTPS relies on an independent signing authority and requires no private key from the client, there is no embedded way for it to determine the identity of the client. In secure applications that want to verify the identity of the client, it is typically required that the client provide some signature dependent on an agreed-upon secret key as a parameter in the URL. This accomplishes the same function as an SSL connection with two private keys but stays within the HTTPS framework.

OAuth

The rise of social media and social-assisted apps brought a surge of interest into standardizing and securing app-assisted login. A cohort of open source developers created OAuth. OAuth verifies the identity of the user and the third-party application through the API provider, allowing the user to permit the application to access the API on its behalf without the user disclosing its password to the application.

This process went a step above HTTPS with non-SSL private keys and was rapidly adopted by many API providers. It serves the same function as HTTPS with non-SSL private keys if the user and third-party application are considered the same person, all while reserving the extensibility to open the application to anonymous users in the future.

OAuth is a great development for the retail trading industry because it allows brokerages to create one API with one authentication system that serves the needs of both automated traders and platform developers.

Feasibility Analysis for Trading APIs

We can accomplish almost anything with R because it can call low-level languages. For this section, keep in mind *possible* is not the same as *easy*. Some APIs are easy to integrate with our platform, while others are not. In our platform, we keep trade execution separate from all other components including order generation. Developers will naturally find different ways of accomplishing trade execution in ways that leverage their programming skills and brokerage APIs.

Feasibility of Custom R Packages

Any brokerage that requires an SSL connection through its SDK will require the developer to build an R package around it to use it directly from R. Creating an R package from C++ or Java is a well-documented and doable process for developers familiar with C++ or Java.

Note that R uses the GNU-C++ compiler (GCC) for compiling C/C++ code, so C/C++ code built in/for the VC++ or .NET framework will likely fail to compile in R. On Windows, R uses a GCC compiler within a MinGW environment even on machines with working VC++ and .NET compilers.

Brokerages that offer APIs through DLLs can also be compiled into R packages through C++ wrapper code.

Developers familiar with C/C++ or Java may want to compile broker SDKs for easy use in their R code. We will explore other means of executing trades that may be more feasible even to experienced low-level programmers.

HTTPS + OAuth Through Existing R Packages

The ROAuth, RJSONIO, and XML packages provide users with everything they need to execute trades directly from R with no other programming languages. Opening up APIs to high-level languages is a new concept aimed at stimulating web-based platform development and high-volume automated trading from retail clients. It is an exciting prospect for traders looking to automate orders at a frequency of a few times per second or less.

The biggest downside to this avenue is brokerage selection. Developers are unlikely to have existing accounts with these brokerages and do not have a lot of opportunity to shop for competitive rates.

Fortunately, these brokerages tend to have large and active communities of like-minded developers.

FIX Engines

FIX is an open source protocol for communicating orders in a minimal number of bytes using integer parameters and pipes. Many FIX engines exist that communicate over SSL connections with the brokerage. FIX engine compatibility is more common at the institutional level, but some retail brokerage APIs offer it. Traders familiar with FIX engines or with existing accounts in a brokerage that support pure FIX communication may find it favorable to export trade directions from R to the FIX engine.

Exporting Directions to a Supported Language

Developers familiar with any language explicitly supported by their brokerage should try exporting trading directions from R to their language of choice for execution. There is a strong chance the SDK in their language of choice is well-supported with plenty of sample code, making it more practical to read from a text file of trading directions rather than wrap the SDK in an R package.

Planning and Executing Trades

Planning our trades ahead of time and running automated execution algorithms are distinct, straightforward, and lightweight processes. We will outline heuristics for planning and executing trades. These heuristics cover two of four distinct processes that our platform will automate, the PLAN and TRADE jobs, respectively. The remaining two jobs, MODEL and UPDATE, are outlined in Chapter 10 and Appendix A but do not deal with networking concepts specific to this chapter.

The PLAN Job

We are planning to trade in the morning of the coming trading day based on information from the last trading day. The PLAN job must be executed between the time when information from the prior day becomes available and the market opens the coming morning. Practically, running the job between 6 p.m. the night before and 8 a.m. the following morning (EST) should ensure the information is available for trading when the market opens.

1. Compute only the last row, or most recent observation, of ENTRY, EXIT, and FAVOR.

2. Fetch current positions from the brokerage. Compute that last row of P, the matrix of position directions. Place 1s in the positions of stocks currently held long and -1s in the positions of stocks currently held short.

3. Execute steps 4 through 8 of the "Listing 7-1: Pseudocode" section from Chapter 7. In Listing 9-1, these correspond to steps 4 through 8 of the Listing 7-1 code but treat zoo objects ENTRY, EXIT, FAVOR, and P as named vectors.

4. Output the list of trades-to-exit and the manner in which to exit them. Output the list of trades-to-enter and the manner in which to enter them. Store these in a location accessible by the TRADE job.

Listing 9-1 shows a modification of our simulator function to plan trades based on steps 4 through 8 of the "Listing 7-1: Pseudocode" section from Chapter 7. Most importantly, this is consistent with the way we have simulated strategy performance in this text.

Listing 9-1. The PLAN Job

```
# Normally declared by your strategy
FAVOR <- rnorm(ncol(DATA[["Close"]]))
ENTRY <- rbinom(ncol(DATA[["Close"]]), 1, .005) -
  rbinom(ncol(DATA[["Close"]]), 1, .005)
EXIT <- rbinom(ncol(DATA[["Close"]]), 1, .8) -
  rbinom(ncol(DATA[["Close"]]), 1, .8)

# Normally fetched from brokerage
currentlyLong <- c("AA", "AAL", "AAPL")
currentlyShort <- c("RAI", "RCL", "REGN")
S <- names(DATA[["Close"]])
initP <- (S %in% currentlyLong) - (S %in% currentlyShort)

names(initP) <-
  names(FAVOR) <-
  names(ENTRY) <-
  names(EXIT) <-
  names(DATA[["Close"]])

# At this point we have established everything normally
# taken care of by your trading strategy.
# Given named vectors of length ncol(DATA[["Close"]])
# initP, FAVOR, ENTRY, and EXIT, we proceed.

maxAssets <- 10
startingCash <- 100000
```

```
K <- maxAssets
k <- 0
C <- c(startingCash, NA)
S <- names(DATA[["Close"]])
P <- initP

# Step 4
longS <- S[which(P > 0)]
shortS <- S[which(P < 0)]
k <- length(longS) + length(shortS)

# Step 5
longTrigger <- setdiff(S[which(ENTRY == 1)], longS)
shortTrigger <- setdiff(S[which(ENTRY == -1)], shortS)
trigger <- c(longTrigger, shortTrigger)

if( length(trigger) > K ) {

  keepTrigger <- trigger[order(c(as.numeric(FAVOR[longTrigger]),
                              -as.numeric(FAVOR[shortTrigger])),
                          decreasing = TRUE)][1:K]

  longTrigger <- longTrigger[longTrigger %in% keepTrigger]
  shortTrigger <- shortTrigger[shortTrigger %in% keepTrigger]

  trigger <- c(longTrigger, shortTrigger)

}

triggerType <- c(rep(1, length(longTrigger)), rep(-1, length(shortTrigger)))

# Step 6
longExitTrigger <- longS[longS %in% S[which(EXIT == 1 | EXIT == 999)]]

shortExitTrigger <- shortS[shortS %in% S[which(EXIT == -1 | EXIT == 999)]]

exitTrigger <- c(longExitTrigger, shortExitTrigger)

# Step 7
needToExit <- max( (length(trigger) - length(exitTrigger)) - (K - k), 0)

if( needToExit > 0 ){

  toExitLongS <- setdiff(longS, exitTrigger)
  toExitShortS <- setdiff(shortS, exitTrigger)

  toExit <- character(0)

  for( counter in 1:needToExit ){
    if( length(toExitLongS) > 0 & length(toExitShortS) > 0 ){
```

```
    if( min(FAVOR[toExitLongS]) < min(-FAVOR[toExitShortS]) ){
      pullMin <- which.min(FAVOR[toExitLongS])
      toExit <- c(toExit, toExitLongS[pullMin])
      toExitLongS <- toExitLongS[-pullMin]
    } else {
      pullMin <- which.min(-FAVOR[toExitShortS])
      toExit <- c(toExit, toExitShortS[pullMin])
      toExitShortS <- toExitShortS[-pullMin]
    }
  } else if( length(toExitLongS) > 0 & length(toExitShortS) == 0 ){
    pullMin <- which.min(FAVOR[toExitLongS])
    toExit <- c(toExit, toExitLongS[pullMin])
    toExitLongS <- toExitLongS[-pullMin]
  } else if( length(toExitLongS) == 0 & length(toExitShortS) > 0 ){
    pullMin <- which.min(-FAVOR[toExitShortS])
    toExit <- c(toExit, toExitShortS[pullMin])
    toExitShortS <- toExitShortS[-pullMin]
  }
}

longExitTrigger <- c(longExitTrigger, longS[longS %in% toExit])
shortExitTrigger <- c(shortExitTrigger, shortS[shortS %in% toExit])

}

# Step 8
exitTrigger <- c(longExitTrigger, shortExitTrigger)
exitTriggerType <- c(rep(1, length(longExitTrigger)),
                     rep(-1, length(shortExitTrigger)))

# Output planned trades
setwd(rootdir)

# First exit these
write.csv(file = "stocksToExit.csv",
          data.frame(list(sym = exitTrigger, type = exitTriggerType)))

# Then enter these
write.csv(file = "stocksToEnter.csv",
          data.frame(list(sym = trigger, type = triggerType)))
```

The TRADE Job

We separate trading into the planning and executing phases for two reasons. First, we cannot allow compute times to delay our trading. Second, we want to give developers the option of executing trades in a programming language that makes sense for them and their brokerage. In many cases, this language will be R, but often it will be more feasible to execute in a language expressly supported by the brokerage.

The following heuristic will apply to any language implementing our portfolio management framework:

1. Initiate the program anywhere from 60 to 300 seconds before market open and attempt to establish a connection with the brokerage. If successful, maintain this connection. If unsuccessful, re-attempt the connection until successful.

2. Read in trades to exit and trades to enter. Prepare necessary variables in advance of market open.

3. At market open, send exit orders at market in rapid succession.

4. As soon as, or if initially, cash is available, send entry orders in rapid succession. Buy the most shares of a stock possible with $\dfrac{C}{K-k}$ dollars, where C represents cash on hand, K represents the maximum number of unique assets to hold, and k represents the number of assets currently held.

5. (Optional) At any point before, during, or after execution, adjust behavior based on user-defined fail safes and risk-avoidance criteria. This may include avoiding stocks that took adverse overnight price moves or halting activity if account equity reaches a certain point.

Code for this process cannot be explicitly defined without tying us to a specific broker. Specific source code will not be provided for the TRADE job in this chapter and in Appendix A. The rest of this chapter will discuss a host of communication protocols and data formats. We will give special attention to R methods for handling and manipulating these connections and formats. By the end of the chapter, you should be well-equipped to digest API documentation from a variety of brokerages.

Common Data Formats

We will discuss eXtensible Markup Language (XML), JavaScript Object Notation (JSON), Financial Information eXchange (FIX), and a hybrid FIX and XML (FIXML).

Data manipulation of XML is handled by XPath, which is language-independent. There are XPath analogs for JSON data, but they are nonstandard. Handling JSON combines language-dependent packages and the general assumption of well-formed JSON data.

A JSON document can almost always convey the same information as the equivalent XML document in fewer characters, sparking many debates concerning whether XML will be completely phased out in the future. XML has advantages in readability, accessibility, and standardization. Users will typically see XML used in scenarios where there is highly variable formatting and small message sizes, barring direct dependencies on JavaScript technologies in which JSON is likely to be used.

Manipulating XML

XPath is the universal language for manipulating XML. It can be thought of as the XML analog to regular expressions for readers familiar with string manipulation. Much like regular expressions, almost every language has an interface for standard XPath, but interfaces vary by language and often by package/library.

The most robust XPath library for R is simply called XML. We have used it in this text to organize data from Yahoo! Query Language. We will use an example from YQL to give an introduction to XPath and discuss some practical methods for handling XML in R.

First, we will grab a small XML document from YQL using a slight modification of a code piece from Chapter 2. This will pull two days each of Apple and Yahoo! stock prices. The xmlParse() function can take a file path or URL. It will return an XML document organized internally in a C-level Document Object Model (DOM), which is a special C object that stores the nodes of an XML tree as objects. This means if we want to efficiently manipulate XML documents, we will use XPath to organize them within C-level DOMs before we map the data to an R object. DOMs can be directly mapped to R list objects because of their similar tree structure. The XML package provides the ability to do this, but we will refrain from taking advantage of XPath's efficiency and avoid losing details of DOM.

See the help file of `xmlParse()` for variations and arguments for more exotic XML files.

```
library(XML)

base <- "http://query.yahooapis.com/v1/public/yql?"
begQuery <- "q=select * from yahoo.finance.historicaldata where symbol in "
midQuery <- "('YHOO', 'AAPL') "
endQuery <- "and startDate = '2016-01-11' and endDate = '2016-01-12'"
endParams <- "&diagnostics=false&env=store://datatables.org/alltableswithkeys"

urlstr <- paste0(base, begQuery, midQuery, endQuery, endParams)

doc <- xmlParse(urlstr)
```

The variable doc is now a reference to a C-level DOM. If we print the variable to the R console, we can see the XML document. Listing 9-2 shows the output of printing the variable doc. We will use this to variable to give examples of XPath in R. Further, Listing 9-3 provides a list of common XPath field types for reference.

Listing 9-2. YQL XML Output Sample

```
<?xml version="1.0" encoding="UTF-8"?>
<query xmlns:yahoo="http://www.yahooapis.com/v1/base.rng" yahoo:count="4"
yahoo:created="2016-06-25T22:09:50Z" yahoo:lang="en-US">
  <results>
    <quote Symbol="YHOO">
      <Date>2016-01-12</Date>
      <Open>30.58</Open>
      <High>30.969999</High>
      <Low>30.209999</Low>
      <Close>30.690001</Close>
      <Volume>12635300</Volume>
      <Adj_Close>30.690001</Adj_Close>
    </quote>
    <quote Symbol="YHOO">
      <Date>2016-01-11</Date>
      <Open>30.65</Open>
      <High>30.75</High>
      <Low>29.74</Low>
      <Close>30.17</Close>
      <Volume>16676500</Volume>
      <Adj_Close>30.17</Adj_Close>
    </quote>
    <quote Symbol="AAPL">
      <Date>2016-01-12</Date>
      <Open>100.550003</Open>
      <High>100.690002</High>
      <Low>98.839996</Low>
      <Close>99.959999</Close>
      <Volume>49154200</Volume>
      <Adj_Close>98.818866</Adj_Close>
    </quote>
    <quote Symbol="AAPL">
```

```
        <Date>2016-01-11</Date>
        <Open>98.970001</Open>
        <High>99.059998</High>
        <Low>97.339996</Low>
        <Close>98.529999</Close>
        <Volume>49739400</Volume>
        <Adj_Close>97.40519</Adj_Close>
    </quote>
  </results>
</query>
<!-- total: 89 -->
<!-- main-9ec5d772-3a4c-11e6-a4df-d4ae52974c31 -->
```

Listing 9-3. Common XML Field Types

```
# Opening and closing XML tags, empty
<Date></Date>

# Opening and closing XML tags, with value
<Date>2016-01-11</Date>

# Opening and closing XML tags, with value and attribute
<Date format="YYYY-MM-DD">2016-01-11</Date>

# Self-closing XML tag
<Date />

# Self-closing XML tag with attributes
<Date format="YYYY-MM-DD" value="2016-01-11" />

# XML Comment
<!-- some comment or explanation -->

# XML Declaration
<?xml version="1.0" encoding="UTF-8"?>

# Processing Instruction
<?xml-stylesheet type="text/xsl" href="XLS/Todo.xsl" ?>

# Character Data Entity (Escapes symbolic characters)
<codeSnippet><![CDATA[ y < x | z > sqrt(y) ]]></codeSnippet>
# Document Type Declaration
<!DOCTYPE html>
```

XPath examines XML documents like a filesystem with extra control structures. An XPath query consists of one or more statements of the following format separated by forward slashes. We will explain the meaning of axis, node-test, and predicate in this context.

```
axis::node-test[predicate]
```

The axis argument has many abbreviations, so we will rarely specify it explicitly. Many XPath axes work the same way as filesystem axes in the UNIX and MS-DOS command lines. We can use a single period to specify the self axis or two periods to specify the parent axis. Table 9-2 details common XPath axes.

Table 9-2. *Common XPath Axes*

Axis	Symbol	Description
Child	Default	Specifies nodes in the level below the reference node. This is the default.
Attribute	@	Specifies attributes of the reference node.
Parent	..	Specifies the level of the context node. /someNode/../anotherNode searches for anotherNode in the DOM level of someNode.
Descendent	None	Any child, child of a child, and so on, relative to the reference node.
Descendent-or-self	/	Same as descendent, except includes the reference node. In context, this looks like someNode//descendentNode, as in it adds one forward slash to the typical separator.
Ancestor	None	All levels above reference node.
Ancestor-or-self	None	All levels above the reference node including itself.
Following	None	Nodes that lie below the reference node in the document.
Preceding	None	Nodes that lie above the reference node in the document.
Following-sibling	None	All nodes on the same level as the reference node and below the reference node in the document.
Preceding-sibling	None	All nodes on the same level as the reference node and above the reference node in the document.
Namespace	None	Specifies node with the document namespace.

XPath axes with abbreviations are the most commonly used. See Listing 9-4 for examples of abbreviations and their equivalent long-form expressions.

Listing 9-4. XPath Abbreviations

```
# Child node
child::someNode
someNode

# Attribute value
attribute::someAttr
@someAttr

# Parent node
someNode/parent::*/someSibling
someNode/../someSibling

# Descendent-or-self
someNode/descendent-or-self::node()/someDescendent
someNode//someDescendent
```

```
# Ancestor (has no abbreviation)
someNode/ancestor::someAncestorNode
```

The node-test argument is most commonly the name of a node. Specifying only a node name defaults to testing equality between the name specified and the nodes of the tree. Other arguments, like asterisks and conditional symbols, can enter the mix. These will typically be made obsolete by points of flexibility in the XML package for R. XML attributes can also be accessed in the node-test but are also best manipulated by functions in the XML package.

Predicates are conditional statements attached to the node-test. In addition to meeting the requirements of the node-test, nodes must meet the requirements of the predicate. Predicates can contain conditional tests and native XPath functions capable of referencing any piece of information in an XML document, making them much more powerful than the node-test for selecting specific sets of nodes. In general, node-tests can be thought as having the regular capabilities of a UNIX directory engine for flexibly accessing files. Predicates can be thought of as extra functionalities specific to XPath. Axes have many functionalities native to UNIX filesystems and many specific to XPath. Table 9-3 details common XPath predicate function for reference.

Table 9-3. *Common XPath Predicate Functions*

Function	Input	Description
last()	None	Number of elements in the reference node set.
position()	None	Position number of reference node.
count()	None	Number of elements in the node set.
name()	None	Name of the first node in the reference node set.
concat()	One of more strings	Returns concatenation of string arguments supplied.
starts-with()	Target and search string	Returns true if first string starts with second.
contains()	Target and search string	Returns true if first string contains the second.
substring()	Position *a* and length *b*	Portion of string starting at a for the length of b.
string-length()	Single string	Number of characters in supplied string.
Arithmetic operators	As implied	Add, subtract, multiply, divide, modulus (+ - * div mod).
Comparative operators	As implied	<, <=, >, >=, = as implied.
not()	Single Boolean	not(a = b) is the functional equivalent of a != b.
Logical operators	As implied	and and or spelled in all lowercase.

Listing 9-5 will give a handful of examples on the doc variable of XML data pulled earlier in this section. Supplying minimal parameters to the getNodeSet() function is a great way to test XML queries. We will supply more parameters to it and call xpathSApply() within it in practice.

Listing 9-5. XPath Examples on YQL Data

```
# Descend the tree to each individual stock quote
getNodeSet(doc, "/query/results/quote")

# Get the second quote
getNodeSet(doc, "/query/results/quote[2]")
```

```
# Descend to the third level of the tree, get second element
getNodeSet(doc, "/*/*/*[2]")

# Get all nodes named "quote" regardless of level
getNodeSet(doc, "//quote")

# Get all node with Symbol = AAPL attribute
getNodeSet(doc, "/query/results/quote[@Symbol = 'AAPL']")

# Get the last quote
getNodeSet(doc, "/query/results/quote[last()]")

# Get the first 3 quotes
getNodeSet(doc, "/query/results/quote[position() <= 3]")

# Get all quotes with closing price less than 40
getNodeSet(doc, "/query/results/quote[./Close < 40]")

# Get all closing prices less than 40
getNodeSet(doc, "/query/results/quote[./Close < 40]/Close")
```

In practice, we will have XML with a known structure. We will use knowledge of this structure to convert the XML directly into R objects we are comfortable with. Most often, these will be data frames and lists.

The YQL output used in our examples can easily be mapped to a data frame with each row containing the price information, the date, and the corresponding stock symbol. We want to first descend the tree to the quote level where we have four nodes. Descending the tree can take a considerable amount of time for large or complex XML data, so we want to make a point of descending it as few times as possible. We will supply the xpathSApply() function and the xmlValue() function to getNodeSet() to accomplish this. This makes use of a quirk in the R XML package that allows us to make multiple queries, descend the tree once, and not copy pieces of the tree in separate variables. This is very computationally efficient with compact code. We will descend the tree twice, first using xmlValue() to get the price data and then using xmlAttrs() to get the attributes from the nodes. Notice how we do not use the @ symbol to access the attributes. There is an equivalent but less robust way to handle this using the @ symbol given in Listing 9-6. Listing 9-6 converts the YQL XML data to a data frame in a logical and compact fashion.

Listing 9-6. XPath Converting YQL to Data Frame

```
# Descend the tree to this point
root <- "/query/results/quote"

# Descend to each of these leaves for every node in root
leaves <- c("./Date", "./Open", "./High", "./Low",
            "./Close", "./Volume", "./Adj_Close")

# Get data in list
df <- getNodeSet(doc, root, fun = function(v) xpathSApply(v, leaves, xmlValue))

# Get symbols as attributes
sym <- getNodeSet(doc, root, fun = function(v) xpathSApply(v, ".", xmlAttrs))

# This is equivalent to the above line in this case
# sym <- as.character(getNodeSet(doc, "/query/results/quote/@Symbol"))
```

```r
# Organize as data frame
df <- data.frame(t(data.frame(df)), stringsAsFactors = FALSE)

# Append stock symbols
df <- cbind(unlist(sym), df)
df[,3:8] <- lapply(df[3:8], as.numeric)
df[,1] <- as.character(df[,1])

# Fix names
rownames(df) <- NULL
colnames(df) <- c("Symbol", substring(leaves, 3))
```

Generating XML Documents

We will be using XML to transmit and receive data. There are great functionalities in the XML package for intuitively generating XML documents. The most common XML document traders will generate is a FIXML message. We will discuss FIX and FIXML in the following sections, but for now we will give a simple example and generate it using the XML package. Listing 9-7 gives a simple FIXML sample message, and Listing 9-8 generates the same message using the XML package.

We notice a few things. XML namespaces are similar to attributes but must be declared using a different argument.

Listing 9-7. FIXML Sample Message

```xml
<FIXML xmlns="http://www.fixprotocol.org/FIXML-5-0-SP2">
  <Order TmInForce="0" Typ="1" Side="1" Acct="999999">
    <Instrmt SecTyp="CS" Sym="AAPL"/>
    <OrdQty Qty="100"/>
  </Order>
</FIXML>
```

Listing 9-8. Generating XML Data

```r
library(XML)

# Generate the XML message in Listing 9-7
out <- newXMLNode("FIXML",
                  namespaceDefinitions =
                    "http://www.fixprotocol.org/FIXML-5-0-SP2")

newXMLNode("Order",
           attrs = c(TmInForce = 0, Typ = 1, Side = 1, Acct=999999),
           parent = out)

newXMLNode("Instrmt",
           attrs = c(SecTyp = "CS", Sym = "AAPL"),
           parent = out["Order"])

newXMLNode("OrdQty",
           attrs = c(Qty = 100),
           parent = out["Order"])
```

```
print(out)

# Extra example for how to insert content in non-self-closing nodes
newXMLNode("extraInfo", "invalid content.", parent = out["Order"])
print(out)
```

Manipulating JSON Data

JSON data can handle the delivery of all the information that an XML document can handle in fewer characters. Unfortunately, this reduces standardization and the range of facilities available for manipulating it. JSON does not have a natural ability to handle attributes, so translation of attributes from XML creates fields named attr:{} or a similar abbreviation. Sometimes an API decides that certain XML attributes should not be treated as attributes in JSON, so it treats attributes like normal data fields. This is the case with the Symbol attribute when YQL outputs JSON.

We will request the same data as used in our XML examples as JSON from YQL. JSON is simple enough that it can be losslessly mapped to an R list object. We do not have a standard analog for efficiently accessing JSON like XPath, so we go straight to R lists and work from there. R lists can easily replicate the tree-descending behavior of XPath with many double-bracket subsetting operations.

Listing 9-9 loads JSON data from YQL and organizes the same data frame as in Listing 9-6. It is relatively simple to do so because the quote level of the tree has four sets of seven data points. This enables the default behavior of data.frame() to generate useful output. It is easy to see how poorly structured or incomplete JSON data can lead to complicated tree-descent procedures.

Listing 9-9. Manipulating JSON Data

```
library(RJSONIO)

base <- "http://query.yahooapis.com/v1/public/yql?"
begQuery <- "q=select * from yahoo.finance.historicaldata where symbol in "
midQuery <- "('YHOO', 'AAPL') "
endQuery <- "and startDate = '2016-01-11' and endDate = '2016-01-12'"

# Supply "format=json" argument to URL
endParams <-
  "&diagnostics=false&format=json&env=store://datatables.org/alltableswithkeys"

urlstr <- paste0(base, begQuery, midQuery, endQuery, endParams)

# Encode URL before requesting
# This is normally handled automatically by the XML package
jdoc <- fromJSON(URLencode(urlstr))

# Format and output data frame as in Listing 9-6
df <- data.frame(t(data.frame(jdoc[["query"]][["results"]][["quote"]])),
                 stringsAsFactors = FALSE)
df[,3:8] <- lapply(df[3:8], as.numeric)
df[,1] <- as.character(df[,1])
rownames(df) <- NULL
```

It is worth discussing how the fromJSON() function maps JSON to R lists. You may have noticed that the leaves of our R list jdoc were named vectors. This is a simplification performed by fromJSON() when the default argument simplify = Strict is used. This greatly simplifies visualization and manipulation of the R list into other formats. Technically, mapping a JSON document to an R list should be a strict list of lists rather than a list of named vectors. This may be useful to have in cases where the JSON structure is variable. For this we specify the argument simplify = FALSE. See the documentation for fromJSON() for options to simplify singular or multiple specific data types.

Generating JSON output is simple because any R list can be instantly converted to JSON. The JSON document will be of a similar form to str(jdoc) in R. Be wary if R list attributes need to be passed to the JSON output. Behaviors vary across attributes and package-specific classes. Users passing R list attributes to JSON documents are encouraged to manually verify the output is as intended during development.

```
# Outputs JSON representation of list object as string
jout <- toJSON(jdoc)
```

Note on URL Encoding

Listing 9-9 required URLencode() because HTTP requests through the RJSONIO package do not automatically encode. *Encoding* is the process of replacing unsafe characters with ASCII-encoded values. These values are percent signs followed by two hexadecimal characters. Various web security practices and HTTP protocol specifications justify URL encoding. It is important to know that transmitting unsafe characters over HTTP/HTTPS is forbidden and typically results in the error code "400: Bad Request" from the intended target. Browsers and software packages will often automatically encode URLs, but some like RJSONIO do not. This requires that we manually call the URLencode() function.

Some common unsafe characters include the spacebar and the following: < > # % { } | [ ] ' .

The Financial Information eXchange Protocol

The FIX protocol is a widely accepted and independently maintained protocol for financial communication. The protocol is normally communicated over low-level languages that establish proprietary FIX-compliant connections on top of standard TCP connections. These are the types of connections established by proprietary SDKs offered by retail brokerages.

A FIX engine is a program that establishes and maintains the FIX connection between two parties. Many FIX engines exist to provide out-of-the-box compatibility with brokerages supporting pure FIX implementations.

FIX is a very low-latency protocol most commonly used in order management systems between brokers or funds and electronic exchanges. Only ultra-low-latency strategies can significantly benefit from the efficiency of pure FIX. All other strategies will not significantly benefit from the minimal latency of FIX messages. Our strategy only involves daily adjustments and therefore does not require the minimal latency of FIX. It is important to understand FIX nonetheless because typical client-to-broker communications will be more verbose versions or analogs of FIX. The prime example of this is FIXML, which is an XML adaptation of FIX. FIXML sacrifices latency advantages of FIX but is easier to read and manipulate.

The nonprofit FIX maintenance body FIX Trading Community is developing FIXT as well. FIXT stands for Transport-Independent FIX. It is currently in version 1.1 and seeks to make FIX independent of FIX-compliant TCP connections. This opens up the opportunity for brokerages to extend connection options other than FIX-compliant TCP, including web services (HTTP/HTTPS mainly) and message queues (Amazon SQS, Microsoft Message Queueing, and so on). This is an important development for bringing us into the language-independent standardization of financial messaging. Brokers may offer the ability to transmit such FIXT messages over HTTPS in the future, opening up ultra-low-latency trading to all languages that can transmit secure HTTP requests.

A comprehensive treatment of FIX format is beyond the scope of this text, but there are a few key facts to know. FIX messages comprise key-value pairs of mostly integer parameters separated by the ASCII control code known as the start-of-header character (SOH). SOH can be expressed as A in ASCII or 0x01 in hexadecimal. In almost every character representation, it is represented as the second character of a zero-indexed set. In FIX documentation, it is often replaced with a pipe character for readability.

It is important to note that while exchanges may support most FIX capabilities, retail brokerages provide a deliberately limited set of FIX capabilities. This practice is necessary to shield them from certain risks, and it consequentially dictates the most efficient way to learn FIX. Since FIX capabilities are dependent on the brokerage itself, the best way to learn FIX is almost always from the brokerage's documentation. Examples given by the brokerage are guaranteed to be supported. Traders are wise to follow these examples and guidelines rather than expecting the broker to support a capability of FIX it is not familiar with.

The following is an arbitrary example of a FIX message to buy shares of the symbol TESTA. Pure FIX distinguishes itself from other communication protocols through minimalism. FIX messages are not self-documenting like FIXML messages. Parameter names are arbitrary integer values.

```
8=FIX.4.2|9=153|35=D|49=BLP|56=SCHB|34=1|50=30737|97=Y|
52=20000809-20:20:50|11=90001008|1=10030003|21=2|55=TESTA|54=1|38=4000|
40=2|59=0|44=30|47=I|60=20000809-18:20:32|10=061|
```

It is worth noting that the authoritative body on FIX runs a very slow, confusing, and unreliable web site at www.fixtradingcommunity.org/ (noted as of June 2016). Documentation can be located with some perseverance, but many links are dead and/or hang. This is an additional reason to learn from your brokerage's documentation.

The FIX eXtensible Markup Language

FIXML is both XML and self-explaining, meaning the knowledge of the acronyms and abbreviations used within it can fully explain the content and purpose of a message. FIXML deliberately sacrifices the minimal latency of FIX for easier readability and adoptability. As with the FIX protocol, it is best to learn from examples provided by the brokerages themselves because they will offer fewer features than the creators of FIXML make possible to communicate.

The placement of parameters is important in FIXML. Parameters are placed as attributes in the appropriate node. Table 9-4 discusses some common FIXML attributes. There are many more parameters available to options, complex orders, foreign exchange, fixed income, and so on. These are the most commonly used attributes for stock trading. We will discuss the node structure as well.

Table 9-4. *Common FIXML Attributes*

Attribute	Node	Description
Acct	Order	The account number needs to be passed with all order requests.
AcctTyp	Order	Only for buy-to-cover short positions. Mark AcctTyp="5".
OrigID	OrdCxlReq	Order ID that needs to be passed for any change or cancel requests.
Px	Order	Limit price for limit orders.
SecTyp	Instrmt	Security type. CS for common stock.
Side	Order	Specifies order. 1 = buy or buy to cover, 2 = sell, 5 = sell short.
Sym	Instrmt	Ticker symbol of underlying security.
TmInForce	Order	Time in force. 0 = Day, 1 = GTC, 7 = Market On Close. Not applicable when Typ = 1.
Typ	Order	Order type. 1 = Market, 2 = Limit, 3 = Stop, 4 = Stop Limit, P = trailing stop.
Qty	OrdQty	Specifies number of shares on which to execute the corresponding order.

The following is a copy of Listing 9-7. This FIXML message is a market buy order for 100 shares of Apple stock on account 999999.

```
<FIXML xmlns="http://www.fixprotocol.org/FIXML-5-0-SP2">
  <Order TmInForce="0" Typ="1" Side="1" Acct="999999">
    <Instrmt SecTyp="CS" Sym="AAPL"/>
    <OrdQty Qty="100"/>
  </Order>
</FIXML>
```

The following is a sell-short limit-day order at $690 for 100 shares of Google stock:

```
<FIXML xmlns="http://www.fixprotocol.org/FIXML-5-0-SP2">
  <Order TmInForce="0" Typ="2" Side="5" Px="690" Acct="999999">
    <Instrmt SecTyp="CS" Sym="GOOGL"/>
    <OrdQty Qty="100"/>
  </Order>
</FIXML>
```

This is a FIXML order for replacing existing order SVI-888888 with a buy limit-day order for 100 shares of Caterpillar stock:

```
<FIXML xmlns="http://www.fixprotocol.org/FIXML-5-0-SP2">
  <OrdCxlRplcReq TmInForce="0" Typ="2" Side="1" Px="75" Acct="999999"
    OrigID="SVI-888888">
      <Instrmt SecTyp="CS" Sym="CAT"/>
      <OrdQty Qty="100"/>
  </OrdCxlRplcReq>
</FIXML>
```

FIXML messages are most often transmitted over HTTPS and FIX SSL connections. When transmitting over HTTPS, the FIXML message will be supplied as a lengthy HTML parameter in a POST request. We will discuss this further when covering OAuth.

OAuth in R

We have discussed the dynamics of OAuth in detail. R has a simple ROAuth package that wraps many of the complicated communication steps of OAuth with a single R object. Within this R object, users can manage the connection and make GET/POST requests.

There are a lot of ways to initiate OAuth depending on the user's security clearance for a specific project. We mentioned before that OAuth for client-brokerage communications in client-built systems often treats the client's trading program as both the end user and the third party within the OAuth framework. In this case, the client will receive both a consumer key-secret pair and an OAuth key-secret pair. In the case where the client is acting as a third party authenticating on behalf of an end user, the third party will need a single key-secret pair and a single access-request URL pair.

Depending on your brokerage and the key-secret pairs available, you may consider using various pieces of Listings 9-10 and 9-11. The code presented shows different scenarios the ROAuth package can handle.

Listing 9-10. ROAuth with Secret-Key and Access-Request Pairs

```r
# Example is not executable.
# For example purposes only.
library(ROAuth)

# Requesting with key-secret and access-request pair
reqURL <- "requestUrl"
accessURL <- "accessUrl"
authURL <- "authenticationUrl"
cKey <- "consumerKey"
cSecret <- "consumerSecret"

credentials <- OAuthFactory$new(consumerKey=cKey,
                                consumerSecret=cSecret,
                                requestURL=reqURL,
                                accessURL=accessURL,
                                authURL=authURL,
                                needsVerifier=FALSE)
credentials$handshake()

# Send GET Request to URL
testURL <- "http://someurl.com/some parameters"
credentials$OAuthRequest(testURL, "GET")

# Send GET Request to URL
testURL <- "http://someurl.com/some un-encoded parameters"
credentials$OAuthRequest(testURL, "GET")
```

Listing 9-11. ROAuth with Two Secret-Key Pairs, FIXML Message, and No Verifier

```r
oKey <- "oauthKey"
oSecret <- "oauthSecret"
cKey <- "consumerKey"
cSecret <- "consumerSecret"
credentials <- OAuthFactory$new(consumerKey = cKey,
                                consumerSecret = cSecret,
                                oauthKey = oKey,
                                oauthSecret = oSecret,
                                needsVerifier=FALSE)

# Manually declare authentication as complete
credentials$handshakeComplete <- TRUE

# Send a FIXML message through OAuth to testURL with POST request
aFIXMLmessage <- c("<FIXML xmlns=...>content</FIXML>")
testURL <- "https://testurl.com/"
credentials$OAuthRequest(testURL, "POST", aFIXMLmessage)
```

POST requests deliver information in the same URL format as other APIs that use purely GET requests. POST requests have different headers and can handle substantially longer URLs.

As of ROAuth version 0.9.2, APIs that require verification-on-request or nonpersistent OAuth sessions will need manual override of the handshake verifier. This allows the ROAuth package to pass the verification information on request rather than rely on a persistent OAuth session. This may change in future releases of ROAuth. Watch out for documentation and package updates from both CRAN and your brokerage for users relying on this method of ROAuth.

Conclusion

Programming client-brokerage communication is the most open-ended element of this text. Until now, we have provided a precise framework and set of examples for developing trading strategies. In this chapter, you have been asked to assess your abilities, connections, and financial needs to choose the best method for client-brokerage communication. We will move through the end of this book assuming this has been achieved to some degree. You are encouraged to read through the remaining chapters to see how our platform is fully prepared and executed from a home computer, even if you do not have client-brokerage communications fully developed.

The next chapter will discuss how to automate different R jobs from the command line of a Windows or UNIX machine. This is the final step to bringing a trading platform into production.

Production Trading

CHAPTER 10

■ ■ ■

Organizing and Automating Scripts

This chapter will cover CRON jobs for UNIX machines and task scheduling for Windows machines to automate routine execution of trading scripts. We will discuss which jobs should be run when, frequently referencing Appendix A for production-ready code examples.

Organizing Scripts into Jobs

There are four possible jobs we may want to automate on a schedule. We will call these jobs UPDATE, PLAN, TRADE, and MODEL.

The UPDATE job will need to be run once per day after Yahoo! Finance has updated trade data. This can be around 5 to 6 p.m. EST. This script will update the data in our stock data directory for use in other scripts.

The PLAN job will run after we update the data but before the start of the trading day. This job will run the strategy on the most recently available data and output trading directions for use by the TRADE job.

The TRADE job is the most open-ended in terms of execution. It can be written in the most appropriate language for the job, as discussed in Chapter 9. This script will be run right when the trading day starts at 9:30 a.m. EST. It will rely purely on the output of the PLAN job to execute trades.

The MODEL job has the most flexible schedule. This job is responsible for updating the parameters utilized by the strategy implemented in the TRADE job. Depending on the trader's simulation and optimization framework, this may have time to run every night, every weekend, or once per month. Running the MODEL job more frequently is not necessarily better, and this decision should depend on results of the trader's research into his strategy. It may be desirable to only update the strategy manually, in which the MODEL job would not be used.

Calling Jobs with the Source Function

The source() function in R allows us to call scripts from files like R functions, but with a few important differences.

- The source() function does not pass information by parameters. It passes information through the parent R environment.

- R functions create in-memory copies of their parameters in a local environment that are deleted upon function termination.

- All scripts called with the source() function share the scope of the parent environment, while independent R function calls do not share or maintain scope.

© Chris Conlan 2016
C. Conlan, *Automated Trading with R*, DOI 10.1007/978-1-4842-2178-5_10

In short, the source() function allows us to effortlessly break up pieces of existing scripts for on-demand use. Nesting calls to the source() function allows us to easily perform our four jobs as described previously.

The remainder of this section will describe the four jobs as nested calls to the source() function, as defined in the source code of Appendix A.

Calling Jobs via Sourcing

Users who have arranged the source code of this text as in Appendix A are able to call jobs via the source() function, as in Listing 10-1.

Listing 10-1. Calling Jobs via Sourcing

```
# Warning: These are not to be run concurrently

# UPDATE Job
source("~/Platform/update.R")

# PLAN Job
source("~/Platform/plan.R")

# TRADE Job
source("~/Platform/trade.R")

# MODEL Job
source("~/Platform/model.R")
```

Listing 10-1 is a trivial example to illustrate the power of the source() function. In practice, we intend to call these scripts independently of one other in an automated fashion. We will introduce CRON jobs and the Windows Task Scheduler for this reason.

Task Scheduling in Windows

Task scheduling is the Windows equivalent of UNIX CRON jobs for running programs on a schedule. Some MS-DOS basics are required to understand how to get our R scripts to run with the Windows Task Scheduler. The code discussed here will work with Windows 7, 8, and 10. Some previous versions of Windows may successfully execute the code as well, particularly Vista.

Running R from the Command Line in Windows

R installations contain utilities for running the R console from the command line and running scripts as programs from the command line. To do so, we must let Windows know where the R binaries exist. R installations contain a /bin/ directory with R and Rscript executables. Windows R installations may contain a /bin/x64/ directory with 64-bit copies of R and Rscript executables. The most efficient way to access these executables is to declare the /bin/ or /bin/x64/ directory as part of the path variable. The contents of the path variable can be observed by simply typing it at the command prompt and hitting the Enter key.

Windows users may have trouble locating the R installation in their machine. If default paths are used upon install, it should be in C:/Program Files/R/R-3.x.x/bin/ with or without /x64/ at the end, depending of your architecture. If users have a different flavor or R installed, it will be in a different place. For example, if users have Microsoft R Open (MRO), the binaries will be in C:/Program Files/Microsoft/MRO/R-3.x.x/bin/.

Listing 10-2 shows the special format required to add the R binaries to the path variable on a default 64-bit R installation. It is important to respect case and spacing at the command prompt, particularly in path statements.

Listing 10-2. Setting the path Variable in Windows

```
set path= %path%;C:\Program Files\R\R-3.3.0\bin\x64
```

Now we are capable of calling the R and Rscript executables from the command line. If you would like to experiment with using R from the Windows command line, type R and hit the Enter key to start an R session in the terminal. Run the quit function q() with no parameters to exit.

We are more interested in the Rscript executable. This enables us to run scripts from the command line. If we want to run the plan.R script in our platform, we can run Listing 10-3 in the terminal. Be aware that the command line treats spaces as delimiters. If a file path contains spaces, it will need to be placed in double quotes.

Listing 10-3. Running R Scripts from the Command Line

```
Rscript C:\Platform\plan.R
```

Running scripts like this is ambiguous. The only indication that a script completes or terminates is the greater-than sign re-appearing in the terminal. Output from the R console is not sent to the terminal. We can better observe our scripts and diagnose them in the event of failure by sending the R console output to a file.

Listing 10-4 changes the directory with the cd command and then sends the console output of plan.R to a file called planlog.txt. Notice the trailing 2>&1 in this command. This is an interesting console command that is the same across many UNIX and Windows terminals. It sends the stderr stream (stream 2) into the stdout stream (stream 1). The result stores both streams in the same text file, similar to the way we see the actual R console output. The stdout and stderr streams are simply the standard output and standard error streams native to any console. Normally, black console output represents the stdout stream, and red console output represents the stderr stream when using Rgui or RStudio.

Listing 10-4. Sending Console Output to a Text File

```
cd C:\Platform\errorlog
Rscript C:\Platform\plan.R > planlog.txt 2>&1
```

Before we schedule our R scripts, we will store a few commands together in a Windows BAT file (otherwise referred to as a .bat file). These are text files of MS-DOS commands that end in .bat. They can be run from the terminal in a single command. This will make it simple and concise for us to schedule multiple terminal commands at a time. Listing 10-5 combines the concepts we have discussed into a single BAT file. Save this listing in your C:/Platform/ directory using a text editor as plan.bat. Make sure to change the paths to R binaries and logging directories as needed. Generate and save analogs for the UPDATE, TRADE, and possibly MODEL jobs as well.

Listing 10-5. BAT File for Running the PLAN Job (plan.bat)

```
set path= %path%;C:\Program Files\R\R-3.2.3\bin
cd C:\Platform\errorlog\
Rscript C:\Platform\plan.R > planlog.txt 2>&1
```

Setting Up and Managing the Task Scheduler

The Windows Task Scheduler can be accessed from the command-line utility `schtasks`. This utility has many varied and abbreviated parameters that can get confusing. It can accommodate very complex and dozens of parameters. We will focus on what we need as traders. We would like to run scripts at a specific time every weekday. To do this, we execute the `schtasks` utility created in Listing 10-6.

Listing 10-6. Scheduling plan.R with schtasks

```
schtasks /create /tn PLAN /sc weekly /d mon,tue,wed,thu,fri /mo 1 /st 19:00
/tr "C:\Platform\plan.bat"
```

Reading through Listing 10-6, we see that it created (/create) a task with the task name (/tn) PLAN. It runs on a weekly schedule (/sc) on the days (/d) Monday through Friday. We clarify with a modifier (/mo) we will be running every week as opposed to every two, three, four weeks, or so on. Finally, the start time (/st) is 1900 hours, and the command is simply to run (/tr) C:/Platform/plan.bat. This will run every weekday at 7 p.m. to prepare for trading.

Users will need to build analogs for the other jobs as with the BAT files.

These tasks can be created and managed through the Windows Task Scheduler GUI as well. We have focused on command-line solutions to minimize OS dependency of our tutorial. We will further explain how to manage scheduled tasks from the command line. See Listing 10-7 for common Task Scheduler management commands.

Listing 10-7. Managing Scheduled Tasks with Examples for PLAN

```
# Delete a task
schtasks /delete /tn PLAN

# Run a task
schtasks /run /tn PLAN

# End a currently run task, does not affect scheduling
schtasks /end /tn PLAN

# Get info on a task
schtasks /query /tn PLAN

# Modify a task (this example removes Wednesday from PLAN)
schtasks /change /tn PLAN /d mon,tue,thu,fri

# Disable a task, cancel scheduling
schtasks /change /tn PLAN /disable

# Enable an inactive task, resume scheduling
schtasks /change /tn PLAN /enable
```

Further research into task scheduling in Windows can add features users may be interested in. For example, requiring user authentication on a task run is a good way to prevent trading when the developer is not present to monitor the results in real time.

Task Scheduling in UNIX

UNIX systems have a few advantages that make scheduling tasks very simple. The R and Rscript executables are almost always available without changing the PATH variable in UNIX. Additionally, scheduling jobs is handled by editing a single line of a file already managed your system's native CRON daemon.

The CRON file you will be editing is most likely /etc/crontab but can differ depending on your OS. The CRON daemon in your machine checks /etc/crontab and files in the /etc/cron.*/ directories every minute and runs commands on them at the appropriate times.

The crontab utility enables UNIX users to safely edit and manage often sensitive items in the CRON file. Most importantly, the editing function provides CRON-specific security and error-checking, going above and beyond a typical text editor. Listing 10-8 shows common crontab commands.

Listing 10-8. Managing CRON Jobs

```
# Edit CRON jobs
crontab -e

# Delete all user-specified CRON jobs
crontab -r
```

The following is a useful ASCII graphic for explaining CRON job formatting. We can see from this formatting schema that vanilla CRON cannot handle scheduling tasks at the same level of complexity as Windows Task Scheduler can. Nonetheless, it is sufficient for our purposes.

```
* * * * * command to be executed
- - - - -
| | | | |
| | | | ----- Day of week (0 - 7) (Sunday = 0 or 7)
| | | ------- Month (1 - 12)
| | --------- Day of month (1 - 31)
| ----------- Hour (0 - 23)
------------- Minute (0 - 59)
```

Before we execute commands with CRON jobs, we will wrap our calls to Rscript in bash scripts. Our bash scripts require only one line of code, the call to Rscript, but our console output will be at the CRON level rather than the R level if we call directly from CRON. We would like our output to be at the R console level so that we can capture output in a text file.

The bash script is similar to the Windows analog. Note that the first line of Listing 10-9 is not a comment but the "shebang" symbol (#!) followed by the path to the bash binary (/bin/bash). Save Listing 10-9 as plan.sh in your platform directory to be called by CRON.

Listing 10-9. Bash Script for PLAN Job

```
#!/bin/bash
cd ~/Platform/errorlog
Rscript ~/Platform/plan.R > planlog.txt 2>&1
```

Run the following line in the terminal to make sure the file is executable:

```
chmod +x ~/Platform/plan.sh
```

Add Listing 10-10 to your /etc/crontab file by running `crontab -e`. This will run the PLAN job on weekdays at 7 p.m. EST.

Listing 10-10. CRON Line for PLAN Job

```
0 19 * * 1-5 ~/Platform/plan.sh
```

Conclusion

You are now equipped to schedule and configure trading tasks using R code developed throughout this text. The next chapter will compare our platform to the rest of the automated trading ecosystem, as well as point you in the right direction to access more functionalities and advanced careers in automated trading.

CHAPTER 11

■ ■ ■

Looking Forward

Our platform stands out in transparency and flexibility. R is very legible but generally slow. We have made efforts to speed up our platform but will always be slower than the equivalent multicore program in C/C++.

We have made accommodations for trading with delayed daily data and retail brokerages. These resources are not the height of aspirations for automated traders.

In this chapter, we will talk about how to get to higher frequencies, further streamline automation, and advance a career in automated trading.

Language Considerations

We have discussed in detail the advantages and disadvantages of using R to trade. Please refer to the "Software Overview" section of Chapter 6 if necessary. This section is a continuation of that discussion.

It is uncommon to find a production trading system built end-to-end in R. It is a scripting language that calls lower-level languages. It often sacrifices speed and memory efficient for readability. If traders would like to move to higher frequencies or build faster optimizers, there are languages other than C/C++ that do not sacrifice all of the benefits of R for the sake of speed.

Python

Python is a legible and safe programming language (in other words, not a scripting language) that is commonly used to build end-to-end automated trading systems. It relies on lower-level languages to run, but, unlike R, it can be both compiled and interpreted. R programmers usually have an easier time learning Python than Java or C/C++. Many professionals have been known to use both for different purposes, typically relying on R for exploratory analysis and on Python for the production deployment of complex algorithms.

Python 2.7.x is more common in production environments than Python 3.x.x as of the time of writing and is better supported for most available libraries.

C/C++

It is worth writing programs in C/C++ rather than Python if milliseconds matter. C/C++ has more capability to fine-tune memory management and thread communication in multicore programs. To fine-tune memory management, expert C/C++ programmers can manipulate cache-proximity and typecasting to optimize compute time. For multicore computation, expert C/C++ programmers will benefit from the vast number of CPU directives available for thread communication.

© Chris Conlan 2016
C. Conlan, *Automated Trading with R*, DOI 10.1007/978-1-4842-2178-5_11

C/C++ can be difficult to learn for programmers accustomed to scripted or interpreted languages. Speed is the bigger concern in trading rather than in research. It is common for exploratory analysis and model development to be performed in R and Python, while separate C/C++ programs use the results of the research to make trading decisions in real time.

Hardware Description Languages

Hardware description languages (HDLs) are necessary when microseconds matter. HDLs allow physical electronic circuits to be constructed based on textual input. They are most commonly C-like languages for programmable logic devices.

The most flexible and common programmable logic device for high-frequency trading is the Field-Programmable Gate Array (FPGA). To understand what an FPGA is, we need to discuss application-specific integrated circuit (ASIC) chips. ASIC chips are the small computer chips that run most electronic devices in our daily lives. They are the computer chips that run coffee makers, sound systems, treadmills, and many other electronic devices we interface with regularly. FPGAs are functionally ASIC chips that can be rewired on demand. They are rewired through special devices that interpret HDL languages and physically transform logic gates on the chip to run the desired program.

Expressing a program through digital logic gates makes many components of conventional CPUs unnecessary. For example, FPGAs have no need for schedulers because the schedule is printed on the chip. This substantially speeds up computations.

FPGA's development has a high production cost and presents a unique challenge drawing on electrical engineering knowledge just as much as programming skill. Specializing in FPGA development can open up many interesting career opportunities both inside and outside of high-frequency trading.

Retail Brokerages and Right to Refuse

Retail brokerages trade on behalf of their clients with direct-to-market trading algorithms. The brokerage acts as a counterparty to other direct-to-market participants, including institutional traders, market makers, funds, banks, and other brokerages. Brokerages stay in business by taking commissions and managing risks associated with trading on their clients' behalf.

Direct-to-market participants are institutions that trade at the purest level. These institutions trade with other participants within the exchanges with no middle man.

One of the biggest risks brokerages face is margin default by leveraged and/or short traders. During volatile market conditions, clients run a high risk of getting margin calls. Typically, the brokerage would exit the position on your behalf and bill you or your account for the overage. In volatile market conditions, the brokerage may be unable to exit the security at a desirable price in the event of forced liquidation. This may result in the client's inability to pay margin overages and result in a large loss for the brokerage.

To mitigate this risk, brokerages can disallow initiation of positions. This is known as the *right to refuse*. Brokerages will typically maintain the right to refuse without justification. Reputable brokerages do not abuse this right in an effort to best serve their clients, but the fact remains that no order sent by a client is guaranteed to clear under any circumstances.

Platforms built under our framework are not likely to trigger right to refuse because they are characteristically nonaggressive. Aggressive trading systems that attempt to exploit volatile price moves in real time are more likely to trigger the right to refuse. Funds that trade direct-to-market are at a significant advantage in aggressive trading because they are not subject this provision.

Right to Refuse in the Swiss Currency Crisis

A memorable example of widespread dependence on right to refuse took place during the January 15, 2015, Swiss Currency Crisis. At 9:30 a.m. GMT the Swiss National Bank issued a statement declaring that its currency would be unpegged and its federal deposit interest rate would be -0.75 percent. This caused immediate waves in the currency markets. The USDCHF pair (U.S. dollar against Swiss franc) fell as much as 31 percent in a matter of minutes.

Data feeds from many retail brokerage price charts failed to show any tick-by-tick data from 9:30 a.m. GMT to about 9:36 a.m. GMT. This indicated that retail brokerages were not generating spreads actionable by clients during this time period. This means that, for example, a limit order to buy the USDCHF may have been rejected even when the market price fell below the limit price, regardless of whether the order was first sent before or after 9:30. Orders sent during this time were rejected because the brokerage feared it would result in losses in excess of account values and general defaults by clients.

After the crisis, many retail currency brokerages decreased maximum leverage multiples by 33 percent to 50 percent. Additionally, many foreign exchange branches of mature brokerages sold or merged in an effort to cut losses.

Connection Latency

Institutional traders make great efforts to secure connections and minimize the time it takes to communicate over them.

Ethernet vs. WiFi

As a bare-minimum provision, any computer running automated strategies should be hardwired to a modem through Ethernet. This means that a computer connected to a router wirelessly communicating with the modem will not suffice. The computer can be connected to a router only if the router has a hardwired path to the modem.

Only as a last resort should any automated strategy be communicating over a wireless connection. WiFi connections can be significantly slower than Ethernet when an imperfect connections sends corrupt or partial packets that must be re-sent. Packets are bits of information that comprise pieces of the entire message being communicated over a connection. The router manages packets by checking whether they have been corrupted in transit. If a packet fails to deliver for any reason, it will be re-sent after the router is notified the packet is missing. This checking and notification process takes substantially more time per packet than the successful receipt of a packet.

For example, Voice over IP (VoIP) traffic will suffer negligible loss of speech quality at 1 percent package loss, but speech will be incomprehensible at anywhere from 5 percent to 10 percent packet loss. Packet loss for WiFi can vary substantially depending on the types of physical materials the signal must pass through. Metals and nonorganic objects tend to deflect and corrupt signals the greatest.

Packet loss over Ethernet is typically between 0.01 percent and 0.1 percent depending on the length of the cable and sources of radiation surrounding the cable. Fiber-optic lines, like those used by the modem to communicate with your Internet service provider, typically suffer 0.0001 percent packet loss. Understandably, some large funds have taken to communicating trades over purely fiber-optic lines.

Given a network connection that must deliver content without loss, as is the case with web pages, e-mails, trading messages, and so on, we can estimate connection latency to be proportional to

$$k\left(1+\gamma\frac{p}{1-p}\right)$$

where k is the size of a message in bytes, p is the sum of packet loss proportions over all communication media traversed by the message, and $\gamma>1$ is a constant. The constant γ is equal to the ratio of time taken by the average packet failure to the time taken by the average packet delivery.

If we have a message traveling over a WiFi connection with 10 percent packet loss, an Ethernet connection with 0.1 percent packet loss, and fiber-optic connections with 0.0001 percent packet loss, we have $p=0.101001$. If a packet loss takes approximately 20 times longer than a packet delivery, we have $\gamma=20$.

In this case, a message of size k will take $1+(20)\dfrac{0.101}{1-0.101}=3.246$ times longer than a lossless connection to deliver the message.

Be wary that this formula assumes messages travel at the same speed. Wireless messages take longer to travel over airwaves than wires take to transmit messages electronically. This difference can become substantial if transmitting messages over hundreds of miles, so this formula is most appropriate for comparing communication latency over short distances.

Proximity to Exchanges

Large funds take great pains to make sure they are close to the exchanges to reduce latency. Exchanges operate on a first-come, first-served basis, so proximity can significantly affect performance in high-frequency arenas. This has caused funds to compete over server proximity in exchange buildings. When milliseconds matter, institutional traders co-locate servers in the same data warehouses used by financial exchanges. At this point, they try to shave microseconds and nanoseconds off of connection latency by making sure their servers are closer to the exchange servers than the competition's servers.

High-frequency trading is as much of a networking problem as it is a strategy development problem. As frequency increases, funds take more expensive and more drastic measures to reduce compute time and connection latency.

Prime Brokerages

We have spoken about trading through retail brokerages and direct-to-market. These represent two extremes of dependence and freedom for traders. Prime brokerages lie in between these two options but a little toward the "freedom" end of the spectrum. Prime brokerages act just like retail brokerages in that they can provide leverage and execution. They differ in that they provide much more power and flexibility to execute orders on the client's terms. These are typically specific execution algorithms for exotic order types that mix limit, stop, and market orders to attain some desired discretion, speed, or market impact.

Relationships with prime brokerages are often stronger and more personal than those established with retail brokerages. With increased personal attention and lower commissions per dollar traded come increased minimum account sizes. These brokerages cater to wealthy individuals and funds rather than retail traders.

Digesting News and Fundamentals

We have spent the bulk of this chapter discussing how to increase trade frequency. Advancing capabilities in automated trading is hardly limited to increasing trade frequency. Automated trading systems of all frequencies can benefit from automatically digesting news and fundamentals. Some expensive services will automatically assess the significance of and direction of the market impact of news breaks, but it is also well within the capabilities of programmers to measure market sentiment with news.

Chapter 9 discussed ways to digest and organize XML data. Developers can organize HTML data using these methods. Relatively simple natural-language processing (NLP) can be used to determine sentiment from news. The methods in Chapter 9 can also be used to digest fundamental information on assets. History of asset fundamentals can be easily incorporated into indicators and optimizations to great effect.

Conclusion

There are a lot of opportunities to learn about different fields in automated trading and advance a career in it. There are equally as many opportunities to build on the platform created in this book within or outside of the R language. I hope you will continue to increase your knowledge and advance the field.

APPENDIX A

■ ■ ■

Source Code

This appendix will include all the production code covered in this book organized into an R project directory. An R project directory is a traditional file hierarchy of source code files that will be called by delegating scripts in the root of the project directory. In our case, we will continue using the root directory named in variable `rootdir` in the "Setting Up Directories" section of Chapter 2. We will create some new directories for holding source code and declare all of our directories in a list format to keep them organized.

Every script will be named by its file path in this appendix. You are expected to copy and save these files in the proper locations with the proper names for the platform to work. Initial commentary will be given, and new project-level code comments will be included. You are encouraged to go back to the section in which the code was introduced if more specific explanation is needed.

It is important to distinguish *delegating* scripts from *job* scripts. A delegating script may call other scripts but will be dependent on previous scripts to run properly. Job scripts scripts are the highest-level scripts meant to be run independently. This can be done from the command line, another call to `source()`, or manually in Rgui or RStudio.

Platform/config.R

Everything in this document is meant to be editable. It will be called at the beginning of each delegating script to set important global configuration variables. If there are other values within the platform a user would like to edit frequently, it should be declared here in the `CONFIG` list. The declaration of the variable within the source code should then be modified to the proper entry in the `CONFIG` list.

We use lists to hold configuration variables because they can be extended to hold any number of variables. Our code will frequently use the `rm()` function to clean up the R environment of every variable but a few select ones. Lists like `DIR`, `CONFIG`, and `DATA` will frequently be excluded from cleanup. By default, we will use `CONFIG` to store function objects used in multicore `rollapply()` calls.

Users will want to again edit file paths in this section if they differ from my defaults. The root directory can change without consequence, but you need to keep the same directory structure to ensure functionality.

```
DIR <- list()
DIR[["root"]] <- "~/Platform/"
DIR[["data"]] <- "~/Platform/stockdata/"
DIR[["function"]] <- "~/Platform/functions/"
DIR[["load"]] <- "~/Platform/load/"
DIR[["compute"]] <- "~/Platform/compute/"
DIR[["plan"]] <- "~/Platform/plan/"
DIR[["model"]] <- "~/Platform/model/"
```

C. Conlan, *Automated Trading with R*, DOI 10.1007/978-1-4842-2178-5_12

```
CONFIG <- list()

# Windows users should set to FALSE

CONFIG[["isUNIX"]] <- TRUE

# Set to the desired number of multicore
# processes. Windows users need to be conscious
# of memory requirements of these processes.
CONFIG[["workers"]] <- 4

# Max assets to be held in simulation, optimization,
# and potentially trade execution.
CONFIG[["maxAssets"]] <- 10

# Max iterations in optimization function
# for MODEL job. All users need to be conscious of
# time constraints.
CONFIG[["maxIter"]] <- 100

# Range or scalar value of years
# to train strategy on for MODEL job
CONFIG[["y"]] <- 2016

CONFIG[["minVal"]] <- c(n1 = 1, nFact = 1, nSharpe = 1, shThresh = .01)
CONFIG[["maxVal"]] <- c(n1 = 150, nFact = 5, nSharpe = 200, shThresh = .99)

CONFIG[["PARAMnaught"]] <- c(n1 = -2, nFact = -2, nSharpe = -2, shThresh = 0)

setwd(DIR[["root"]])
```

Platform/load

This section will cover all scripts pertaining to fetching, updating, storing, and preparing data for analysis. It will include most of the content from Chapters 2 and 3.

Platform/load.R

This is the delegating script for loading our data into memory and preparing it for analysis. Top-level delegating scripts called from the command line will run this script to load data.

```
setwd(DIR[["load"]])
cat("initial.R\n\n")
source("initial.R")

setwd(DIR[["load"]])
cat("loadToMemory.R\n\n")
source("loadToMemory.R")
```

```
setwd(DIR[["load"]])
cat("updateStocks.R\n\n")
source("updateStocks.R")

setwd(DIR[["load"]])
cat("dateUnif.R\n\n")
source("dateUnif.R")

setwd(DIR[["load"]])
cat("spClean.R\n\n")
source("spClean.R")

setwd(DIR[["load"]])
cat("adjustClose.R\n\n")
source("adjustClose.R")

setwd(DIR[["load"]])
cat("return.R\n\n")
source("return.R")

setwd(DIR[["load"]])
cat("fillInactive.R\n\n")
source("fillInactive.R")

cat("\n")
```

Platform/update.R

This is the job script for the UPDATE job. This job updates data in our stock data directory. Running this script in advance of analysis will allow the load.R script to skip update steps and load stock data straight into memory.

```
source("~/Platform/config.R")

setwd(DIR[["load"]])
cat("initial.R\n\n")
source("initial.R")

setwd(DIR[["load"]])
cat("loadToMemory.R\n\n")
source("loadToMemory.R")

setwd(DIR[["load"]])
cat("updateStocks.R\n\n")
source("updateStocks.R")

cat("\n")
```

Platform/functions/yahoo.R

You can skip this if you have already used the dump() function in Listing 2-2 to save the function yahoo() as an R object. Here we will save the function declaration as an R script. It will work the same either way when called by source() in other scripts.

```r
# Listing 2-2

yahoo <- function(sym, current = TRUE,
                  a = 0, b = 1, c = 2000, d, e, f,
                  g = "d")
{

  if(current){
    f <- as.numeric(substr(as.character(Sys.time()), start = 1, stop = 4))
    d <- as.numeric(substr(as.character(Sys.time()), start = 6, stop = 7)) - 1
    e <- as.numeric(substr(as.character(Sys.time()), start = 9, stop = 10))
  }

  require(data.table)

  tryCatch(
  suppressWarnings(
  fread(paste0("http://ichart.yahoo.com/table.csv",
                "?s=", sym,
                "&a=", a,
                "&b=", b,
                "&c=", c,
                "&d=", d,
                "&e=", e,
                "&f=", f,
                "&g=", g,
                "&ignore=.csv"), sep = ",")),
  error = function(e) NULL
  )
}
```

Platform/load/initial.R

This script makes the initial request for complete stock history of symbols that are without a .csv file in the data directory. It also checks for invalid symbols in a vector of symbols S and stores them to prevent repeated failed HTTP requests to Yahoo!

```r
# Listing 2-3 and 2-4

setwd(DIR[["function"]])
source("yahoo.R")

setwd(DIR[["root"]])
if("S.R" %in% list.files()) {
  source("S.R")
```

```
} else {
  url <- "http://trading.chrisconlan.com/SPstocks.csv"
  S <- as.character(read.csv(url, header = FALSE)[,1])
  dump(list = "S", "S.R")
}

invalid <- character(0)
if("invalid.R" %in% list.files()) source("invalid.R")

setwd(DIR[["data"]])
toload <- setdiff(S[!paste0(S, ".csv") %in% list.files()], invalid)

if(length(toload) != 0){
  for(i in 1:length(toload)){

  df <- yahoo(toload[i])

  if(!is.null(df)) {
    write.csv(df[nrow(df):1], file = paste0(toload[i], ".csv"),
              row.names = FALSE)
  } else {
    invalid <- c(invalid, toload[i])
  }

}
}

setwd(DIR[["root"]])
dump(list = c("invalid"), "invalid.R")

rm(list = setdiff(ls(), c("CONFIG", "DIR", "yahoo")))
gc()
```

Platform/load/loadToMemory.R

This script loads the data directory into memory, making sure they are in date-ascending order in memory. This script will take less than ten seconds if the data is stored in the data directory in date-ascending order. You may want to investigate the data directory for incorrectly formatted files if this script takes unduly long.

```
# Listing 2-5

setwd(DIR[["data"]])
S <- sub(".csv", "", list.files())

library(data.table)

DATA <- list()
for(i in S){
  suppressWarnings(
  DATA[[i]] <- fread(paste0(i, ".csv"), sep = ","))
  DATA[[i]] <- (DATA[[i]])[order(DATA[[i]][["Date"]], decreasing = FALSE)]
}
```

Platform/load/updateStocks.R

This script updates data in memory and in the data directory. It will attempt to update using the YQL method introduced in Listing 2-7 but will default to the CSV method introduced in Listing 2-6 if the data has not been updated for more than 20 days to avoid receiving incomplete XML requests from YQL.

This differs from the original scripts in Chapter 2 in that it includes a verification mechanism for the adjusted close. If the adjusted close has been retroactively changed because of dividends or splits, we download the entire history of the symbol again from Yahoo! Finance. About 350 of our stocks are regular dividend distributors, so this should trigger a re-download of an average of $\frac{350}{252/4}$ stocks per day.

```
# Listing 2-7

setwd(DIR[["data"]])
library(XML)

batchsize <- 51

redownload <- character(0)

for(i in 1:(ceiling(length(S) / batchsize)) ){

  midQuery <- " ("
  maxdate <- character(0)

startIndex <- ((i - 1) * batchsize + 1)

endIndex <- min(i * batchsize, length(S))

for(s in S[startIndex:(endIndex - 1)]){
  maxdate <- c(maxdate, DATA[[s]][[1]][nrow(DATA[[s]])])
  midQuery <- paste0(midQuery, "'", s, "', ")
}

maxdate <- c(maxdate, DATA[[S[endIndex]]][[1]]
            [nrow(DATA[[S[endIndex]]])])

startDate <- max(maxdate)

useCSV <- FALSE
if( startDate <
    substr(strptime(substr(Sys.time(), 0, 10), "%Y-%m-%d")
          - 20 * 86400, 0, 10) ){
  cat("Query is greater than 20 days. Updating with csv method.")
  useCSV <- TRUE
  break
}
startDate <- substr(as.character(strptime(startDate, "%Y-%m-%d") + 86400), 0, 10)
endDate <- substr(Sys.time(), 0, 10)

isUpdated <- as.numeric(difftime(Sys.time(), startDate, units = "hours")) >= 40.25
```

```r
weekend <- sum(c("Saturday", "Sunday") %in%
                    weekdays(c(strptime(endDate, "%Y-%m-%d"),
                            c(strptime(startDate, "%Y-%m-%d"))))) == 2

span <- as.numeric(difftime(Sys.time(), startDate, units = "hours")) < 48

runXMLupdate <- startDate <= endDate & !weekend & !span & isUpdated

# Push back query date to validate extra days against adj. close
startDateQuery <- substr(as.character(
    strptime(startDate, "%Y-%m-%d") - 7 * 86400
    ), 0, 10)

if( runXMLupdate ){
base <- "http://query.yahooapis.com/v1/public/yql?"
begQuery <- "q=select * from yahoo.finance.historicaldata where symbol in "
midQuery <- paste0(midQuery, "'", S[min(i * batchsize, length(S))], "') ")
endQuery <- paste0("and startDate = '", startDateQuery,
                    "' and endDate = '", endDate, "'")
endParams <- "&diagnostics=true&env=store://datatables.org/alltableswithkeys"

urlstr <- paste0(base, begQuery, midQuery, endQuery, endParams)

doc <- xmlParse(urlstr)

df <- getNodeSet(doc, c("//query/results/quote"),
                    fun = function(v) xpathSApply(v,
                                                    c("./Date",
                                                      "./Open",
                                                      "./High",
                                                      "./Low",
                                                      "./Close",
                                                      "./Volume",
                                                      "./Adj_Close"),
                                                    xmlValue))

if(length(df) != 0){

symbols <- unname(sapply(
    getNodeSet(doc, c("//query/results/quote")), xmlAttrs))

df <- cbind(symbols, data.frame(t(data.frame(df, stringsAsFactors = FALSE)),
                stringsAsFactors = FALSE, row.names = NULL))

names(df) <- c("Symbol", "Date",
                "Open", "High", "Low", "Close", "Volume", "Adj Close")

df[,3:8] <- lapply(df[,3:8], as.numeric)
df <- df[order(df[,1], decreasing = FALSE),]
```

```
sym <- as.character(unique(df$Symbol))

for(s in sym){

  temp <- df[df$Symbol == s, 2:8]
  temp <- temp[order(temp[,1], decreasing = FALSE),]

  # Check if the Adj. Close data is equal for matching dates
  # if not, save symbol to redownload later
  if(any( !DATA[[s]][DATA[[s]][["Date"]] %in% temp[,1]]$"Adj Close" ==
    temp[temp[,1] %in% DATA[[s]][["Date"]],7] ))
  {

    redownload <- c(redownload, s)

  } else {

    startDate <- DATA[[s]][["Date"]][nrow(DATA[[s]])]

    DATA[[s]] <- DATA[[s]][order(DATA[[s]][[1]], decreasing = FALSE)]
    DATA[[s]] <- rbind(DATA[[s]], temp[temp$Date > startDate,])
    write.table(DATA[[s]][DATA[[s]][["Date"]] > startDate],
                    file = paste0(s, ".csv"), sep = ",",
                    row.names = FALSE, col.names = FALSE, append = TRUE)
  }

}
}
}
}

# Listing 2-6
if( useCSV ){
for(i in S){
  maxdate <- DATA[[i]][["Date"]][nrow(DATA[[i]])]
  isUpdated <- as.numeric(difftime(Sys.time(), maxdate, units = "hours")) >= 40.25
  if( isUpdated ){

    maxdate <- strptime(maxdate, "%Y-%m-%d") + 86400

    weekend <- sum(c("Saturday", "Sunday") %in%
                    weekdays(c(maxdate, Sys.time()))) == 2

    span <- FALSE
    if( weekend ){
      span <- as.numeric(difftime(Sys.time(), maxdate, units = "hours")) < 48
    }

    # Push back query date to validate extra days against adj. close
    startDateQuery <- maxdate - 7 * 86400
```

```r
    if(!weekend & !span){
      c <- as.numeric(substr(startDateQuery, start = 1, stop = 4))
      a <- as.numeric(substr(startDateQuery, start = 6, stop = 7)) - 1
      b <- as.numeric(substr(startDateQuery, start = 9, stop = 10))
      df <- yahoo(i, a = a, b = b, c = c)
      if(!is.null(df)){
        if(all(!is.na(df)) & nrow(df) > 0){

          df <- df[nrow(df):1]

          if( any(!DATA[[i]][DATA[[i]][["Date"]] %in% df[["Date"]]]$"Adj Close" ==
            df[["Adj Close"]][df[["Date"]] %in% DATA[[i]][["Date"]]]) )
            {

              redownload <- c(redownload, i)

            } else {
              write.table(df, file = paste0(i, ".csv"), sep = ",",
                row.names = FALSE, col.names = FALSE, append = TRUE)
              DATA[[i]] <- rbind(DATA[[i]], df)
            }
        }
      }
    }
  }
}

# Re-download, store, and load into memory the symbols with
# altered adj. close data
setwd(DIR[["data"]])
if(length(redownload) != 0){
  for( i in redownload ){

  df <- yahoo(i)
  if(!is.null(df)) {
    write.csv(df[nrow(df):1], file = paste0(i, ".csv"),
            row.names = FALSE)
  }

  suppressWarnings(
  DATA[[i]] <- fread(paste0(i, ".csv"), sep = ","))
  DATA[[i]] <- (DATA[[i]])[order(DATA[[i]][["Date"]], decreasing = FALSE)]

}
}

rm(list = setdiff(ls(), c("S", "DATA", "DIR", "CONFIG")))
gc()
```

Platform/load/dateUnif.R

This script will organize the data as date-uniform zoo objects, ensuring all data is numeric with dates stored as order.by attributed in zoo data frames. Additionally, it reorganizes the data into six data frames (Open, High, Low, Close, Adjusted Close, Volume) instead of one data frame for each symbol.

```r
# Listing 2-8

library(zoo)

datetemp <- sort(unique(unlist(sapply(DATA, function(v) v[["Date"]]))))
datetemp <- data.frame(datetemp, stringsAsFactors = FALSE)
names(datetemp) <- "Date"

DATA <- lapply(DATA, function(v) unique(v[order(v$Date),]))

DATA[["Open"]] <- DATA[["High"]] <- DATA[["Low"]] <-
  DATA[["Close"]] <- DATA[["Adj Close"]] <- DATA[["Volume"]] <- datetemp

for(s in S){
  for(i in rev(c("Open", "High", "Low", "Close", "Adj Close", "Volume"))){
    temp <- data.frame(cbind(DATA[[s]][["Date"]], DATA[[s]][[i]]),
                       stringsAsFactors = FALSE)
    names(temp) <- c("Date", s)
    temp[,2] <- as.numeric(temp[,2])

    if(!any(!DATA[[i]][["Date"]][(nrow(DATA[[i]]) - nrow(temp)+1):nrow(DATA[[i]])]
            == temp[,1])){
      temp <- rbind(t(matrix(nrow = 2, ncol = nrow(DATA[[i]]) - nrow(temp),
                             dimnames = list(names(temp)))), temp)
      DATA[[i]] <- cbind(DATA[[i]], temp[,2])
    } else {
      DATA[[i]] <- merge(DATA[[i]], temp, all.x = TRUE, by = "Date")
    }

    names(DATA[[i]]) <- c(names(DATA[[i]]))[-(ncol(DATA[[i]]))], s)
  }
  DATA[[s]] <- NULL

  # Update user on progress
  if( which( S == s ) %% 25 == 0 ){
    cat( paste0(round(100 * which( S == s ) / length(S), 1), "% Complete\n") )
  }

}

DATA <- lapply(DATA, function(v) zoo(v[,2:ncol(v)], strptime(v[,1], "%Y-%m-%d")))

rm(list = setdiff(ls(), c("DATA", "DIR", "CONFIG")))
gc()
```

Platform/load/spClean.R

 # Listing 3-1

```
setwd(DIR[["root"]])

if( "SPdates.R" %in% list.files() ){
  source("SPdates.R")
} else {
  url <- "http://trading.chrisconlan.com/SPdates.csv"
  S <- read.csv(url, header = FALSE, stringsAsFactors = FALSE)
  dump(list = "S", "SPdates.R")
}

names(S) <- c("Symbol", "Date")
S$Date <- strptime(S$Date, "%m/%d/%Y")


for(s in names(DATA[["Close"]])){
  for(i in c("Open", "High", "Low", "Close", "Adj Close", "Volume")){
    Sindex <- which(S[,1] == s)
    if(S[Sindex, "Date"] != "1900-01-01 EST" &
      S[Sindex, "Date"] >= "2000-01-01 EST"){
        DATA[[i]][index(DATA[[i]]) <= S[Sindex, "Date"], s] <- NA
    }
  }
}
```

Platform/load/adjustClose.R

 # Listing 3-6

```
MULT <- DATA[["Adj Close"]] / DATA[["Close"]]


DATA[["Price"]] <- DATA[["Close"]]
DATA[["OpenPrice"]] <- DATA[["Open"]]

DATA[["Open"]] <- DATA[["Open"]] * MULT
DATA[["High"]] <- DATA[["High"]] * MULT
DATA[["Low"]] <- DATA[["Low"]] * MULT
DATA[["Close"]] <- DATA[["Adj Close"]]

DATA[["Adj Close"]] <- NULL
```

Platform/load/return.R

 # Listing 3-8

```
NAPAD <- zoo(matrix(NA, nrow = 1, ncol = ncol(DATA[["Close"]])), order.by =
index(DATA[["Close"]])[names(NAPAD) <- names(DATA[["Close"]])

RETURN <- rbind( NAPAD, ( DATA[["Close"]] / lag(DATA[["Close"]], k = -1) ) - 1 )

OVERNIGHT <- rbind( NAPAD, ( DATA[["Open"]] / lag(DATA[["Close"]], k = -1) ) - 1 )
```

Platform/load/fillInactive.R

 # Listing 3-7

```
for( s in names(DATA[["Close"]]) ){
  if(is.na(DATA[["Close"]][nrow(DATA[["Close"]]), s])){
    maxInd <- max(which(!is.na(DATA[["Close"]][,s])))
    for( i in c("Close", "Open", "High", "Low")){
      DATA[[i]][(maxInd+1):nrow(DATA[["Close"]]),s] <- DATA[["Close"]][maxInd,s]
    }
    for( i in c("Price", "OpenPrice") ){
      DATA[[i]][(maxInd+1):nrow(DATA[["Close"]]),s] <- DATA[["Price"]][maxInd,s]
    }
    DATA[["Volume"]][(maxInd+1):nrow(DATA[["Close"]]),s] <- 0
  }
}
```

Platform/compute

This directory will hold files associated with multicore wrappers, indicator functions, and simulation functions.

Platform/compute/MCinit.R

```
if( CONFIG[["isUNIX"]] ){
  library(doMC)
  workers <- CONFIG[["workers"]]
  registerDoMC( cores = workers )
} else {
  library(doParallel)
  workers <- CONFIG[["workers"]]
  registerDoParallel( cores = workers )
}
```

Platform/compute/functions.R

 # Listing 6-9

```
library(foreach)

delegate <- function( i = i, n = n, k = k, p = workers ){
  nOut <- n - k + 1
  nProc <- ceiling( nOut / p )
  return( (( i - 1 ) * nProc + 1) : min(i * nProc + k - 1, n) )
}
```

 # Listing 6-12

```
mcTimeSeries <- function( data, tsfunc, byColumn, windowSize, workers, … ){

  args <- names(mget(ls()))
  export <- ls(.GlobalEnv)
  export <- export[!export %in% args]
```

```r
  SERIES <- foreach( i = 1:workers, .combine = rbind,
                     .packages = loadedNamespaces(), .export = export) %dopar% {
    jRange <- delegate( i = i, n = nrow(data), k = windowSize, p = workers)

    rollapply(data[jRange,],
      width = windowSize,
      FUN = tsfunc,
      align = "right",
      by.column = byColumn)

  }

  names(SERIES) <- gsub("\\..+", "", names(SERIES))
  if( windowSize > 1){
    PAD <- zoo(matrix(nrow = windowSize-1, ncol = ncol(SERIES), NA),
               order.by = index(data)[1:(windowSize-1)])
    names(PAD) <- names(SERIES)
    SERIES <- rbind(PAD, SERIES)
  }

  if(is.null(names(SERIES))){
    names(SERIES) <- gsub("\\..+", "", names(data)[1:ncol(SERIES)])
  }

  return(SERIES)

}

equNA <- function(v){
   o <- which(!is.na(v))[1]
   return(ifelse(is.na(o), length(v)+1, o))
}

# Listing 7-1

simulate <- function(OPEN, CLOSE,
                     ENTRY, EXIT, FAVOR,
                     maxLookback, maxAssets, startingCash,
                     slipFactor, spreadAdjust, flatCommission, perShareCommission,
                     verbose = FALSE, failThresh = 0,
                     initP = NULL, initp = NULL){

# Step 1
if( any( dim(ENTRY) != dim(EXIT) )  |
    any( dim(EXIT)  != dim(FAVOR) ) |
    any( dim(FAVOR) != dim(CLOSE) ) |
    any( dim(CLOSE) != dim(OPEN)) )
  stop( "Mismatching dimensions in ENTRY, EXIT, FAVOR, CLOSE, or OPEN.")

if( any( names(ENTRY) != names(EXIT))   |
  any( names(EXIT)    != names(FAVOR) ) |
  any( names(FAVOR)   != names(CLOSE) ) |
  any( names(CLOSE)   != names(OPEN) ) |
```

```
  is.null(names(ENTRY)) | is.null(names(EXIT)) |
  is.null(names(FAVOR)) | is.null(names(CLOSE)) |
  is.null(names(OPEN)) )
  stop( "Mismatching or missing column names in ENTRY, EXIT, FAVOR, CLOSE, or OPEN.")

FAVOR <- zoo(t(apply(FAVOR, 1, function(v) ifelse(is.nan(v) | is.na(v), 0, v) )),
             order.by = index(CLOSE))

# Step 2
K <- maxAssets
k <- 0
C <- rep(startingCash, times = nrow(CLOSE))
S <- names(CLOSE)

P <- p <- zoo( matrix(0, ncol=ncol(CLOSE), nrow=nrow(CLOSE)),
               order.by = index(CLOSE) )

if( !is.null( initP ) & !is.null( initp ) ){
  P[1:maxLookback,] <-
    matrix(initP, ncol=length(initP), nrow=maxLookback, byrow = TRUE)
  p[1:maxLookback,] <-
    matrix(initp, ncol=length(initp), nrow=maxLookback, byrow = TRUE)
}

names(P) <- names(p) <- S

equity <- rep(NA, nrow(CLOSE))

rmNA <- pmax(unlist(lapply(FAVOR, equNA)),
    unlist(lapply(ENTRY, equNA)),
    unlist(lapply(EXIT, equNA)))

for( j in 1:ncol(ENTRY) ){
  toRm <- rmNA[j]
  if( toRm > (maxLookback + 1) &
      toRm < nrow(ENTRY) ){
    FAVOR[1:(toRm-1),j] <- NA
    ENTRY[1:(toRm-1),j] <- NA
    EXIT[1:(toRm-1),j] <- NA
  }
}

# Step 3
for( i in maxLookback:(nrow(CLOSE)-1) ){

  # Step 4
  C[i+1] <- C[i]
  P[i+1,] <- as.numeric(P[i,])
  p[i+1,] <- as.numeric(p[i,])
```

```
longS <- S[which(P[i,] > 0)]
shortS <- S[which(P[i,] < 0)]
k <- length(longS) + length(shortS)

# Step 5
longTrigger <- setdiff(S[which(ENTRY[i,] == 1)], longS)
shortTrigger <- setdiff(S[which(ENTRY[i,] == -1)], shortS)
trigger <- c(longTrigger, shortTrigger)

if( length(trigger) > K ) {

  keepTrigger <- trigger[order(c(as.numeric(FAVOR[i,longTrigger]),
                               -as.numeric(FAVOR[i,shortTrigger])),
                             decreasing = TRUE)][1:K]
  longTrigger <- longTrigger[longTrigger %in% keepTrigger]
  shortTrigger <- shortTrigger[shortTrigger %in% keepTrigger]

  trigger <- c(longTrigger, shortTrigger)

}

triggerType <- c(rep(1, length(longTrigger)), rep(-1, length(shortTrigger)))

# Step 6
longExitTrigger <- longS[longS %in%
                         S[which(EXIT[i,] == 1 | EXIT[i,] == 999)]]

shortExitTrigger <- shortS[shortS %in%
                           S[which(EXIT[i,] == -1 | EXIT[i,] == 999)]]

exitTrigger <- c(longExitTrigger, shortExitTrigger)

# Step 7
needToExit <- max( (length(trigger) - length(exitTrigger)) - (K - k), 0)

if( needToExit > 0 ){

  toExitLongS <- setdiff(longS, exitTrigger)
  toExitShortS <- setdiff(shortS, exitTrigger)

  toExit <- character(0)
  for( counter in 1:needToExit ){
    if( length(toExitLongS) > 0 & length(toExitShortS) > 0 ){
      if( min(FAVOR[i,toExitLongS]) < min(-FAVOR[i,toExitShortS]) ){
        pullMin <- which.min(FAVOR[i,toExitLongS])
        toExit <- c(toExit, toExitLongS[pullMin])
        toExitLongS <- toExitLongS[-pullMin]
      } else {
        pullMin <- which.min(-FAVOR[i,toExitShortS])
        toExit <- c(toExit, toExitShortS[pullMin])
        toExitShortS <- toExitShortS[-pullMin]
      }
```

```
    } else if( length(toExitLongS) > 0 & length(toExitShortS) == 0 ){
      pullMin <- which.min(FAVOR[i,toExitLongS])
      toExit <- c(toExit, toExitLongS[pullMin])
      toExitLongS <- toExitLongS[-pullMin]
    } else if( length(toExitLongS) == 0 & length(toExitShortS) > 0 ){
      pullMin <- which.min(-FAVOR[i,toExitShortS])
      toExit <- c(toExit, toExitShortS[pullMin])
      toExitShortS <- toExitShortS[-pullMin]
    }
  }

  longExitTrigger <- c(longExitTrigger, longS[longS %in% toExit])
  shortExitTrigger <- c(shortExitTrigger, shortS[shortS %in% toExit])

}

# Step 8
exitTrigger <- c(longExitTrigger, shortExitTrigger)
exitTriggerType <- c(rep(1, length(longExitTrigger)),
                     rep(-1, length(shortExitTrigger)))

# Step 9
if( length(exitTrigger) > 0 ){
  for( j in 1:length(exitTrigger) ){

    exitPrice <- as.numeric(OPEN[i+1,exitTrigger[j]])

    effectivePrice <- exitPrice * (1 - exitTriggerType[j] * slipFactor) -
      exitTriggerType[j] * (perShareCommission + spreadAdjust)

    if( exitTriggerType[j] == 1 ){

      C[i+1] <- C[i+1] +
        ( as.numeric( P[i,exitTrigger[j]] ) * effectivePrice )
      - flatCommission
    } else {
      C[i+1] <- C[i+1] -
        ( as.numeric( P[i,exitTrigger[j]] ) *
            ( 2 * as.numeric(p[i, exitTrigger[j]]) - effectivePrice ) )
      - flatCommission
    }

    P[i+1, exitTrigger[j]] <- 0
    p[i+1, exitTrigger[j]] <- 0

    k <- k - 1

  }
}
```

```
# Step 10
if( length(trigger) > 0 ){
  for( j in 1:length(trigger) ){

    entryPrice <- as.numeric(OPEN[i+1,trigger[j]])

    effectivePrice <- entryPrice * (1 + triggerType[j] * slipFactor) +
      triggerType[j] * (perShareCommission + spreadAdjust)

    P[i+1,trigger[j]] <- triggerType[j] *
      floor( ( (C[i+1] - flatCommission) / (K - k) ) / effectivePrice )

    p[i+1,trigger[j]] <- effectivePrice

    C[i+1] <- C[i+1] -
      ( triggerType[j] * as.numeric(P[i+1,trigger[j]]) * effectivePrice )
      - flatCommission

    k <- k + 1

  }
}

# Step 11
equity[i] <- C[i+1]
for( s in S[which(P[i+1,] > 0)] ){
  equity[i] <- equity[i] +
    as.numeric(P[i+1,s]) *
    as.numeric(OPEN[i+1,s])
}

for( s in S[which(P[i+1,] < 0)] ){
  equity[i] <- equity[i] -
    as.numeric(P[i+1,s]) *
    ( 2 * as.numeric(p[i+1,s]) - as.numeric(OPEN[i+1,s]) )
}

if( equity[i] < failThresh ){
  warning("\n*** Failure Threshold Breached ***\n")
  break
}

# Step 12
if( verbose ){
  if( i %% 21 == 0 ){
    cat(paste0("############################## ",
               round(100 * (i - maxLookback) /
                       (nrow(CLOSE) - 1 - maxLookback), 1), "%",
               " ##############################\n"))
    cat(paste("Date:\t",as.character(index(CLOSE)[i])), "\n")
    cat(paste0("Equity:\t", " $", signif(equity[i], 5), "\n"))
    cat(paste0("CAGR:\t ",
```

```
                 round(100 * ((equity[i] / (equity[maxLookback]))^
                             (252/(i - maxLookback + 1)) - 1), 2),
                "%"))
    cat("\n")
    cat("Assets:\t", S[P[i+1,] != 0])
    cat("\n\n")
  }
 }

}
# Step 13
return(list(equity = equity, C = C, P = P, p = p))

}
```

Platform/plan

This directory will hold files associated with the PLAN job. Much of the code in this section is meant to be modified for production use by you. We randomly initialize some trading and indicator data for the sake of example.

Platform/plan.R

This is the job script for the PLAN job.

```
source("~/Platform/config.R")

setwd(DIR[["root"]])
cat("load.R\n\n")
source("load.R")

setwd(DIR[["compute"]])
cat("MCinit.R\n\n")
source("MCinit.R")

cat("functions.R\n\n")
source("functions.R")

setwd(DIR[["plan"]])
cat("decisionGen.R\n\n")
source("decisionGen.R")

cat("\n")
```

Platform/plan/decisionGen.R

This is the main script called by the PLAN job. In this script or another, users should declare necessary variables through their trading strategies and information from their brokerages. The default in this code is for the long-only MACD.

```r
# Listing 9-1

# See Chapter 9
setwd(DIR[["plan"]])

# Normally declared by your strategy.
# Long-only MACD is computed with rollapply()
# here for sake of example.
n1 <- 5
n2 <- 34
nSharpe <- 20
shThresh <- 0.50

INDIC <- rollapply(DATA[["Close"]][nrow(DATA[["Close"]]) - n2:0, ],
                width = n2,
                FUN = function(v) mean(v[(n2 - n1 + 1):n2]) - mean(v),
                by.column = TRUE,
                align = "right")

FAVOR <- rollapply(DATA[["Close"]][nrow(DATA[["Close"]]) - nSharpe:0, ],
                FUN = function(v) mean(v, na.rm = TRUE)/sd(v, na.rm = TRUE),
                by.column = TRUE,
                width = nSharpe,
                align = "right")

entryfunc <- function(v, shThresh){
  cols <- ncol(v) / 2
  as.numeric(v[1,1:cols] <= 0 &
            v[2,1:cols] > 0 &
            v[2,(cols+1):(2*cols)] >
            quantile(v[2,(cols+1):(2*cols)],
                    shThresh, na.rm = TRUE)
          )
}

cols <- ncol(INDIC)

ENTRY <- rollapply(cbind(INDIC, FAVOR),
                function(v) entryfunc(v, cols),
                by.column = FALSE,
                width = 2,
                align = "right")

# ***IMPORTANT***
# The quick version used in the PLAN job accepts named vectors
# representing the most recent single row of ENTRY, FAVOR, and EXIT.
# These lines convert the zoo/data frame/matrix objects computed
# in the above lines to named vectors of the last row of data.
```

```
FAVOR <- as.numeric(FAVOR[nrow(FAVOR),])
names(FAVOR) <- names(DATA[["Close"]])

ENTRY <- as.numeric(ENTRY[nrow(ENTRY),])
names(ENTRY) <- names(DATA[["Close"]])

EXIT <- zoo(matrix(0, ncol=ncol(DATA[["Close"]]), nrow = 1),
            order.by = index(DATA[["Close"]]))
names(EXIT) <- names(DATA[["Close"]])

# Normally fetched from brokerage.
# These are arbitrarily declared here.
# Users need to fetch this information from the brokerage
# for production use.
currentlyLong <- c("AA", "AAL", "AAPL")
currentlyShort <- c("")
S <- names(DATA[["Close"]])
initP <- (S %in% currentlyLong) - (S %in% currentlyShort)
cashOnHand <- 54353.54

names(initP) <-
  names(FAVOR) <-
  names(ENTRY) <-
  names(EXIT) <-
  names(DATA[["Close"]])

# At this point we have established everything normally
# taken care of by your strategy.
# Given named vectors of length ncol(DATA[["Close"]])
# initP, FAVOR, ENTRY, and EXIT

maxAssets <- CONFIG[["maxAssets"]]

K <- maxAssets
k <- 0
C <- c(cashOnHand, NA)
S <- names(DATA[["Close"]])
P <- initP

# Normally declared by your strategy
FAVOR <- rnorm(ncol(DATA[["Close"]]))
ENTRY <- rbinom(ncol(DATA[["Close"]]), 1, .005) -
  rbinom(ncol(DATA[["Close"]]), 1, .005)
EXIT <- rbinom(ncol(DATA[["Close"]]), 1, .8) -
  rbinom(ncol(DATA[["Close"]]), 1, .8)

# Normally fetched from brokerage
currentlyLong <- c("AA", "AAL", "AAPL")
currentlyShort <- c("RAI", "RCL", "REGN")
S <- names(DATA[["Close"]])
initP <- (S %in% currentlyLong) - (S %in% currentlyShort)
```

```r
names(initP) <-
  names(FAVOR) <-
  names(ENTRY) <-
  names(EXIT) <-
  names(DATA[["Close"]])

# At this point we have established everything normally
# taken care of by your strategy.
# Given named vectors of length ncol(DATA[["Close"]])
# initP, FAVOR, ENTRY, and EXIT

maxAssets <- 10
startingCash <- 100000

K <- maxAssets
k <- 0
C <- c(startingCash, NA)
S <- names(DATA[["Close"]])
P <- initP

# Step 4
longS <- S[which(P > 0)]
shortS <- S[which(P < 0)]
k <- length(longS) + length(shortS)

# Step 5
longTrigger <- setdiff(S[which(ENTRY == 1)], longS)
shortTrigger <- setdiff(S[which(ENTRY == -1)], shortS)
trigger <- c(longTrigger, shortTrigger)

if( length(trigger) > K ) {

  keepTrigger <- trigger[order(c(as.numeric(FAVOR[longTrigger]),
                        -as.numeric(FAVOR[shortTrigger])),
                      decreasing = TRUE)][1:K]

  longTrigger <- longTrigger[longTrigger %in% keepTrigger]
  shortTrigger <- shortTrigger[shortTrigger %in% keepTrigger]

  trigger <- c(longTrigger, shortTrigger)

}

triggerType <- c(rep(1, length(longTrigger)), rep(-1, length(shortTrigger)))

# Step 6
longExitTrigger <- longS[longS %in% S[which(EXIT == 1 | EXIT == 999)]]

shortExitTrigger <- shortS[shortS %in% S[which(EXIT == -1 | EXIT == 999)]]

exitTrigger <- c(longExitTrigger, shortExitTrigger)
```

```r
# Step 7
needToExit <- max( (length(trigger) - length(exitTrigger)) - (K - k), 0)

if( needToExit > 0 ){

  toExitLongS <- setdiff(longS, exitTrigger)
  toExitShortS <- setdiff(shortS, exitTrigger)

  toExit <- character(0)

  for( counter in 1:needToExit ){
    if( length(toExitLongS) > 0 & length(toExitShortS) > 0 ){
      if( min(FAVOR[toExitLongS]) < min(-FAVOR[toExitShortS]) ){
        pullMin <- which.min(FAVOR[toExitLongS])
        toExit <- c(toExit, toExitLongS[pullMin])
        toExitLongS <- toExitLongS[-pullMin]
      } else {
        pullMin <- which.min(-FAVOR[toExitShortS])
        toExit <- c(toExit, toExitShortS[pullMin])
        toExitShortS <- toExitShortS[-pullMin]
      }
    } else if( length(toExitLongS) > 0 & length(toExitShortS) == 0 ){
      pullMin <- which.min(FAVOR[toExitLongS])
      toExit <- c(toExit, toExitLongS[pullMin])
      toExitLongS <- toExitLongS[-pullMin]
    } else if( length(toExitLongS) == 0 & length(toExitShortS) > 0 ){
      pullMin <- which.min(-FAVOR[toExitShortS])
      toExit <- c(toExit, toExitShortS[pullMin])
      toExitShortS <- toExitShortS[-pullMin]
    }
  }

  longExitTrigger <- c(longExitTrigger, longS[longS %in% toExit])
  shortExitTrigger <- c(shortExitTrigger, shortS[shortS %in% toExit])

}

# Step 8
exitTrigger <- c(longExitTrigger, shortExitTrigger)
exitTriggerType <- c(rep(1, length(longExitTrigger)),
                     rep(-1, length(shortExitTrigger)))

setwd(DIR[["plan"]])

# First exit these
write.csv(file = "stocksToExit.csv",
          data.frame(list(sym = exitTrigger, type = exitTriggerType)))

# Then enter these
write.csv(file = "stocksToEnter.csv",
          data.frame(list(sym = trigger, type = triggerType)))
```

Platform/trade

This directory will hold files associated with the PLAN job. Much of the code in this section is meant to be modified for production use by you. We randomly initialize some trading and indicator data for the sake of example.

Platform/trade.R

```
# First exit these
toExit <- read.csv(file = "stocksToExit.csv")

# Then enter these
toEnter <- read.csv(file = "stocksToEnter.csv")

# This is open-ended...
# This may be done inside or outside R depending on choice of brokerage and API
```

Platform/model

This directory will hold files associated with the MODEL job. Much of the code in this section is meant to be modified for production use by you. The long-only MACD is shown here with generalized pattern search optimization.

Platform/model.R

```
source("~/Platform/config.R")

setwd(DIR[["root"]])
cat("load.R\n\n")
source("load.R")

setwd(DIR[["compute"]])
cat("MCinit.R\n\n")
source("MCinit.R")

cat("functions.R\n\n")
source("functions.R")

setwd(DIR[["model"]])
cat("optimize.R\n\n")
source("optimize.R")

cat("\n")
```

Platform/model/optimize.R

```r
setwd(DIR[["model"]])

minVal <- CONFIG[["minVal"]]
maxVal <- CONFIG[["maxVal"]]
PARAM <- CONFIG[["PARAMnaught"]]

source("evaluateFunc.R")
source("optimizeFunc.R")

PARAMout <- optimize(y = CONFIG[["y"]], minVal, maxVal)

setwd(DIR[["plan"]])

write.csv(data.frame(PARAMout), "stratParams.csv")
```

Platform/model/evaluateFunc.R

```r
# Listing 8-1

# Declare entry function for use inside evaluator
entryfunc <- function(v, shThresh){
  cols <- ncol(v) / 2
  as.numeric(v[1,1:cols] <= 0 &
          v[2,1:cols] > 0 &
          v[2,(cols+1):(2*cols)] >
          quantile(v[2,(cols+1):(2*cols)],
              shThresh, na.rm = TRUE)
          )
}

evaluate <- function(PARAM, minVal = NA, maxVal = NA, y = 2014,
                  transform = TRUE, verbose = FALSE,
                  negative = FALSE, transformOnly = FALSE,
                  returnData = FALSE, accountParams = NULL){

  # Convert and declare parameters if they exist on domain (-inf,inf) domain
  if( transform | transformOnly ){
    PARAM <- minVal +
      (maxVal - minVal) * unlist(lapply( PARAM, function(v) (1 + exp(-v))^(-1) ))
    if( transformOnly ){
    return(PARAM)
    }
  }

  # Max shares to hold
  K <- CONFIG[["maxAssets"]]
```

```
# Declare n1 as itself, n2 as a multiple of n1 defined by nFact,
# and declare the length and threshold in sharpe ratio for FAVOR
n1 <- max(round(PARAM[["n1"]]), 2)
n2 <- max(round(PARAM[["nFact"]] * PARAM[["n1"]]), 3, n1+1)
nSharpe <- max(round(PARAM[["nSharpe"]]), 2)
shThresh <- max(0, min(PARAM[["shThresh"]], .99))
maxLookback <- max(n1, n2, nSharpe) + 1

# Subset data according to year, y
period <-
  index(DATA[["Close"]]) >= strptime(paste0("01-01-", y[1]), "%d-%m-%Y") &
  index(DATA[["Close"]]) < strptime(paste0("01-01-", y[length(y)]+1), "%d-%m-%Y")

period <- period |
  ((1:nrow(DATA[["Close"]]) > (which(period)[1] - maxLookback)) &
  (1:nrow(DATA[["Close"]]) <= (which(period)[sum(period)]) + 1))

CLOSE <- DATA[["Close"]][period,]
OPEN <- DATA[["Open"]][period,]
SUBRETURN <- RETURN[period,]

# Compute inputs for long-only MACD as in Listing 7.2
# Code is optimized for speed using functions from caTools and zoo
require(caTools)

INDIC <- zoo(runmean(CLOSE, n1, endrule = "NA", align = "right") -
             runmean(CLOSE, n2, endrule = "NA", align = "right"),
          order.by = index(CLOSE))
names(INDIC) <- names(CLOSE)

RMEAN <- zoo(runmean(SUBRETURN, n1, endrule = "NA", align = "right"),
          order.by = index(SUBRETURN))

FAVOR <- RMEAN / runmean( (SUBRETURN - RMEAN)^2, nSharpe,
                          endrule = "NA", align = "right" )
names(FAVOR) <- names(CLOSE)

ENTRY <- rollapply(cbind(INDIC, FAVOR),
                   FUN = function(v) entryfunc(v, shThresh),
                   width = 2,
                   fill = NA,
                   align = "right",
                   by.column = FALSE)
names(ENTRY) <- names(CLOSE)

EXIT <- zoo(matrix(0, ncol=ncol(CLOSE), nrow=nrow(CLOSE)),
          order.by = index(CLOSE))
names(EXIT) <- names(CLOSE)

# Simulate and store results
if( is.null(accountParams) ){
```

```
    RESULTS <- simulate(OPEN, CLOSE,
            ENTRY, EXIT, FAVOR,
            maxLookback, K, 100000,
            0.001, 0.01, 3.5, 0,
            verbose, 0)
  } else {
    RESULTS <- simulate(OPEN, CLOSE,
        ENTRY, EXIT, FAVOR,
        maxLookback, K, accountParams[["C"]],
        0.001, 0.01, 3.5, 0,
        verbose, 0,
        initP = accountParams[["P"]], initp = accountParams[["p"]])
  }

  if(!returnData){
    # Compute and return sharpe ratio
    v <- RESULTS[["equity"]]
    returns <- ( v[-1] / v[-length(v)] ) - 1
    out <- mean(returns, na.rm = T) / sd(returns, na.rm = T)
    if(!is.nan(out)){
      if( negative ){
        return( -out )
      } else {
        return( out )
      }
    } else {
      return(0)
    }

  } else {
    return(RESULTS)
  }

}
```

Platform/model/optimizeFunc.R

```
# See Chapter 8
# Example optimization function coded for
# Generalized pattern search
optimize <- function(y, minVal, maxVal){

# Maximum iterations
# Max possible calls to evaluator is K * (4 * n + 1)
K <- CONFIG[["maxIter"]]

# Restart with random init when delta is below threshold
deltaThresh <- 0.05

# Set initial delta
delta <- deltaNaught <- 1
```

```r
# Scale factor
sigma <- 2

# Vector theta_0
PARAM <- PARAMNaught <- CONFIG[["PARAMnaught"]]
np <- length(PARAM)

OPTIM <- data.frame(matrix(NA, nrow = K * (4 * np + 1), ncol = np + 1))
names(OPTIM) <- c(names(PARAM), "obj"); o <- 1

fmin <- fminNaught <- evaluate(PARAM, minVal, maxVal, negative = TRUE, y = y)
OPTIM[o,] <- c(PARAM, fmin); o <- o + 1

# Print function for reporting progress in loop
printUpdate <- function(step){
  if(step == "search"){
    cat(paste0("Search step: ", k,"|",l,"|",m, "\n"))
  } else if (step == "poll"){
    cat(paste0("Poll step: ", k,"|",l,"|",m, "\n"))
  }
  names(OPTIM)
  cat("\t", paste0(strtrim(names(OPTIM), 6), "\t"), "\n")
  cat("Best:\t", paste0(round(unlist(OPTIM[which.min(OPTIM$obj),]),3), "\t"), "\n")
  cat("Theta:\t", paste0(round(unlist(c(PARAM, fmin)),3), "\t"), "\n")
  cat("Trial:\t", paste0(round(as.numeric(OPTIM[o-1,]), 3), "\t"), "\n")
  cat(paste0("Delta: ", round(delta,3) , "\t"), "\n\n")
}

for( k in 1:K ){

  # SEARCH subroutine
  for( l in 1:np ){
    net <- (2 * rbinom(np, 1, .5) - 1) * runif(np, delta, sigma * delta)
    for( m in c(-1,1) ){

      testpoint <- PARAM + m * net
      ftest <- evaluate(testpoint, minVal, maxVal, negative = TRUE, y = y)
      OPTIM[o,] <- c(testpoint, ftest); o <- o + 1
      printUpdate("search")

    }
  }

  if( any(OPTIM$obj[(o-(2*np)):(o-1)] < fmin ) ){

    minPos <- which.min(OPTIM$obj[(o-(2*np)):(o-1)])
    PARAM <- (OPTIM[(o-(2*np)):(o-1),1:np])[minPos,]
    fmin <- (OPTIM[(o-(2*np)):(o-1),np+1])[minPos]
    delta <- sigma * delta
  } else {
```

```r
    # POLL Subroutine
    for( l in 1:np ){
      net <- delta * as.numeric(1:np == l)
      for( m in c(-1,1) ){
        testpoint <- PARAM + m * net
        ftest <- evaluate(testpoint, minVal, maxVal, negative = TRUE, y = y)
        OPTIM[o,] <- c(testpoint, ftest); o <- o + 1
        printUpdate("poll")
      }
    }

    if( any(OPTIM$obj[(o-(2*np)):(o-1)] < fmin ) ){

      minPos <- which.min(OPTIM$obj[(o-(2*np)):(o-1)])
      PARAM <- (OPTIM[(o-(2*np)):(o-1),1:np])[minPos,]
      fmin <- (OPTIM[(o-(2*np)):(o-1),np+1])[minPos]
      delta <- sigma * delta

    } else {

      delta <- delta / sigma

    }

  }

  cat(paste0("\nCompleted Full Iteration: ", k, "\n\n"))

  # Restart with random initiate
  if( delta < deltaThresh ) {

    delta <- deltaNaught
    fmin <- fminNaught
    PARAM <- PARAMNaught + runif(n = np, min = -delta * sigma,
                                 max = delta * sigma)

    ftest <- evaluate(PARAM, minVal, maxVal,
                      negative = TRUE, y = y)
    OPTIM[o,] <- c(PARAM, ftest); o <- o + 1

    cat(paste0("\nDelta Threshold Breached, Restarting with Random Initiate\n\n"))
  }
}

# Return the best optimization in untransformed parameters
return(
  evaluate(OPTIM[which.min(OPTIM$obj),1:np],
           minVal, maxVal, transformOnly = TRUE)
)
}
```

■ ■ ■

Scoping in Multicore R

This book makes frequent use of the foreach package in R to parallelize computations. This package, developed by Steve Weston of Revolution Analytics, allows users to write operating system–independent (OS-independent) multicore code. It works by acting as a single OS-independent interface to different OS-dependent parallel back ends.

At face value, the package seems to implement this idea well. Windows users rely on doParallel for a parallel back end, and UNIX users rely on doMC for a parallel back end. All of the examples in the official package documentation run without problems.

Before we discuss the problems associated with foreach and instance replication, we will have a general discussion about scoping in R. The purpose of this discussion is to clarify how and why Windows users face significant setbacks to extensibility in multicore R.

Scoping Rules in R

The R language follows easy-to-use scoping rules. In general, R is lexically scoped, meaning functions have their own environments. In a stricter sense, scoping rules in R cannot be fully explained by labeling them as lexical.

A variable declared in a function cannot be then called from the global environment. At the end of function execution, the variables in the function environment can no longer be accessed. The function environment is disengaged and subject to overwriting or deletion according to the R language's memory management protocols.

If a function calls for a variable x that is not present in the function environment, the function will search for a variable named x in the next highest scope, whether that scope is in another function or the global environment. In other words, when any process needs the variable x, it will start at its current scope and move up until it finds it, throwing an error if it reaches the global environment and still cannot locate x.

These are the major tenants of scoping in R. These are all standard behaviors of lexically scoped languages. The R language cannot be classified as strictly lexical because it allows other means of traversing environments in a nonlexical manner. These behaviors are typically obviously deliberate by the programmer. This is important because it ensures that programmers will not accidentally encounter exceptions to lexical scoping rules.

Using Lexical Scoping

We make great use of lexical scoping in this text. Listing B-1 gives a concrete example. This exhibit may be rudimentary to skilled R developers, but we encourage you to follow along to better understand comparisons to multicore scoping rules covered later in this appendix.

© Chris Conlan 2016
C. Conlan, *Automated Trading with R*, DOI 10.1007/978-1-4842-2178-5_13

Listing B-1. Lexical Scoping

```r
# Declare global variables a and b
a <- 2
b <- 3

# Declare functions
f <- function(){
  a
}

g <-function(){
  f() + b
}

h <- function(b){
  f() + b
}

# a = 2 throughout.
# b = 3 when not supplied as a parameter.
f() # f() = 2
g() # g() = 5
h(5) # h(5) = 7
```

Takeaways

Throughout R literature, there are many examples of complicated scoping procedures and specific exceptions to the lexical scoping paradigm. These are instructive in explaining the more technical semantics of the R language, but the typical developer will not have to confront these issues in practice. More important than the jargon and fringe exceptions that can dominate discussion is the notion that R scoping is intuitive. Most R users will never have to think about it because it is logical.

We present here the major tenants of scoping in R functions:

- If a function requires an object not supplied as a parameter, R will find it in the global environment.

- If a function modifies an object from the global environment in the function scope, the object will remain unchanged in the global environment.

- The only way a function can affect the global environment is through the single object returned by the function.

Exceptions to these rules can occur in the case where users modify system variables, options, and working directories; intentionally fetch the global environment; and so on. In the vast majority of cases, functions will not perform such operations and can be coded casually without much thought to scoping.

These rules have important implications for the way we modify, share, and extend R code. We have taken them for granted in this text up to this point, because we only sacrifice the luxuries of lexical scoping when performing multicore computations in Windows. As we will observe in the following sections, Windows users who want to perform certain computations will need to follow stricter scoping rules.

The UNIX fork System Call

We touched on some of the low-level differences between foreach in Windows and UNIX in Chapter 6. The main difference is that foreach in UNIX creates R instances with the system call fork. The UNIX fork call is very powerful and has been standard in UNIX and UNIX-like OSs for at least 25 years. The call works at the kernel level to give multiple memory address spaces to the same set of data and enforce copy-on-write semantics.

The kernel is the lowest-level interface between the OS and the hardware, including the RAM, disk, I/O, and CPU. The kernel is specific to the OS. In many ways, the kernel is the bare-bones version of the operating system.

A memory address space is the range of binary values from which a program can access data in memory. The fork call gives R instances access to the same data without copying the physical memory. In this manner, programs can have explicitly defined nonoverlapping address spaces while accessing the same data in the same physical memory.

The fork Call and Memory Management

The fork call enforces copy-on-write semantics to give programs flexibility while maintaining the efficiency of shared physical memory. To *copy on write* is to create a copy of a variable if any process writes to it rather than purely reads from it. With copy-on-write semantics, any variable that a forked process manipulates will automatically get a process-specific copy made in physical memory on the address space of that forked process. For example, if a foreach loop is computing an indicator based on DATA while continually changing the value of an iterator i and a matrix indic, the forked process will share DATA, but each gets independent copies of i and indic.

If DATA is 110MB, indic is 3MB, and i is negligibly small, a four-process fork call would take 110MB + 4(3MB) = 122MB of memory. If forked processes were to inefficiently copy entire environments without copy-on-write semantics, the call would take 4(110MB + 3MB) = 452MB to complete. Of course, this is the theoretical case for a perfectly efficient language. In reality, both processes will take much more memory because of scoping and copy semantics specific to the programming language. In any case, the proportionality stands. A forked multicore program running *n* processes on large read-only data will take just shy of *n* times less memory to complete.

Scoping Implications for R

There are no atypical scoping implications for multicore R in UNIX. This is logical considering the nature of forked processes as described in this section.

For our platform, this means mcTimeSeries() can be called liberally from any location and will follow the same scoping rules as any normal R function. For reasons that will become apparent as we discuss foreach in Windows, the .packages and .exports arguments of foreach() are ignored in UNIX systems. Our original declaration of mcTimeSeries() includes a handful of lines for Windows compatibility that are not required in UNIX. Removing these lines will result in marginal performance increases in the function and allow both Windows and UNIX users to better understand the content of it.

Listing B-2 declares a pure UNIX version of mcTimeSeries(). It is the same as the OS-independent version declared in Listing 6-12, less a few bells and whistles. We list and explain the differences here:

- The ellipsis (...) has been removed from the end of the argument list. This ellipsis is unneeded for UNIX users because they can take advantage of lexical scoping rather than explicitly passing extra values and functions.

- The first three lines of the function body are removed. These lines constructed a character vector export of object names that existed in the global environment but not the function environment. The vector was passed to foreach() in the .export argument to enforce lexical scoping at a maximum of two levels. Performing this calculation was a means of manually implementing lexical scoping in the case that only the global and a single function environment mattered. The .export argument is completely ignored in the UNIX implementation of foreach().

- The .packages argument is removed. This argument was supplied with loadedNamespace() in order to export all packages loaded in the main environment. The .packages argument is not ignored in UNIX foreach() but is altogether redundant because R instances share the packages under fork. The R instances would still attempt to load the existing packages every time mcTimeSeries() is run only to find them already loaded, much in the same way running library() repeatedly would have no effect. There is the possibility that conditional loading of a package across instances can necessitate this argument in UNIX but would be unlikely and in poor developmental style. There is a strong chance that reloading all of the active packages in the order supplied by loadedNamespaces() can result in unintended masking in packages that have conflicting function names. This is unlikely to hinder development but is another nuisance that can be avoided with this version of our function.

Listing B-2. Pure UNIX mcTimeSeries()

```
mcTimeSeries <- function( data, tsfunc, byColumn, windowSize, workers ){

  SERIES <- foreach( i = 1:workers, .combine = rbind ) %dopar% {

  jRange <- delegate( i = i, n = nrow(data), k = windowSize, p = workers)

  rollapply(data[jRange,],
    width = windowSize,
    FUN = tsfunc,
    align = "right",
    by.column = byColumn)

  }
  names(SERIES) <- gsub("\\..+", "", names(SERIES))

  if( windowSize > 1){
    PAD <- zoo(matrix(nrow = windowSize-1, ncol = ncol(SERIES), NA),
            order.by = index(data)[1:(windowSize-1)])
    names(PAD) <- names(SERIES)
    SERIES <- rbind(PAD, SERIES)
  }

  if(is.null(names(SERIES))){
    names(SERIES) <- gsub("\\..+", "", names(data)[1:ncol(SERIES)])
  }

  return(SERIES)

}
```

UNIX users are highly encouraged to adopt this as a pure replacement over Listing 6-12. It will allow for smoother development, higher performance, and greater extensibility of our source code. The importance of extensibility cannot be stressed enough. For example, in exploring the source code, we have programmed a function called entryfunc() into many of our indicators, evaluators, and optimizers. Say a developer was looking to extend our platform and wanted to program in his own new function, exitfunc(). He then found that this function performed best run through mcTimeSeries(). A UNIX user can run an optimization with this new function by simply declaring exitfunc() in the global environment and using it in the evaluator to alter the EXIT object. Listing B-3 gives a nonexecutable outline of how this might look.

Listing B-3. Multicore Extensibility in UNIX

```
exitfunc <- function(v) {
  # Body of developer's new exit function
}

evaluate(…) <- function(…){

  # Body of the evaluate function

  EXIT <- mcTimeSeries(CLOSE, exitfunc, TRUE, 20, workers)

  # Remainder of the evaluate function

}
```

All the UNIX developer needs to do to extend our platform to optimize his strategy with multicore R is declare his exit function and alter one line of code in the evaluator. This is the case for normal single-core functions in R, and it is a major reason why R is great for research. As we will see, this is not the case for multicore R in Windows.

Instance Replication in Windows

Windows does not have a native fork equivalent. The foreach package works with doParallel to create *n* independent R instances to run an *n*-core process. In simple cases, the foreach package allows for OS-independent development of multicore code. When we begin depending on lexical scoping for objects lying in between the function scope and global scope, the R instances will see them as missing and throw errors.

Instance Replication and Memory Management

The foreach implementation in Windows creates *n* independent R instances for an *n*-core process. These instances are GUI-less R run-time environments instantiated and maintained via calls to the Windows command prompt through the R function system(). This creates problems because each R instance contains a remotely maintained persistent global environment.

The call to foreach() attempts to mimic UNIX's fork and R's lexical scoping by treating the global environment of each R instance as the function environment of the foreach() call. This is confusing because the environments claim to exist at the function level but do not the follow scoping protocol expected from a temporary and subglobal R environment. This is additionally inefficient because large objects are not subject to normal removal and garbage collection protocol. Function-level objects exported to these instances persist in memory when unused, which can quickly lead to out-of-memory errors in systems that are otherwise capable of handling multicore computations of similar size.

Scoping Implications for R

As a means of maintaining efficiency under instance replication, the foreach() function has us explicitly declare all packages and objects we would like loaded in our instances. This behavior is not an attempt at mimicry of fork; rather, it is a non-R programming paradigm introduced out of necessity for Windows compatibility. We declare these packages and objects through the .packages and .export arguments to foreach(), respectively. Since the objects referenced in these arguments may not be present in the function scope, we supply a character vector of object names. The requirement to supply a character vector of names rather than a list of objects to .export prevents us from dynamically exporting objects that lie in between the global environment and the mcTimeSeries() environment.

The OS-independent declaration of mcTimeSeries() in Listing 6-12 contains an ellipsis (...) at the end of the argument list to allow users to supply extra objects from in-between environments directly into mcTimeSeries(). If a user wants to dynamically declare a function within a call to mcTimeSeries(), as is typically done with apply-style functions, he must pass constituent function objects through all nested function calls. This is a technically viable solution but greatly inhibits extensibility when compared to the standard lexical scoping protocol of R.

We will take the example given in Listing B-3 where a user would like to incorporate his new exitfunc() using multicore R into the optimizer. We will walk through this process for a Windows user.

First, it must be noted that most functions need arguments other than just data, and this matters for multicore in Windows. If the user wants to pass a parameter to his function, he must declare it as a parameter to exitfunc() rather than relying on lexical scoping. Moving along, we see the repeated pains of passing this function object from the highest function that depends on it, the optimizer, all the way down to the lowest, mcTimeSeries().

Listing B-4. Multicore Extensibility in Windows

```
# Declare parameter alpha as function parameter
exitfunc <- function(v, alpha) {
  # Body of developer's new exit function
}

# Declare function object exitfunc as
# function parameter to evaluator
evaluate <- function(… , exitfunc){

  # Body of the evaluate function

  # alpha exists in the function scope
  # of the evaluator
  alpha <- 0.5

  # Dynamically declare function object in
  # mcTimeSeries. Pass exitfunc and alpha
  # in the ellipses of the call because
  # the second argument depends on them.
  EXIT <- mcTimeSeries(CLOSE,
                       function(v) exitfunc(v, alpha),
                       TRUE, 20, workers,
                       exitfunc, alpha)
  # Remainder of the evaluate function

}
```

```
optimize <- function(… , exitfunc){

  # Alter all calls to evaluate to include
  # new function object parameter exitfunc

  # Body of the optimizer

  evaluate( … , exitfunc )

  # Body of the optimizer

  evaluate( … , exitfunc )

  # And so on. There are typically many calls
  # to evaluate() within the optimizer.

}
```

Aside from extensibility issues as they pertain to our platform, there are a few behaviors developers need to be aware of in regard to reproducibility, instance management, and development testing.

- By default, foreach() exports all required nonfunction data objects in the environment from which it was called. This is a notable efficiency optimization. It makes efforts to copy only the necessary objects.

- Once any function object is exported either explicitly or implicitly through foreach(), it persists in the global environment for an unspecified amount of time or until terminated. This can cause reproduceability issues when exporting functions. If two independent calls to foreach() need the same user-defined function exported, the second call to be executed will run without error if the function is exported in the first call. Once the user-defined function has been exported a single time, it is available to all future functions as long as the instances are up.

- Once any data object is exported either explicitly or implicitly through foreach(), it persists in the global environment for an unspecified amount of time. Letting large data objects pile up will eventually cause an out-of-memory error.

Windows users face significant setbacks to extensibility with regard to multicore R. Ultimately, many production strategies will not depend on multicore R but rather the creative use of existing binaries.

Index

© Chris Conlan 2016
C. Conlan, *Automated Trading with R*, DOI 10.1007/978-1-4842-2178-5

Get the eBook for only $5!

Why limit yourself?

Now you can take the weightless companion with you wherever you go and access your content on your PC, phone, tablet, or reader.

Since you've purchased this print book, we're happy to offer you the eBook in all 3 formats for just $5.

Convenient and fully searchable, the PDF version enables you to easily find and copy code—or perform examples by quickly toggling between instructions and applications. The MOBI format is ideal for your Kindle, while the ePUB can be utilized on a variety of mobile devices.

To learn more, go to www.apress.com/companion or contact support@apress.com.

Printed in the United States
By Bookmasters